1

BASIC GUIDE TO
Environmental Compliance

VNR BASIC GUIDE SERIES

Each volume in Van Nostrand Reinhold's Basic Guide Series introduces environmental and occupational health and safety professionals to topics they need to be familiar with, but may not need to specialize in.

Titles in the series include:

Basic Guide to Accident Investigation
Basic Guide to Environmental Compliance
Basic Guide to System Safety

Also Available from Van Nostrand Reinhold:

Environmental Auditing and Compliance Manual
by the Environmental Resource Center

Hazardous Waste Management Compliance Handbook
by the Environmental Resource Center

SARA Title III: Intent and Implementation of Hazardous Materials Regulations
by Frank L. Fire, Nancy K. Grant, and David H. Hoover

VNR BASIC GUIDE SERIES

BASIC GUIDE TO
Environmental Compliance

Jeffrey W. Vincoli, CSP

VNR VAN NOSTRAND REINHOLD
_____ New York

Copyright © 1993 by Van Nostrand Reinhold

Library of Congress Catalog Card Number 93-14969
ISBN 0-442-01472-4

I(T)P Van Nostrand Reinhold is an International Thomson Publishing company.
       ITP logo is a trademark under license.

Printed in the United States of America.

Van Nostrand Reinhold   International Thomson Publishing GmbH
115 Fifth Avenue   Königswinterer Str. 518
New York, New York 10003   5300 Bonn 3
                                      Germany
International Thomson Publishing
Berkshire House, 168-173   International Thomson Publishing Asia
High Holborn   38 Kim Tian Rd., #0105
London WC1V7AA   Kim Tian Plaza
England   Singapore

Thomas Nelson Australia   International Thomson Publishing Japan
102 Dodds Street   Kyowa Building, 3F
South Melbourne 3205   2-2-1 Hirakawacho
Victoria, Australia   Chiyada-Ku, Tokyo 102
                                      Japan
Nelson Canada
1120 Birchmount Road
Scarborough, Ontario
M1K 5G4, Canada

16 15 14 13 12 11 10 9 8 7 6 5 4 3 2 1

Library of Congress Cataloging-in-Publication Data

Vincoli, Jeffrey W.
    Basic guide to environmental compliance / Jeffrey W. Vincoli.
        p.   cm. — (VNR basic guide series)
    Includes bibliographical references (p.   ) and index.
    ISBN 0-442-01472-4
    1. Environmental protection—United States.   2. Environmental law-
United States.   I. Title.   II. Series.
TD171.V56   1993
363.7′056′0973—dc20   93-14969
                                                           CIP

To my parents, Joe and Carmela, with much love and great appreciation for all that I am and could have ever aspired to be.

Contents

Preface

The *Basic Guide to Environmental Compliance* is the second in a series of *Basic Guide* books that focus upon topics of interest to today's safety and/or health professional. As with the other books of this series, this text is designed to provide the reader with a fundamental understanding of the subject and, it is hoped, foster a desire for additional training and information.

It should be noted from the onset that it is not the intention of the *Basic Guide to Environmental Compliance* to provide or impart any level of expertise in the field of environmental compliance beyond that of novice. Those practitioners who desire more comprehensive instruction in this most complex subject will not be satisfied with the information presented in the following pages. It is not practical or feasible to expect a basic guidebook to contain all possible information on any subject, especially one as dynamic and changing as environmental compliance. However, those readers that require or perhaps only desire a basic understanding of the environmental profession will find this *Basic Guide to Environmental Compliance* a valuable source of information. It is also hoped that those professionals currently involved in the environmental arena might find this material somewhat enjoyable and, at the very least, refreshing. Other professionals who are not directly involved with environmental issues, but who must work with those who are, will also find this text useful.

In short, safety, health, and environmental professionals, as well as managers, engineers, technicians, and trainers should obtain some benefit from the information contained in this text.

Acknowledgments

The author wishes to acknowledge the individuals and organizations who have assisted in the development of this publication.

First, the author would like to thank Douglas Tomlin, Susie Adkins, and George Brunner for their advice, suggestions, and input.

Second, thanks to Jennifer Scarpino for her valuable contribution of reference materials.

Finally, thanks to the engineering and professional environmental consulting services firm of O'Brien & Gere, Inc. and, in particular, Al Kauper, Paul R. Seavy, Steve Garver, Cheryl L. Cundall, and Matthew Traister for their very competent technical assistance.

I

Environmental Compliance— An Introduction

INTRODUCTION TO PART I

The process of environmental compliance is, by most definitions, extremely complex, tedious, and, with very few exceptions, expensive. The practicing safety and health professional has, in recent years, been exposed to an ever-increasing level of responsibility in the environmental arena as well. In most cases, this *combining* of responsibilities may be the result of direct budgetary constraints or other forced cost-control actions, such as manpower reductions. Whatever the specific reason for the addition of environmental responsibilities to the already cumbersome task of safety and health compliance, many safety and health professionals find themselves behind the power curve of knowledge with regard to the basic requirements associated with environmental compliance.

- Therefore, the first part of this *Basic Guide to Environmental Compliance* is intended as an introduction to the compliance process in terms of the most basic and fundamental concepts associated with the preservation of environmental health and resources. In order for the reader to understand the various complex rules and regulations that have been enacted during the past two decades, a brief explanation of the history behind the environmental rule-making process will first be provided.

Part I of this text will focus on the historical development of environmental policy in the United States. An analysis of the events and circumstances that eventually resulted in the environmental awareness of the U.S. population will also be provided. The formation and intended purpose of the U.S. Environmental Protection Agency (EPA) and the process of environmental rule making will be topics of discussion in the early chapters of this part. It should also be understood from the beginning that, although the EPA sets regulatory requirements on the federal level, many states and some local municipalities have similar and, in many cases, more strict environmental plans that must be complied with in conjunction with federal requirements. Part I provides a brief summary explanation of the relationship between state plans and federal environmental compliance schemes. However, because so many state plans now exist, it is not feasible to fully detail each plan in this limited volume. For the most part, federal requirements are the *minimum* standards, and existing state plans are either more stringent or at least as stringent as federal environmental protection strategies. For specific information on individual state plans, the reader is directed to the state agency of their concern, as listed in the Appendices to this text.

Finally, Chapter 4 will provide an extensive discussion and explanation on the process of environmental audits. The various types and phases of audits, the audit report, and the importance of proper documentation and follow-up will be examined.

Upon completion of Part I, the reader will have developed a basic understanding of the environmental movement in the United States and, it is hoped, be better able to appreciate, interpret, and understand those laws discussed in Part II and the many more environmental laws and regulations that now exist and are yet to come.

1

History of U.S. Environmental Policy

INTRODUCTION

In discussing the development of formal environmental policy in the United States, it seems most logical to approach the issue based upon a division in time: that which occurred *prior* to 1970 (when the U.S. Environmental Protection Agency was created) and that which occurred *after* 1970. Such a demarcation will facilitate the presentation of information dealing with those actions that ultimately led to the Presidential creation of a federal agency with a stated purpose to protect and preserve the national environment and maintain it for future generations. Chapter 2 will focus on the agency itself and the changes in U.S. environmental policy that have occurred since the inception of the EPA.

BACKGROUND

There is no real documented evidence that positively identifies an exact point in our nation's history where the level of environmental awareness of the population reached a point that demanded governmental intervention. It has been suggested that the *environmental movement* may have its roots as far back as the Industrial Revolution (circa 1800 in the United States, even earlier in England), although there is little indication in the literature to validate this theory. It may be feasible, however, to assume that the tremendous changes caused by the Industrial Revolution, which was marked by an abrupt shift in both social and economic organization, could very well have influenced some broader-minded individuals and heightened their concern over the effects of such changes on the environment and the abundant supply of natural resources that existed in late eighteenth and early nineteenth century America. Changes resulting from the replacement of hand tools with machines and power tools and the development of large-scale industrial production would have obviously also introduced new and dramatic levels and methods of environmental pollution and abuse. In their eagerness to take full advantage of these new and exciting changes, it is entirely possible that our industrial predecessors also took extreme advantage of our country's environment.

All this, however, is historical speculation and can not be verified as absolute fact in the literature of the period. Still, one can not simply overlook the suggestion that, as our nation progressed forward with dramatic industrial, scientific, and technological advancements and achievements, the environment inevitably suffered as a direct result of such progress.

OVERVIEW OF U.S. ENVIRONMENTAL POLICY

Whatever the exact roots of the environmental movement in the United States, it is a fact that by the end of the nineteenth century national concern over the frequent dumping of solid wastes into navigable waterways led to the enactment of the very first law to positively address any form of environmental abuse: the Rivers and Harbors Act of 1899. Although its primary intent was to prohibit the disposal into waterways of solid objects that could create a *hazard to navigation* and did not specifically address waste disposal as an issue in and of itself, the Act is still considered the very first attempt to regulate solid wastes. The Act also prohibited the *creation* of any object that could possibly interfere with the navigability of any United States waterway. For example, it was illegal to build a wharf, pier, breakwater, jetty, or any similar structure without federal permission. It also became illegal to alter a waterway's course, location, condition, or capacity without government approval. Perhaps of greatest significance in terms of environmental policy, the Act also established a permit system that applied to dredge-and-fill projects and to projects that involved possible obstructions to navigation (Wentz 1989). The idea of a permitting system that required written government permission/approval under the Rivers and Harbors Act set a precedence for future, similar environmental permitting systems that eventually became a part of almost every environmental regulation enacted during this century.

Even though the Rivers and Harbors Act of 1899 is considered to be the first real legislation directed at placing controls on the introduction of waste products into the natural environment, no significant regulatory actions were to follow during the first half of the twentieth century. In fact, the disposal of industrial waste at the turn of the century was not perceived as a serious problem by the majority in both the public and private sectors. Individual industrial plants and factories of the period were relatively small scale, extremely localized facilities. There were very few "large" cities, and the population in the United States in 1900 was approximately half of what it was in 1950. Disposal of several forms of industrial wastes and by-products by dumping into streams, piling in isolated and remote areas, or discharging into the atmosphere created no recognized problems (Simonds and Grimaldi 1963). In fact, the pollution volume from both city wastes and industrial processes, with few exceptions, was considered to be well within the ability of nature to dilute to safe limits. The primary pollution problem during those early years was sewage and disposal. Little thought was given to the idea of wastewater treatment before disposal, other than some minor attempts at chlorination. Generally, an engineer would design a system that essentially consisted of a network of collecting pipelines that conducted the liquid wastes into a river or other large body of water. Very simply stated, the assurance of a fresh water supply system in early twentieth century industrial America revolved around the ignorance of the population, which led to an unwritten policy of deliberate environmental abuse. Water was taken into a city from an upstream location and discharged with sewage and other wastes back into the downstream flow far below the city. Other cities and towns were so far apart in those days that the stream could be expected to correct the contamination by natural methods before waters reached the next downstream town (Simonds and Grimaldi 1963). Of course, there is no way to verify the accuracy of this *natural dilution* theory, since little if any known or documented health sampling of water supplies occurred during this period in our nation's history. Perhaps an examination of the life expectancy rate, incidence of birth defects and miscarriages, and the frequent occurrence of many life-threatening diseases that existed at the time might provide some indication that natural dilution was not as successful as the industrialists had led themselves to believe.

It would appear that the statement "... *the solution to pollution is dilution,*" which is professed quite often today by many non-environmentalists, is not a new concept at all. Turn-of-the-century American polluters had the same idea. The difference is that those early environmental abusers did not realize the possibility that there are limits as to just how much pollution the environment could swallow before regurgitation occurs.

Throughout the first few decades of the twentieth century, national attention and government priorities focused on one dramatic event after another. From the beginning of the 1900s through and including World War II, pollution control concerns took a back seat to the more pressing issues of the day. Such events as the invention of the aircraft and the dawn of flight, World War I, the mass development of the automobile, Prohibition, and the Great Depression made the idea of pollution control seem somewhat trivial by comparison. It is not difficult to understand, in retrospect, why so much time was to pass between the enactment of the Rivers and Harbors Act in 1899 and the next environmentally significant piece of legislation more than 50 years later.

MILESTONES IN ENVIRONMENTAL POLICY

As stated earlier, by the 1950s the population in the United States had almost doubled that of the early 1900s. As the population level grew, so did the size of cities and towns needed to accommodate the expanding populace. Small cities became large cities, and the distance between major population areas began to gradually shrink. Throughout the decade of the 1950s people slowly became generally aware of the population explosion, and the need to eventually ensure the safe disposal of industrial and domestic wastes was gradually introduced.

First Steps Toward National Awareness

The process of environmental awareness was, perhaps, aided by the enactment of the Atomic Energy Act in 1954. Intended as a revision to the Atomic Energy Act of 1946, which created the now defunct Atomic Energy Commission (AEC), the new Act's purpose was to provide for civilian participation in such programs as research and development and the production of nuclear power. For the first time in history, the general population could take part in the development of regulatory policy in the United States. The Act also broadened the Commission's power to include the regulation of all programs involving the use of atomic energy. This included, but was not limited to, regulation concerning the construction of nuclear power plants, medical and scientific research, medical treatment, and the mining and milling of uranium and other radioactive minerals. However, such civil uses of nuclear energy were also viewed as a double-edged sword: There were obviously tremendous benefits in such programs for the general population. But, these processes also generated radioactive wastes that would pose a serious hazard to humans and the environment if their disposal was an unregulated activity. Hence, because it drew attention to the issue of unregulated waste disposal and its potential effects on humans and the environment, the Atomic Energy Act of 1954 is considered a significant milestone in the history of U.S. environmental policy development.

Focus on Air Pollution

The next event affecting environmental policy development, which also occurred in the 1950s, was the enactment of the Air Pollution Control Act of

1955. To understand how our nation reached a point in its history where it realized a need for federal regulation designed to control air pollution, the history of air pollution itself requires brief examination.

Although the many different types of air pollution to which man has been exposed has changed throughout history, man has actually been *aware* of air pollution problems in larger cities from at least the fourteenth century, when coal was first used for domestic heating. Air pollution has been defined as any undesirable substance mixed with open air (Simonds and Grimaldi 1963). Therefore, any objectionable material (gas, particulate, aerosol, etc.) in the air is an atmospheric pollutant, whether it is harmful or merely unpleasant. The main focus of this explanation of air pollution seems to rest on the level of *objectionability* of the contaminant. In fact, this idea has been the basis of air pollution awareness since well before the discovery of America. In England, during the reign of Edward I (1272–1307), there is a recorded protest by the nobility about the use of "sea" coal, which must have burned in an unusually smoky manner. Under his successor, Edward II (1307–1327), a man was put to torture for filling the air with a "pestilential odor" through the use of coal. Under both Henry V (1413–1422) and Richard III (1483–1485), England attempted to restrict the use of coal fuel through taxation. The situation continued to grow worse and, finally, under the reign of Elizabeth I (1533–1603), the English parliament passed the first known law pertaining to air pollution control, which forbid the use of coal in the city of London while parliament was in session (Traister 1990). Granted, the scope of this law ignored the health and welfare of the general public and was only concerned with that of the parliamentarians. However, the law still stands as an indication of early historical concerns over the hazards associated with air pollutants.

These concerns were obviously transferred to the English colonies in the United States along with other English customs, philosophies, principles, and life-style practices. In fact, air pollution problems in the United States were first attributed to coal smoke. As early as 1881, the city of Chicago had adopted a smoke control ordinance. In the years that followed, large cities such as St. Louis, Cincinnati, and Pittsburgh also adopted similar ordinances. During these early years of the U.S. Industrial Revolution, it was an established principle that the responsibility for air pollution controls rested with those states and local (city) governments where such pollution was considered to be of concern (Traister 1990).

From 1930 to 1941, the focus of air pollution was on attempts to regulate and control the emission of smoke rather than on the basic cause of the emissions. However, air pollution was still not recognized as the health hazard we know it to be today, and little progress was made during this period. When the United States declared war on Japan in December 1941, there was a national call to defeat the countries of Germany and Japan once and for all. As a result, any efforts to curb air pollution during this period were virtually nonexistent.

However, an environmentally significant event did surface during the years of World War II. A new type of air pollutant was discovered in the atmosphere over Los Angeles, California. The population began to experience eye and skin irritation, and evidence of plant and foliage damage was discovered throughout the city and surrounding areas. These problems had never been evident from simple exposure to smoke pollution. Studies revealed the presence of a *photochemical smog* and was at first attributed to the oil refineries and storage facilities that had increased productivity to support the war effort. However, when control of these facilities did not result in a significant reduction of the problem, it was then discovered that the internal combustion engine was a major cause of this new type of pollution (Traister 1990). In simple terms, *smog* occurs as a result of two primary actions: the presence of a high level of atmospheric smoke/pollutants in a concentrated area, and the occurrence of a temperature inversion that causes the cooler air in the upper atmosphere to quickly descend and remain close to the earth's surface (carrying the suspended, highly concentrated air pollutants with it). Since the discovery of photochemical smog as an air pollutant, several unfortunate tragedies, referred to as *air pollution episodes* by the EPA, have occurred in large industrial cities in the United States and throughout the world that have been attributed to the presence of high levels of smog in the atmosphere. Such events ultimately led to the enactment of some of the first legislation in the world to deal directly with environmental concerns. Some of the more famous of these regrettable events are described below:

- Donora, Pennsylvania: October 1948. An industrial city located approximately 20 miles southeast of Pittsburgh that produced excessive amounts of smoke pollution from steel, zinc, and sulfuric acid plants. Smoke pollution in this area occurred over a period of many years, and the local population grew accustomed to its presence. However, a temperature inversion in the atmosphere over Donora in the fall of 1948 caused air pollution to accumulate to such high levels that several thousand people became ill. A great many required hospitalization and 20 people died (Traister 1990).
- Poza Rica, Mexico: November 1950. A new plant designed to recover sulfur from natural gas put a portion of its equipment into operation. One of the steps in the process was the removal of hydrogen sulfide from the natural gas. A large amount of concentrated hydrogen sulfide escaped into the air on a morning when winds were calm and a thermal inversion enclosed the area. 320 people were hospitalized and 22 died (Traister 1990).

- London, England: December 1952. For several days the British Isles were covered with a thick fog and thermal inversion. The windless weather prevented the dispersion of air pollutants which were most heavily concentrated over London. The resulting accumulation of smog caused the most devastating smog-related human disaster in modern history. London hospitals were overwhelmed with admissions for heart disease problems and respiratory ailments. In the end, over 4,000 deaths were attributed to the smog condition (Traister 1990). However, since deaths continued for weeks after the weather improved, some accounts have estimated that nearly 8,000 people died as a direct result of the previous winter's smog episode (Simonds and Grimaldi 1963).

  London experienced a similar event in 1956 when a killer smog took the lives of 1,000 people in an 18-hour period. In November 1962, even after implementing a serious and comprehensive smog control scheme, London again fell victim to a smog episode that claimed another 750 lives.

- New York City: November 1953. The most severe smog-related disaster in the United States occurred during an 11-day period in the Fall of 1953. Again, the conditions were perfect for catastrophe. New York City was engulfed in a windless, thermal inversion. The slow drift of this huge stagnant air mass resulted in an accumulation of air pollutants over an area that included the industrial regions of Ohio, Pennsylvania, New Jersey, and New England. In this case, the effects of the smog exposure were gradual, as compared to the immediate results experienced in London and Donora. However, official reports attributed between 175 and 260 deaths to the smog event of 1953.

These are just a few examples of the many documented incidents that have occurred during the last half of this century. It is assumed that many more deaths occurred that could not be attributed directly to these incidents because of the time (sometimes many years) it takes for certain diseases to manifest after an exposure. As a result of these examples of man-caused environmental disasters, there are some lessons to be learned. For instance, automobiles have been prevalent in the modern world since the 1920s. However, we did not fully realize the effect of the internal combustion engine on our fragile atmosphere until many years later. The frightening lesson to be learned from this history requires us to consider what types of damage we are causing ourselves and our environment today, through new chemical processes currently being practiced and/or developed. The ozone issue, the greenhouse dilemma/global warming, and so on are modern-day concerns that threaten disaster on a scale perhaps several orders of magnitude greater than those caused by the smog events of previous years.

In an effort to gain some control over the early concerns of smog and air pollution, Congress enacted the Air Pollution Control Act of 1955. The Act required the U.S. Public Health Service (PHS) to carry out extensive research and to assist the states and local communities in the control of air pollution. Even though the Act did not go further by attacking the actual source of air pollution, it was the first real attempt in this country to address the problem on a national level. The Air Pollution Control Act of 1955 is seen as the predecessor of today's Clean Air Act.

In 1963, Congress enacted the first version of a Clean Air Act to enlarge the duties of the PHS by providing for an accelerated research and training program. The Act also provided for the development of specific air quality criteria and established a program of matching grants to state and local agencies that initiate their own air pollution control mandates.

Then, with the enactment of the Clean Air Act of 1967, regulatory concentration finally began to focus on the actual cause and effects of pollution. Under the provisions of this second version of the Clean Air Act, the PHS was required to study *cause and effect aspects* and designate those pollutants considered to be of major concern. After its studies, the PHS was required to issue Criteria Documents on individual pollutants citing actual levels of concentration in ambient air at which point unfavorable effects would result. The PHS would then have to identify known methods for emission control. Also, PHS was to study those regions in the nation where common or uniform pollution control regulations should be established. These areas became known as Air Quality Control Regions. Finally, the Clean Air Act of 1967 required states to adopt air quality standards compatible with the PHS-established Criteria Documents.

By 1970, it was obvious to the federal legislators that additional changes had to be made in the existing Clean Air Act based almost entirely on the fact that the EPA was created that same year. An explanation of the changes in national air pollution control strategies from 1970 onward is not within the scope of this chapter, but will be addressed later in this text.

Final Stages Toward a Definitive Environmental Strategy

On January 1, 1970, President Richard Nixon signed into law the National Environmental Policy Act (NEPA), which ushered in a decade of legislative activity in the field of environmental protection (Wentz 1989). Responsibility for coordinating and implementing the various provisions of NEPA was given to a new executive branch agency called the Council on Environmental Quality (CEQ). Chapter 5 will provide a detailed discussion on the requirements contained in NEPA. By the end of that same year, the EPA was created

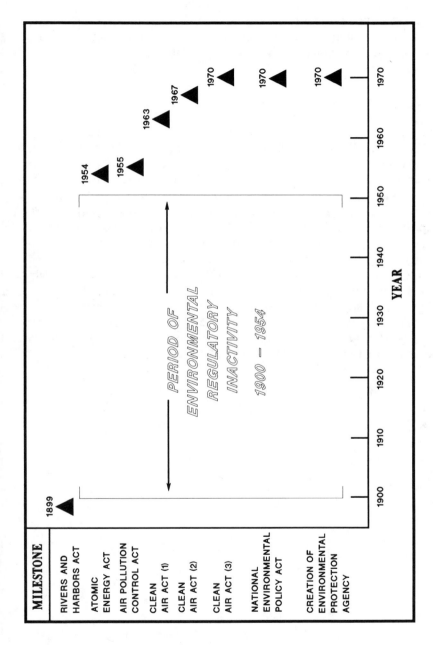

FIGURE 1-1. Pre-1970 environmental regulation milestones. (Source: EPA)

11

by Presidential Executive Order. Figure 1-1 summarizes the milestones in environmental policy as discussed in this chapter.

During the two decades that followed the creation of the EPA this country would witness a dramatic increase in environmental awareness and concern, as well as a proliferation of environmental regulatory actions on the federal, state, and local levels.

SUMMARY

Although the history of environmental awareness can be traced back hundreds of years, the establishment of formal environmental policy in the United States did not occur until the beginning of this century, with the enactment of the Rivers and Harbors Act of 1899. However, until the 1950s, the Rivers and Harbors Act remained the only significant piece of legislation to address the issue of environmental pollution, even though it was indirect.

During and immediately following World War II, attention on a newly discovered pollutant called *photochemical smog* heightened public awareness of the disastrous effects of man's endless assault on the environment and also, for the first time, indicated the possibility that Earth's atmosphere might be more fragile than few could have ever anticipated or imagined.

From 1950 through 1970, the primary focus of environmental policy development centered on the highly visible issue of *air pollution*. During these years, Congress enacted several key pieces of legislation that eventually lead to the creation of the EPA at the end of 1970.

2

The U.S. Environmental Protection Agency

INTRODUCTION

The *U.S. Environmental Protection Agency ("USEPA" or "EPA")* was created as an independent agency of the U.S. government by President Richard M. Nixon as a result of an Executive Order entitled "Reorganization Plan 3 of 1970." The "creation" of a federal agency by executive order rather than by an act of the legislative branch is somewhat of an exception to the rule. This process will be discussed in greater detail in Chapter 3, "The Regulatory Process."

It is important to note that the EPA is certainly not the only federal regulatory agency involved in national environmental policy formation, but it is in fact the primary one. For example, the U.S. Department of Transportation (DOT), the U.S. Department of Labor (DOL) under the Occupational Safety and Health Administration (OSHA), and the U.S. Department of Energy (DOE) have all promulgated regulations aimed at environmental protection and the control of environmental hazards. However, detailed analysis of each of these organizations is beyond the scope of this *Basic Guide to Environmental Compliance*. For the purpose and intent of this text, the concentration shall primarily be on the EPA. Chapter 12 will present a brief discussion on the environmental activities of other federal agencies.

The EPA became an executive branch on December 2, 1970, and was originally designed to consolidate a variety of activities, including environmental research, monitoring, and enforcement activities into one agency. In general, it superseded and assumed most all of the activities of the former Environmental Health Service (an agency of the then Department of Health, Education and Welfare). The EPA is headed by an Administrator who, at the time of this publication, is not part of the President's Cabinet. The EPA reports to the President through the Office of Management and Budget (OMB). In recent years, proposals have been put forward to include the EPA on the President's Cabinet. Based upon the growing importance and visibility of environmental policy in the United States (and the world), there is a high probability that such proposals will eventually succeed.

Initially, the idea of a federal agency designed to ensure the protection of national environmental health did not win a great deal of meaningful support from the majority of the bureaucrats on Capitol Hill. Early budgets were meager and, in fact, as of this writing, the EPA's main headquarters in Washington, D.C. is still located in the same old condominium once owned by Vice President Spiro Agnew (who had trouble selling it through normal real estate channels).

During the two decades following its creation, the EPA has witnessed a gradual and steady growth in public concern for the environment, and, today, such concern has never held a higher place on the country's social, economic, and political agendas. This heightened awareness continues, amplified sporadically by such events as the massive oil spill in Alaska's Prince William Sound and the *environmental terrorism* of Saddam Hussein in the Persian Gulf. Appalling disasters such as these draw international attention to the serious environmental damage and long-lasting consequences of man-caused pollution extremes.

Throughout its first decade, the EPA focused primarily on the implementation of major environmental legislation enacted by Congress during the 1970s. Once implemented, so much of its limited resources were concentrated on interpretation and applicability that very little actual enforcement or compliance-assurance activities took place. During its second decade of existence, the EPA began to finally turn its attention to the problem of enforcing the many statutes. However, critics then and now believe that during the 1980s the EPA did not demonstrate a serious commitment to enforcement. As with all issues of this nature, the desired level of government commitment is typically based upon the particular special interests of individual legislators and their constituents rather than on genuine concern. Evidence of this can be seen in a cursory review of the variety of platform statements and political controversies during the 1988 Presidential campaign (then Vice-President Bush wished to be referred to as the *Environmental Candidate* at a high point during the campaign). By 1991 and early 1992, the issue of the environment and environmental health had become an issue of such national and, therefore, political importance that all the 1992 Presidential candidates had prepared carefully constructed position statements concerning U.S. environmental policy. These events are quite remarkable considering the fact that, in just 20 years, concern for the environment has moved from being viewed as a *national fad* to a national political and social issue that a new generation of American voters insist be addressed by candidates for the Presidency of the United States.

The vigorous political debates during these campaigns, coupled with the actions of President Bush concerning the Clean Air Act and the accelerated phase-out of *chlorofluorocarbons (CFCs)* in the United States, indicate that the decade of the 1990s will be a period of even greater emphasis on civil as well as criminal environmental policy enforcement. Enforcement will also be on the rise on the state and local levels, where environmental regulations are often much stricter than federally mandated requirements.

Even federal agencies, such as the National Aeronautics and Space Administration (NASA), the U.S. Department of Defense (DOD), and the U.S. Department of Energy (DOE), have discovered in recent years that their once professed (and often abused) *sovereign immunity* does not apply in most cases involving violations of federally mandated environmental law.

The private sector, recovering from a devastating economic recession, responded to the concern over heightened environmental enforcement in a variety of ways. From one extreme to the other, examples can be found of corporate actions (or inactions) in response to EPA requirements. Some have created new departments within their respective organizations to focus entirely on environmental compliance. Others have chosen to ignore the issue completely in the failing hope that *it just won't happen to them.* The most common attempt to address this issue, without a significant direct impact on operating costs, has been to combine environmental compliance activities with that of occupational safety and health functions, thereby avoiding any increase in necessary manpower levels. Unfortunately, this management option has placed a tremendous burden on those practicing safety and health professionals who have very little, if any, substantive training in the area of environmental compliance. To make this complicated development worse, the task of environmental management has evolved and expanded almost beyond reasonable comprehension during the past 20 years. Simply ensuring that all required permits are obtained is no longer sufficient. In order to avoid substantial environmental liability, the practicing environmental professional must pursue an aggressive, proactive approach to environmental compliance. Hence, a poorly advised individual or organizational element responsible for environmental regulatory awareness and compliance could create a significant amount of economic, social, and political damage to a firm by either taking no action when such is required or, possibly even worse, taking the wrong action.

ORGANIZATIONAL STRUCTURE
OF THE EPA

The current organizational structure of the EPA can be summarized as follows (Figure 2-1, Source: EPA):

- Administrator—Heads the EPA. Appointed by the President, with consent of the Senate.
- Associate Administrator: Office of Regional Operations and State/Local Relations—Serves as a link between EPA headquarters and the regional administrators.
- Associate Administrator: Office of Communications and Public Affairs— The liaison between the public sector and the agency. Releases all official EPA communications regarding policy and activity.
- Associate Administrator: Office of Congressional and Legislative Affairs—Maintains and ensures close coordination between the agency and Congress regarding past, current, and/or proposed rule-making activities.
- Assistant Administrator: Office of International Activities—Coordinates and supervises the EPA's international programs and activities and serves as a liaison with other international environmental organizations.
- Office of the Inspector General—Responsible for audits and investigations relating to the EPA, and reports any serious problems, abuses, and deficiencies relating to EPA programs and operations to the Administrator and to Congress.
- Office of General Counsel—Serves as a legal advisor to the Administrator and provides other legal services to the EPA.

In addition to the above listed positions, the EPA has eight other operational offices, each with its own Assistant Administrator, as shown in Figure 2-1. Also indicated in Figure 2-1, the EPA has ten regional offices throughout the United States. The main functions of the regional offices are to implement the many EPA programs and to coordinate environmental activities with state, interstate, and local agencies. Because they are often required to act on behalf of the Administrator, the regional offices have considerable authority and enforcement powers. Figure 2-2 shows the current geographical location and regional breakdown of each of the ten regional offices.

CONGRESSIONAL ACTIONS:
ENVIRONMENTAL LAWS UNDER THE EPA

In Chapter 1, those laws that were enacted by Congress prior to the 1970 creation of the EPA were briefly examined and discussed. Figure 1-1 showed these laws as major milestones of U.S. environmental policy up to 1970. Since

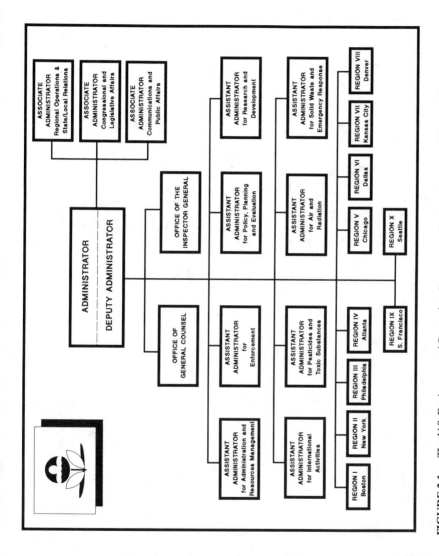

FIGURE 2-1. The U.S. Environmental Protection Agency organizational structure. (Source: EPA)

FIGURE 2-2. Regional boundaries of the U.S. Environmental Protection Agency. (Source: EPA)

STATE	REGION	STATE	REGION	STATE	REGION	STATE	REGION	STATE	REGION
Alabama	4	Hawaii	9	Michigan	5	North Carolina	4	Utah	8
Alaska	10	Idaho	10	Minnesota	5	North Dakota	8	Vermont	1
Arizona	9	Illinois	5	Mississippi	4	Ohio	5	Virginia	3
Arkansas	6	Indiana	5	Missouri	7	Oklahoma	6	Washington	10
California	9	Iowa	7	Montana	8	Oregon	10	West Virginia	3
Colorado	8	Kansas	7	Nebraska	7	Pennsylvania	3	Wisconsin	5
Connecticut	1	Kentucky	4	Nevada	9	Rhode Island	1	Wyoming	8
Delaware	3	Louisiana	6	New Hampshire	1	South Carolina	4	American Samoa	9
D.C.	3	Maine	1	New Jersey	2	South Dakota	8	Guam	9
Florida	4	Maryland	3	New Mexico	6	Tennessee	4	Puerto Rico	2
Georgia	4	Massachusetts	1	New York	2	Texas	6	Virgin Islands	2

its creation, the EPA has become the primary responsible agency for ensuring the enforcement of all federally mandated statutes concerning environmental health and protection. During the past two decades, Congressional activity in this area has steadily increased. Figure 2-3 shows the major milestones in environmental policy that have occurred since 1970, with the individual laws summarized below.

- Clean Air Act (CAA)—Almost immediately after its creation, the EPA was required to implement the provisions of the Clean Air Act of 1970. Essentially, the major focus of this second revision of the Clean Air Act of 1963 (the first revision occurred in 1967) was to transfer responsibility for its implementation to the new Environmental Protection Agency. The Act was again significantly revised and amended in 1990.
- Clean Water Act (CWA)—Basically established in 1972 with the passage of the Federal Water Pollution Control Act (FWPCA) Amendments. The CWA has been the subject of two major amendments—the Clean Water Amendments of 1977 and the Water Quality Act of 1987. The CWA was scheduled for reauthorization in 1992, as this text was being prepared.
- Federal Insecticide, Fungicide and Rodenticide Act (FIFRA)—Originally adopted in 1949, FIFRA was substantially amended in 1972 and again in 1978. It was not viewed as a major source of environmental policy until the 1972 amendments. In general, FIFRA's purpose is to ensure that society reaps the benefits of pesticide use, with minimum risk to human health and the environment.
- Hazardous Material Transportation Act (HMTA)—The HMTA, passed in 1975 and enforced by the U.S. Department of Transportation (DOT), is intended to improve regulatory and enforcement activities by providing the Secretary of Transportation broad authority to set regulations applicable to all aspects concerning the transportation of hazardous materials.
- Toxic Substances Control Act (TSCA)—Signed into law in 1976, TSCA gave the EPA broad and comprehensive authority to regulate and control the introduction and use of new chemicals into or exported out of the United States.
- Resource Conservation and Recovery Act (RCRA)—Enacted in 1976 as an amendment to the Solid Waste Disposal Act (SWDA) and significantly amended in 1980 and again in 1984. The Act addresses the regulation of solid wastes (both hazardous and nonhazardous) and, under the 1984 amendments, the regulation of underground storage tanks (UST).
- Comprehensive Environmental Response, Compensation and Liabilities Act (CERCLA)—Also known as "Superfund," CERCLA was enacted by Congress in 1980 in the wake of a number of well-publicized environmen-

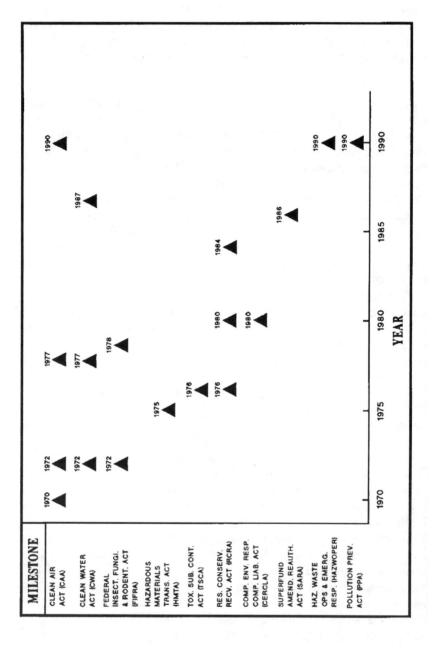

FIGURE 2-3. Post-1970 environmental regulation milestones. (Source: EPA)

tal disasters, such as New York's Love Canal and Kentucky's "Valley of the Drums."

- Superfund Amendments and Reauthorization Act (SARA)—Although actually a 1986 amendment to CERCLA, SARA presented new and challenging requirements to both the EPA, in terms of implementation and enforcement of reporting requirements, and, under its Title III, to industry in terms of compliance.
- Hazardous Waste Operations and Emergency Response (HAZWOPER) —Implemented and enforced by the U.S. DOL under OSHA, this standard, which took effect in March 1990, is intended to address training and qualification requirements for all personnel designated to handle or work with hazardous wastes during the normal course of their assigned duties.
- Pollution Prevention Act (PPA)—In 1990, Congress enacted PPA, whose primary intent is to encourage industry to reduce the amount of hazardous waste generated during the manufacturing process. The Act also contained several important new provisions that expanded the reporting requirements under SARA, Title III (Emergency Planning and Community Right-to-Know Act of 1986).

The particular laws summarized above emphasize the dramatic increase in the formulation of U.S. environmental policy since the creation of the EPA. There is no indication that the pace of such rule-making activities will begin to slow during the third decade of EPA existence.

ENVIRONMENTAL POLICIES
AND PROGRAMS

As an agency of the executive branch of government, the EPA performs legislative, judicial, and enforcement functions. When the EPA engages in the rule-making process, it is actually performing many of the functions normally associated with the legislative process and, therefore, it is actually *making* policy. All organizations and/or individuals that fall within the scope of this policy are automatically required to comply with its requirements. Two primary EPA policies that require close monitoring are the complementary policies of enforcement and compliance inspection. In recent years, the EPA has continued to place increasing emphasis on *criminal enforcement* of environmental law. It is during the inspection process that many violations are uncovered, and enforcement then becomes necessary through a system of fines and penalties. Therefore, each of these two policies shall be examined separately to demonstrate how current enforcement philosophy and inspection policy affects the compliance activities of those involved.

Enforcement of Environmental Policy

In order to ensure compliance with environmental regulatory requirements, the EPA has embarked on a somewhat aggressive enforcement strategy in recent years aimed not only at the serious violators of these requirements, but also at those who are guilty of relatively minor noncompliance activities. An examination of the statistics on environmental crimes during the 1980s supports the fact that the government has directed ever-increasing resources towards criminal enforcement policies. For example, in 1984 the EPA referred only 31 cases to the Department of Justice (DOJ) for criminal prosecution of environmental lawbreakers. Of these, only 14 were successfully prosecuted. Even though 36 defendants were charged, only 26 were actually convicted. These 26 served a cumulative total of only 6 months in jail. However, records show that these numbers have steadily increased. In fact, for the period 1983 to 1990, the DOJ had obtained more than 660 indictments for violations of environmental laws, which resulted in more than 510 convictions. A total of $31.8 million in fines had been collected, and more than 316 cumulative years of imprisonment were imposed. The DOJ has stated that its policy regarding environmental compliance violations is to identify, prosecute, and convict the highest-ranking responsible individuals in the corporate structure. In fact, during 1989 alone, corporate officer defendants were sentenced to a total of 51 years imprisonment and fined approximately $12 million. To make matters worse, Congress has increased the potential fines for all criminal violations, which includes violation of environmental statutes. A felony conviction can cost a corporation up to $500,000 per violation and an individual up to $250,000 (noting that the corporation is not permitted to cover a fine imposed against an individual corporate officer).

There is no indication that the level of attention placed on criminal enforcement policies will decrease in the near future. In fact, after nearly a decade of some of the toughest enforcement activities in EPA history, a demand for even tougher enforcement strategies was issued by the chief executive. In a nationally televised address before Congress in February 1989, President Bush directed both the Attorney General and the Administrator of the EPA to *strengthen the level and speed of environmental law enforcement against those guilty of the disposal of toxic wastes.* He demanded faster cleanups and tougher penalties against environmental polluters. The very next month, the new EPA Administrator, William Reilly, informed the Senate Environment and Public Works Committee that the EPA would place its highest priority on strong enforcement of environmental regulations.

Under current EPA regulatory guidelines, criminal violations of environmental statutes differ from those imposed for other white collar criminal prosecutions in a number of important ways. For example, violations differ dependent upon which environmental statute is involved. The *false statement provision* in the Clean Water Act is not the same as that in RCRA, and both are different than the general false statement provision in Title 18 of the U.S. Code (IAML 1991). Violations also differ depending upon the intent, or *state-of-mind,* of the violator at the time the crime was committed. Basically, there are three levels of violation:

- Negligent violations (i.e., the violator was openly negligent regarding responsibility under the law, either through ignorance or simple carelessness);
- Knowing violations (i.e., those that occur with the full knowledge of responsible individual or parties, with no attempt on their part to prevent the violation; likened to a *willful violation* of OSHA law); and
- Knowing endangerment violations (i.e., those violations, allowed to occur with the violators' full knowledge, that impose a threat of death or serious bodily injury).

Fines and penalties for the various levels of violations are dependent upon the specific regulation or act being violated. For example, monetary fines under the Clean Water Act differ from those under RCRA. In general, however, fines range from a low of $2,500 to $25,000 per day per violation up to a maximum fine against individuals of $250,000, with up to 15 years imprisonment. It is also important to note that the government can establish criminal liability of any employee, regardless of position in the corporation, by demonstrating that the individual took specific action(s) that violated one of the many environmental statutes. This is true for all employees at all organizational levels.

Due to the increasingly complicated issue of the EPA's criminal enforcement of environmental policy, the safety and health professional new to the field of environmental compliance should take all appropriate actions to ensure proper understanding of environmental liability. Focusing compliance efforts on only a portion of applicable statutory requirements due to simple ignorance is a dangerous and potentially career-ending approach to the issue of environmental compliance.

EPA Inspection Policies

One of the EPA's primary methods of uncovering violations that leads to criminal enforcement is that of environmental inspections. An inspection, which differs from the *environmental audit* discussed in Chapter 4, can occur at any time, and organizations should be prepared to respond appropriately. Virtually every major environmental statute contains provisions that authorize the EPA to conduct inspections. Also, when the EPA issues an environmental permit pursuant to any EPA regulations, the permit holder automatically becomes obligated to allow EPA inspections of applicable facilities covered by the permit.

EPA inspections are performed for a variety of reasons, not the least of which is to ensure compliance with environmental law. The EPA may also *target* a particular facility for an inspection as part of its general administrative plan for enforcement of environmental statutes. Inspections provide an excellent method of obtaining data on the various waste-handling and disposal practices throughout the United States. In the past, EPA inspections under RCRA have helped to identify previously unreported Superfund sites for CERCLA.

Currently, the EPA has approximately 2,000 field inspectors and utilizes a *multimedia approach* to its inspection process. By formulating small inspection teams, whose individual members may have expertise in one specific area of environmental compliance, the EPA can effectively cover more than one environmental media during the inspection. For example, while one member of the team is searching for violations and/or compliance with the requirements of RCRA, another may be focusing on Clean Air Act regulations, and still another member may be concentrating on stormwater discharge provisions and other applicable aspects of the Clean Water Act.

Constitutional Considerations

Search Warrants

It is important to note at this point that inspections occurring under the authority of the EPA are not without consideration of Fourth Amendment Constitutional law. In most cases, business establishments and commercial facilities cannot be searched without presentation of an appropriate search warrant. There are three exceptions to this requirement, which require Congressional approval before warrantless inspections can occur:

1. In situations where Congress has expressly determined that warrantless inspections are necessary in order to enforce one of its regulatory goals and where federal regulatory presence is so comprehensive and defined that the owner of the establishment is fully aware of the possibility of a periodic inspection;
2. In those situations where Congress expressly dispensed with the warrant requirement for reasons specific to the individual case; and
3. Those businesses characterized as being *closely regulated* (liquor, firearms, automobile junk yards) for which the federal government has substantial interest in ensuring regulatory compliance.

Administrative Warrants

Administrative warrants are issued to the EPA without the need to demonstrate the existence of probable cause, as opposed to criminal law requirements. Administrative warrants are issued on the specific evidence that an existing violation has or is occurring. The EPA may also obtain an administrative warrant upon showing that reasonable legislative or administrative standards for conducting an inspection are satisfied with respect to a particular establishment. Such warrants, however, are only appropriate if the intended purpose of the inspection is to discover and correct noncompliance with regulatory requirements through civil (not criminal) procedure.

Criminal Search Warrants

If the intent of an inspection is to gather information to be used as evidence in a possible criminal prosecution, then the EPA is required to request that the U.S. Attorney obtain a criminal search warrant. In order to successfully secure a criminal search warrant, the U.S. Attorney must demonstrate that there is sufficient and probable cause to believe that evidence of an environmental crime will be discovered as a result of the requested inspection. Once such a warrant is obtained, the scope of the inspection must strictly adhere to the requirements specified in the warrant. Also, it should be noted that evidence obtained during a valid civil (noncriminal) inspection may be used as admissible evidence subsequent to any future criminal proceedings.

In addition to the three types of warrant searches briefly discussed above, the EPA may also conduct valid inspections without securing a warrant. Inspections where the federal officer remains in a public area and does not enter any facility are considered valid. The use of binoculars and/or telephotographic equipment to enhance such an inspection is not expressly prohibited. Also, aerial photography is within the EPA statutory inspection authority; therefore, no warrant is required.

The EPA Inspection

It is essential for an organization whose business activities could possibly be subject to an EPA environmental inspection to take necessary action to ensure that they are ready for such an occurrence well *before* the inspector arrives at the facility. Assuming that any and all noncompliant conditions have been identified and corrected, the organization should survive a pending EPA inspection with little need for any additional compliance actions. The following is a brief summary of the inspection process, which should provide a basic understanding of the fundamental elements of a simple EPA inspection.

Pre-Inspection Activity

The primary concern prior to an inspection should be the identification of a specific person to accompany the EPA official during the inspection (NOTE: It is understood that many U.S. states with their own environmental plans also conduct inspections and the inspector may, therefore, not always be from the EPA. However, for simplification, only the EPA will be referred to in this explanation.) This person should be identified well in advance and should be made available during the entire inspection. This designated company representative should be congenial, non-adversarial, professional, possess a thorough knowledge of company operations and procedures, and be familiar with the environmental statutes applicable to the organization. If there are any environmental permits in use, the person should know and understand the terms and conditions of each.

Once the designated representative has been selected and agreed upon by management, all appropriate personnel in the organization, including receptionists and security guards (if applicable), should be made aware of his or her identity. This company representative will act as a liaison between the inspector and the organization to ensure, to the greatest extent possible, cooperation during the inspection. When the inspector arrives at the facility, the designated representative should examine the identifying credentials of the federal officer as well as the inspection notice. If the company has legal personnel, they should be contacted as often as necessary during the inspection by the designated representative.

Notification of a Pending Inspection

In general, the EPA will provide advance notice, usually by telephone, for most routine inspections. Only when there is a genuine concern that physical conditions might be altered or documents destroyed if a facility has prior notice will unannounced inspections be conducted. Shortly before an announced inspection is to occur, the company will receive a notification letter from the appropriate EPA office specifying the authority for the inspection and outlining the areas to be covered during the inspection. Safety and health professionals will note that this approach is in marked contrast to the inspection process under OSHA law, where, with few exceptions, advance notification of an OSHA inspection is illegal and punishable by fine, imprisonment, or both.

Preparation

Company environmental personnel should locate all relevant documents and be prepared to make them available during the inspection. Appropriate pre-inspection tours should also be performed by management, environmental personnel, and, if applicable, legal representatives checking for environmental compliance or noncompliance, as the case may be. It is not advisable that quick efforts to rapidly correct long-standing violating conditions be attempted during a pre-inspection tour. Such actions are highly visible to employees, will obviously be discernible to an astute inspector, and could result in an even greater fine for attempting to *cover up* evidence of a long history of noncompliance. Finally, prior to the arrival of the inspecting official, all employees should be notified of the impending inspection.

The Opening Conference

All inspections require an opening conference where introductions take place, official credentials are presented for all members of the inspection team, warrants are provided for inspection by the company, the scope and purpose of the inspection is announced as well as the legal authority to conduct it, and the specific inspection procedures that will be utilized are outlined.

The opening conference is also the point in the inspection process where each side may establish certain ground rules. For example, there may be highly classified areas of a facility where, due to matters of national security, other government agencies (such as the DOD or the DOE) may strictly prohibit inspections. If there are areas where specific *personal protective equipment (PPE)* is required, the company should make arrangements to provide all necessary PPE to the inspection team. It is also important to note that the environmental statutes only give the EPA inspectors authority to conduct a few specific activities. The EPA is authorized to inspect, to have access to and copy documents relating to hazardous wastes, to obtain samples and labels from containers, and to check monitoring equipment for adequacy. Also, it is considered unreasonable for the EPA to force an inspection after normal business hours. Another major difference between the OSHA and EPA inspection process is that EPA inspectors, unlike OSHA's, have no statutory right to interrogate or question production line employees. All questions should be directed to the designated representative in charge of the inspection.

It is also permissible and advisable to ask the inspector if the EPA has received specific complaint allegations regarding the facility and whether the facility is under investigation or if the inspection is simply part of the agency's general administrative plan.

Samples, Photographs, and Company Records

As stated above, the EPA does have authority to take samples. If the inspector chooses to exercise this option during the inspection, the company representative should always take a sample at the same time for analysis and comparison. Also, a facility has the right under both RCRA and CERCLA to receive duplicates of any resultant sample reports. The request should be made during the inspection.

There are no statutory provisions that authorize the EPA to take photographs during an on-site facility inspection. However, if such photographs are to be used as a method of aiding in the inspector's recollection of facility layout and organization, then such photographs have been permitted by the courts in the past. The EPA has no right to take photographs of trade secrets or classified information. The law requires the EPA to ensure that all photographs will be kept confidential. The company should request duplicates and keep a log of any photographs taken by the EPA during the inspection.

The EPA can examine and copy various company records that are determined applicable to the scope of the investigation. Information that the company is not required to maintain by environmental law, such as certain personnel records, should not be divulged during an inspection. Also, if information is considered privileged and confidential to the company, these records should be kept separate from those subject to inspection by the EPA. During the opening conference, the designated representative should assert the claim to confidential or privileged information. If this is not done, then the privilege is considered waived.

The Exit Conference

An exit conference may not always occur under normal procedure. However, the company should always exercise its right to request one in order to ascertain whether or not the inspectors found any compliance problems or areas where improvement would be recommended. The company can also take the opportunity to formally request a copy of the inspection report. It should be noted that, if the individual inspector should refuse, for whatever reason, to release a copy of the report, one may be obtained by filing a Freedom of Information Act request. It is also of utmost importance that no representative of an inspected company should sign or in any way accept or confirm the inspector's report. A signature on the report could be used against the company during any subsequent EPA enforcement proceedings (or by citizens' groups once the report is made public).

Post Inspection

After the inspection is complete, the designated representative should immediately prepare an internal report of everything that took place during the inspection. The results of the inspection should be communicated to management as well as company legal representatives. Management is responsible for ensuring that all necessary corrective actions are properly implemented in a timely manner. Also, management should consider notifying the EPA of those corrective actions and of any errors that may be contained in the inspector's report.

With EPA criminal enforcement policies getting increasingly more complex and compliance inspections occurring more frequently than ever before, it is essential for the environmental professional to have a more-than-adequate understanding of these policies. It is obvious that the possibility of criminal enforcement for environmental noncompliance should never be ignored. If it is, then the lack of proper preparation before an inspection could result in a rather rude introduction to the EPA's enforcement policies.

THE EPA: TODAY AND TOMORROW

The EPA has evolved into an extremely powerful agency of the executive branch of the U.S. government, with a comprehensive authority to implement and enforce numerous environmental regulations. The agency and its activities influence the broad spectrum of our nation's social, economic, and political arenas. During a time when national concern has focused upon budgetary overruns and spending cutbacks, the EPA continues to grow, its enforcement activities expand, and the frequency of environmental compliance inspections are on the rise.

The policies and programs developed and implemented over the years by the EPA have caused such a dramatic increase in the level of national awareness for the environment that the media has coined the phrase *the green initiative*. While this initiative is by no means a direct product of EPA action, it is obvious that the regulatory and enforcement activities of the agency have contributed to the development of the green initiative. Essentially, the green initiative describes the amount of importance placed upon environmental concerns during the daily conduct of business today. For example, *consumers* and the general public can create such pressure on industry for environmental change that companies such as McDonald's have done away with Styrofoam containers and have gone back to wrapping their food items in biodegradable paper. The green initiative also effects the *insurance* industries. Many carriers now demand information on a company's past environmental performance before determining premium levels. *Lending institutions* are now requesting such details during business loan processing. Finally, the *media* is also concentrating heavily on environmental concerns. Nothing draws attention more than headlines or news stories about environmental abuse.

Considering the many dramatic worldwide changes that have occurred during the previous decade (the fall of the communist empire, former *enemies* of democracy wishing to enter the world market, the unification of economic Europe, etc.), it is not inconceivable that the EPA might take on more of a global advisory role in the formulation of worldwide environmental policy.

This is despite the seemingly dismal failure of our nation's representation at the Earth Summit in Rio during the summer of 1992. U.S. environmental responsibilities around the world are more far reaching than any one, single conference event. For example, as the former republics of the Soviet Union begin to experiment with democracy and the freedom to regulate their own futures, it is fact that many have already developed fundamental environmental policies based almost entirely on existing U.S. environmental law. As worldwide concerns for environmental protection increase, other nations may also look to the EPA for examples and initiatives aimed at further reductions and stiffer restrictions on the pollution of the global environment. China recently adapted nearly all existing USEPA regulations as their own.

Based upon the many changes that have occurred during the previous decade, we are not likely to see any reduction in the activities of the EPA in the near future. In fact, it is probably safe to assume that just the opposite is likely to occur. As we approach the end of the twentieth century and the first 30 years of EPA existence, it is almost certain that the strength and authority of this agency will continue to grow in direct proportion to America's ever-increasing awareness of the importance of environmental compliance.

SUMMARY

From the moment it was created, the EPA was charged with the responsibility of protecting our environment and maintaining it for future generations. While the EPA is not the only regulatory agency concerned with environmental policy, it is certainly the primary one. The proliferation of environmental regulations that have emerged during the first two decades of EPA existence is testimony to the increasing level of importance our nation has placed upon the issue of environmental protection during the last half of this century.

Through proactive, comprehensive policies, such as criminal enforcement and compliance inspections, the EPA has demonstrated in recent years that abuse of the environment, whether purposeful or accidental, will no longer be tolerated. Working with the Department of Justice, the EPA has witnessed a remarkable increase in the rate of successful prosecutions and convictions of those who violate environmental law. Neither individuals nor their corporations are immune to the potential threat of EPA criminal enforcement actions. One primary method the EPA uses to gather data and seek out violators is the inspection process. Proper compliance actions, preparation, and subsequent conduct during such an inspection may help a company avoid fines and penalties imposed by the EPA for violation of environmental law.

Awareness has increased to such a level that the efforts of consumers, insurers, lenders, and the media have all focused in recent times on environmental issues. This focus, which has been termed *the green initiative* by the media, affects the way many business decisions are being made today.

Global environmental issues, such as the deterioration of the stratospheric ozone layer, global warming, and subsequent greenhouse effects, have further raised worldwide awareness over the fragile nature of our environment. Many nations continue to look to the EPA for the environmental protection initiatives required to address these concerns on a global level.

3

The Regulatory Process

INTRODUCTION

The EPA functions as an administrative agency whose main purpose is to enforce regulatory statutes as promulgated by the U.S. Congress as *environmental law*. In order to understand how this regulatory process functions, the mechanism upon which it is based—*administrative law*—shall be explored.

Administrative law making is based upon the U.S. Constitution and other federally mandated requirements. Basically, in the United States, government functions are divided into three primary branches. The intent is to ensure the separation of power among the *legislative, executive,* and *judicial* branches of government so that no one individual or group has absolute governing power. This is one of the fundamental concepts of our democratic form of government. The President, in the executive branch, can not exercise total control over the legislative, law-making branch, which consists of the two houses of Congress. The judicial branch, the Supreme Court and the lesser courts, has absolute authority over the adjudication and resolution of conflicts, clarifications, and necessary interpretations that develop from time to time concerning the laws of the land.

Typically, administrative agencies such as OSHA are created by the legislative branch, are managed by the executive branch, and are occasionally audited by the judicial branch. Usually, the administrative process begins with an act of Congress that either creates a new agency or grants new authority and power to an existing agency to address a particular issue or area of concern. For example, to properly address the growing concern for worker safety and health, Congress enacted the Occupational Safety and Health Act of 1970, which is the originating statute, or enabling legislation, that created the Occupational Safety and Health Administration. It is from the originating statute that OSHA derives its rule-making authority, as mandated by the legislative branch. The EPA, however, is an exception to this rule. As noted throughout this text thus far, the EPA was created not by an act of Congress, but by Presidential Executive Order. The EPA obtains its regulating authority from a variety of federally mandated statutes, such as, but not limited to, the Clean Air Act, the Clean Water Act, the Toxic Substances Control Act, and the Resource Conservation and Recovery Act. These and the many other environmental statutes provide exclusive authority to the EPA in the areas of environmental policy formation and enforcement. Since the creation of the EPA was not based upon any legislative actions, the agency can only obtain specific authority in the regulatory process through each act as it is mandated by the Congress.

INFLUENCING FACTORS

In the development of environmental law, there are a variety of influencing factors that either directly or indirectly affect the final outcome of the law-making process. For example, there may be unusually heavy pressure from the public and/or certain special interest groups demanding action regarding a certain area of environmental concern. This is especially true after highly visible environmentally disastrous incidents, such as the Exxon Valdez oil tanker accident. Other sources that may influence the administrative process include specific direction from the executive branch to address an area of concern and accelerate the rule-making process. An example here is President Bush's demand in 1992 that the scheduled phaseout of *chlorofluorocarbons (CFCs)* be accelerated to ensure total phaseout by 1995, 5 years ahead of that which was originally agreed upon. His actions, obviously occurring in a political election year, were reportedly based upon new findings of increased stratospheric ozone depletion. Whatever the reason for his mandate, the President demonstrated the ability of the executive branch to influence the rule-making activities of the EPA. On a more day-to-day basis, the primary influence of the executive branch stems from the President's control over the appointment process. Most statutes that create an agency also permit the President to appoint that agency's top administrators, subject to Senate approval. Even though the EPA has no originating legislation, it still functions as an administrative agency, and the authority for Presidential political appointment appears to be the same. Also, in terms of influence, the Presidential power to appoint is accompanied by the power to remove, which can, under most circumstances, have considerable influence over the direction an administrative agency may take. Since the desired direction of most administrations is typically different and, for the most part, diametrically opposed to that of the legislative branch, an agency is usually caught in the middle of a political tug-of-war between the Congress and the executive branch over a given issue or concern. This is one of the many reasons why *inaction* is often more prevalent than action on the part of many administrative agencies. Still another aspect of executive influence over an administrative agency is the budget process. Under the Constitution, final approval of the national budget, in which that of an administrative agency is contained, is the responsibility of the legislative branch. However, the budget is developed, shaped, and defined in large part by the executive branch. Hence, through this control over budgetary considerations, the executive branch can positively influence those agencies whose regulatory programs it favors and, likewise, adversely affect the budget of those it does not particularly endorse. For the past decade, the vehicle for such control has been the Office of Management and Budget (OMB), which oversees the economic viability of federal agencies and, therefore, has a significant effect on the regulatory initiatives proposed by a given administrative agency.

Of course, the judicial branch can also influence environmental policy through the adjudication of fines and penalties. Many organizations and individuals cited for violations of environmental law can choose to contest these citations and seek justification through the judicial branch. In the absence of a particular or specific statutory or Constitutional amendment, the ultimate interpretive authorities of an administrative policy or provision are the courts. Through its legal and formal interpretation of environmental policy, the judicial branch establishes legal precedence and, in effect, greatly influences the future enforcement and ultimate development of environmental policy. Hence, interpretation of an agency's administrative policy often rests on what the courts decide is correct. Congress does have the authority to amend a given statute in an effort to circumvent a specific judicial interpretation. However, this usually results in a stall rather than an actual avoidance, since most new statutes will ultimately face judicial review by a review court. There is one drawback to the influence of the judicial branch on the regulatory process. The courts can only take action to correct an agency's actions if and when a lawsuit is filed. It can do nothing, even if it believes that an agency's decision is unconstitutional or in violation of a statutory mandate without an initiating action from a party or parties affected by such decisions or violations.

Delegation of Authority

Many of the environmental statutes from which the EPA derives much of its regulating authority give the agency broad powers through purposely non-specific language and vague explanations of responsibility. For example, the

Toxic Substances Control Act (TSCA) directs the EPA to regulate chemicals that pose *an unreasonable risk of injury to health or the environment,* but leaves the agency with a great deal of discretionary power to determine what *unreasonable* actually means.

In empowering the EPA through the enactment of such legislation, Congress exercises a process known as the *delegation doctrine.* However, the doctrine is based upon the constitutional premise that Congress, as the elected representative of the American people, is the repository of all federal legislative power. Hence, Congress can not simply delegate this power to another party, including an administrative agency, because the agency has not been elected by the people (Ashford & Caldart 1991). This issue is of even greater interest when considering the EPA, which was not even created by any legislative action to begin with. Over the years, broad delegation of a substantial amount of authority to administrative agencies has become the rule rather than the exception. This has led some groups to question the entire regulatory process regarding the precise authority of administrative agencies. This complex interpretation of constitutional provisions is beyond the scope of this chapter as well as this text in general. It remains to be seen what effect future interpretations of the delegation doctrine will have on the environmental regulatory process.

Rule Making Under the Administrative Procedure Act

The federal Administrative Procedures Act (APA) provides the rule-making framework that is generally applicable to all federal agencies. Essentially, the APA provides two primary avenues for rule making: formal and informal.

Formal rule making is to be performed only if it is specifically required by Congress in the originating statute. Because formal rule making can be a particularly cumbersome and quite costly process, it is seldom practiced and has actually been required in only relatively few modern regulatory statutes. The formal process requires an agency to conduct a trial-type hearing, where interested parties may present oral or documentary evidence, submit rebuttal evidence, and conduct cross-examinations.

Informal rule making is, by far, the primary method of administrative rule making. Also known as "notice and comment" rule making, the process usually begins with the publication of a *general notice of proposed rule making* in the Federal Register. The notice must state the time, place, and nature of the proceedings, the legal basis of the rule, and the terms of the proposed rule (or at least a description of the rule). The purpose for publishing the proposed rule is to provide interested parties an opportunity to participate in the rule-making process and to satisfy due process require-ments. Constitutional due process does not require an agency to publish all data and information used in formulating a rule, nor does it require that a hearing be held. However, should an agency choose to conduct a hearing anyway, due process allows the agency to consider materials other than those presented at the hearing. Also under informal rule making, when courts review any agency action, the agencies are normally not held to the substan-tial evidence requirements specified under formal rule making (EPA under TSCA and OSHA are exceptions).

Hybrid Rule Making

With regard to proposed EPA rule making, Congress has gone beyond the minimum requirements of the APA. For example, TSCA provides additional opportunities for public input than normally permitted under general APA requirements. When rule-making conditions imposed against an agency consist of a mixture of both formal and informal rule-making requirements, the process is known as *hybrid rule making* (or "notice and comment plus" rule making). Under these provisions, the affected agency may be required to hold a public hearing if requested to do so by any interested party. In some cases, depending upon the statute in question (for example, TSCA), the EPA may also have to allow the cross-examination of witnesses to the extent necessary for a full and true disclosure with respect to the relevant issues. Similarly, the Clean Air Act mandates a disclosure of more information regarding a proposed rule than that required by the APA, and also provides interested parties with an opportunity to orally present data, opinions, and arguments and to submit rebuttal and supplementary information. Even though such provisions are more closely related to the requirements under formal rule making, the hybrid process allows these additional requirements in informal rule making for both the EPA and OSHA.

Participation in the Rule-making Process

Twice a year, the EPA publishes a regulatory agenda in the Federal Register. This agenda provides general information about current, on-going, and/or proposed EPA studies and proposals for future regulatory actions. Persons with considerable expertise are often invited by the EPA to participate in the development of proposed rules. Generally, it is advisable that interested parties monitor these proposed EPA actions so that early participation can be ensured for those actions that are of particular interest to a given party. If possible, interested parties should seek every opportunity to discuss EPA policies and procedures directly with the EPA *before* a regulation is formally proposed. Also, informal contacts with the EPA can be valuable in obtaining information on EPA goals, policies, and perhaps new regulations. Contacts at the regional level should not be overlooked. There is no way to determine the value of an excellent rapport established between an organization and a local EPA regional office.

Participation in the rule-making process also provides the agency with industry-specific information, data, and viewpoints that should probably be considered when promulgating a rule. Public participation is not only persuasive, it also establishes significant record for judicial review should the rule be challenged. There are various levels of public participation in EPA rule making, from the simple submission of written comments up to and including the formal presentation of oral and written materials at public hearings. It should be noted that oral and written communications that are not a part of the public record (commonly known as *ex parte* communications) are strictly prohibited during any formal rule making. Although the APA does not specifically prohibit ex parte communication during informal proceedings, some courts have refused to validate a rule because of the use of ex parte communications. To avoid such a problem, it has been established that ex parte communications will be allowed if all parties knew of its existence, the statements were made in good faith, and no undue influence is shown.

Finally, the APA also gives interested parties a right to *petition for issuance, amendments, or repeal of a rule.* Anyone can exercise this right in the event that a given rule is determined in error by some commonly accepted definition. However, this right does not necessarily mean that the agency will reconsider any rule. It only means that an interested party has some type of recourse when disagreement with a rule occurs. If the agency chooses not to reconsider a given rule, it must still provide prompt notice of denial of the petition with a proper explanation of the reasons for the denial. After a rule becomes final (i.e., becomes a law), the only way to propagate a challenge is to file a lawsuit. This is an extremely time-consuming and expensive process, with no guarantee of success in the courts. To challenge a final rule, a person (or organization) must show that they were actually *injured* by the rule. Attempting to impose a challenge simply because it is felt that the rule is wrong will result in little if any action from the courts.

STATE PLANS

The regulatory process discussed thus far pertains primarily to federal rule-making procedures. However, states are generally governed the same way, and the broad concepts provided here are largely applicable to the various state administrative and legal systems. Of course there are important differences between the specific federal system and many state programs. However, it is important to note that those states operating with approved environmental plans typically have the authority to inspect and enforce federal EPA requirements within their respective states. Also, state agencies can engage in their own rule-making activities and mandate state statutory requirements that are at least as stringent as any similar existing federal statutes.

In most cases, once a state receives full authorization from the EPA to administer all or part of applicable federal environmental policy, the state will maintain requirements that are equivalent to and consistent with the federal regulations. This is usually through state adoption of the federal statutes, either directly or by reference. In those states that do not have approval from the EPA to administer environmental policy, both state and federal provisions generally apply with the more stringent of the two taking precedence. For reference, Appendix A of this text provides a listing of the state agencies involved in environmental regulation for each of the United States and the District of Columbia.

SUMMARY

The regulatory process for administrative agencies such as the EPA is based upon U.S. Constitutional law as well as subsequent federally mandated statutes. As an agency of the *executive branch* of government, the EPA has rule making authority regarding federal environmental policy and enforcement. In addition to the executive branch, the EPA's rule-making decisions are subject to direct and indirect influence from both the *legislative* and *judicial branches* as well. The primary vehicle through which agencies can engage in the process of rule making is the *Administrative Procedures Act (APA)*. The APA establishes the specific criteria that must be followed by all agencies that attempt to revise existing or to develop federal regulations. The APA allows the two basic rule-making methods of *formal* and *informal,* with the latter being the most often practiced approach. The EPA, whose level of authority is not based upon any one single act of legislation, but stems from many Congressional mandates, is often subjected to a mixture of formal and informal rule-making requirements in a process known as *hybrid rule making.* Unlike OSHA, whose *enabling legislation* was the Occupational Safety and Health Act of 1970, the EPA was created by Presidential Executive Order and, therefore, is an exception to the rule regarding congressionally mandated administrative authority to regulate federal policy. This appears in contradiction to the *delegation doctrine,* which portends that Congress, being the duly elected representative of the people, can not simply delegate its legislative authority to nonelected agencies. Therefore, the EPA must look to each of the environmentally related acts of Congress to determine the extent of its regulating authority under the various acts. Hence, the EPA's approach to the regulatory process may differ, depending upon the particular law under which such action has been determined necessary.

Aside from the federal process of environmental regulation, the various states in the United States also have similar if not exact requirements that are implemented and enforced on the state level under authorization from the EPA. Those states without such approval from the EPA must comply with both state and federal requirements simultaneously. Generally speaking, each state that has developed its own regulations has done so either by direct incorporation of the various EPA mandates or through the establishment of their own statutes, which should be at least as stringent as those of the federal EPA.

4

The Environmental Audit

INTRODUCTION

The term "audit" is not unfamiliar to today's practicing safety and health professional. Indeed, safety compliance audits are a fact of life in any responsible industrial endeavor with an interest in ensuring employee safety and health. Such audits can be performed by an outside regulatory agency like OSHA or by unbiased private contracting consultants hired to evaluate the extent and effectiveness of existing programs as well as to determine if additional measures are necessary. Audits can also be performed by internal elements, such as the safety and health organization as a "self-check" of compliance status.

In the practice of environmental compliance, companies are also subjected to a similar auditing process aimed at ensuring that a particular level of compliance is adequate to meet applicable regulatory requirements. This chapter will define the types of environmental audits, explain their specific purpose and stated objectives, and provide a brief and general description of the auditing procedure itself.

What Is an Environmental Audit?

In general, an audit may be described as an established method of verifying that compliance with certain regulatory requirements and company policies are fulfilled, and ensuring that acceptable operating practices are in place. The term *audit* often has different meanings and has, in fact, been interpreted differently, depending upon who is providing the interpretation under what circumstances. The term *environmental audit* is routinely applied to situations

40

ranging in scope from a formal regulatory compliance review to the use of self-help questionnaires and surveys.

So, what exactly is an environmental audit? The EPA has defined an environmental audit as *a systematic, documented, periodic, and objective review by regulated entities of facility operations and practices related to meeting environmental requirements.* Basically, this definition tells us that:

1. An environmental audit must be a *systematic,* organized, consistent approach to ensuring regulatory compliance. Standardized checklists and/or established procedures are often used to ensure that this objective is fulfilled.
2. The audit results must be formally *documented* if the audit is intended to have any positive impact on upper management or other organizational elements whose cooperation is essential to the success of an environmental compliance program.
3. In order to ensure the benefits of the environmental auditing function, the process must be performed on a *periodic*, scheduled basis. Those responsible for areas subjected to audits must be made aware of the possibility of frequent, additional audits and/or follow-up reviews.
4. For an audit to be truly *objective,* it should be conducted by independent, unbiased personnel who have no direct relationship with those functions being audited. While internal audits have some benefit to internal management, an independent audit will, in most cases, be far more objective.

In short, an environmental audit functions as a tool to verify regulatory compliance. However, it can also provide management with certain assurances regarding the status and effectiveness of existing programs, as well as identify those areas of increased risk where improvement is necessary. In addition, when performed properly, the audit process can actually limit or reduce potential environmental liabilities by identifying existing program shortcomings *prior* to their resulting in a financially and environmentally damaging pollution episode. The primary caution with all audits is to understand that the audit represents only a *"snap-shot"* in time for a given facility and may not, in fact, reveal or disclose the true status of a complete environmental compliance program. Still, in most instances such a picture will typically provide some meaningful insight into the adequacy of a particular facility's compliance efforts.

TYPES OF ENVIRONMENTAL AUDITS

There are a number of audits currently being performed in the environmental arena for a variety of reasons. Certainly the most common is known as the *environmental compliance audit,* which is typically conducted to evaluate the adequacy of a facility's compliance with a particular set of regulations and to verify that appropriate compliance systems are in place and functioning properly. Because of the specific nature of this type of audit, it closely resembles the same process as that of a government agency (e.g., EPA, state environmental inspection).

A second type of audit that is sometimes performed in combination with the compliance audit, although it can be conducted independently as well, is the *environmental liability audit*. Also known as a *risk assessment audit*, it is typically performed on an existing facility in an attempt to determine the particular level of liability and/or potential liabilities associated with the facility's current environmental status. Such an audit is usually conducted outside of a facility as a precursor to an impending real estate transaction. When performed for this purpose, this type of audit may also be referred to as a *property transfer audit* or an *environmental site assessment*. The performance of such audits are often essential, since prospective owners of a new property who unknowingly purchase land intended for immediate or future development may become liable for the cleanup of any such properties if, in fact, subsequent evaluations determine levels of contamination at or above predetermined specifications.

When a specific waste disposal site is subjected to a compliance audit under the requirements of RCRA and/or CERCLA and its amendments, it may be called a *waste disposal site audit*. In this case, the very specific compliance requirements contained in RCRA and the Superfund narrow the scope of the audit considerably.

Audits may also be performed as a remedy for previously identified problem areas, as well as to reduce the potential for similar or repeat problems occurring in the future. These type of audits are often proposed as the result of some settlement negotiations or consent degree imposed by the EPA or a state agency and may be known as a *consent audit*. They are essentially the same as the environmental compliance audit discussed above. Environmental auditing provisions are most likely to be proposed in settlement negotiations where:

1. A pattern of previous violations can be attributed in part to either the absence or inadequacy of an environmental management function; and/or
2. The nature of previous violations indicates a serious potential that similar noncompliance problems may exist or occur elsewhere within the subject facility or at other facilities controlled by the same management organization.

PHASES OF ENVIRONMENTAL AUDITS

In cases where there is a concern over existing environmental liabilities with regard to a particular facility or piece of property, environmental audits may be performed in a series of phases, commonly referred to as a *phase audit* or a *phase assessment*. Used most often in conjunction with the property transfer audit, the phased approach offers an existing or, more commonly, a potential property owner a significant option with regard to the degree of detail, the extent of the evaluation, and, of particular importance, the subsequent expense of the audit.

Due to the extreme potential for quite extensive costs associated with the evaluation, abatement, and/or eventual cleanup of sites that may have been "contaminated" due to the ignorance (or negligence) of current or previous owner(s), a three-phase environmental audit may be performed. While there is no set or defined criteria established for the three-phase audit, the usual protocol employed by auditors is described here.

The "Three-Phase Plan"

An environmental audit generally may be divided into three phases. The level of detail will increase with each phase, as does the cost. It is important to note that progression from one phase into the next is not always necessary; thus, the reason for such an approach becomes more evident. Although there are no set or established parameters to this three-phase assessment strategy, the phases typically encountered can be categorized and explained as follows:

- Phase 1: Preliminary assessment/site visit
- Phase 2: Detailed assessment/sample taking
- Phase 3: Site cleanup and abatement actions

Phase 1
Phase 1 audits will provide a quick and general assessment of overall site conditions and liability potential. In a Phase 1 review, all pertinent Federal EPA and state plan regulations are reviewed for their application to the specific site. For example, the requirements in the Clean Water Act for stormwater discharge and runoff should be reviewed if it is determined applicable to the (proposed) facility or site. State and local regulations may be more stringent and, therefore, should also be evaluated.

When a property transaction is involved, all available real estate ownership records must also be reviewed. A great deal of information can be derived based upon the knowledge of any previous owner's activities and processes. A walk-around site visit is typically conducted as part of a visual survey of the property.

Neighboring properties and associated activities should also be considered, especially if the particular site topography would lend itself to intrusion or runoff of contaminants from these neighboring areas. Cleanup of such runoff contamination on a prospective property could be the responsibility of existing or subsequent owners.

Another valuable source of review for historical evidence of past noncompliance practices or possible environmental contamination problems are any old aerial photographs of the subject site. If available, these photographs may reveal evidence of previous land disturbance activities. In many cases, old drum or waste storage (dumping) areas may be visible in a photograph where none exist now. Disturbances in the otherwise natural growth of surrounding vegetation, as evidenced by patches of dead or dried foliage, may also indicate a problem with the soil in the area. When compared with views obtained from an actual aerial assessment of the current site, old photographs will not only validate the existence of such problems, they will also provide approximate time-lines of the pollution condition(s). Actual proximity to existing waterways or natural water accumulation areas, such as ponds, are better surveyed from the air. Natural or forced runoff and drainage paths are best visible from an aerial assessment.

There are usually no sampling or analyses performed during a Phase 1 audit, since the cost of the assessment will increase significantly if extensive sampling is performed. If the results of the audit reveal substantial cause for environmental concern, progression into Phase 2 will then be recommended. The decision to proceed into the Phase 2 audit rests with the management function of the effected organization.

Phase 2

Phase 2 involves actual sampling and analysis of the suspect area(s) of contamination. The purpose is primarily to assess the full extent of any contamination and to determine requirements for cleanup. If Phase 1 resulted in a substantial concern for environmental liability, then a Phase 2 review is usually essential to ensure accurate assessment of the true nature and degree of any such liability. Examples of sampling that may be performed include groundwater testing (monitoring wells may even be used to obtain continuous underground effluent flow data). In order to ensure, to the maximum extent possible, that all environmental liability associated with a specific site is properly considered, Phase 2 audits are usually quite extensive, extremely detailed, and, of course, quite costly, depending on the degree of contamination discovered. A proper Phase 2 assessment should also offer recommended actions for proper cleanup and subsequent abatement of any environmental contamination.

It is important to note at this point that the information obtained during a Phase 2 evaluation may not always remain confidential between the client and the auditor. Assuring the confidentiality of the data collected is often a function of the contractual agreement between the auditor and the party for which the audit has been performed. In most cases, private consultants who perform property transfer audits under contract to a potential buyer will almost always include specific language in the contract stipulating disclosure of data only to the parties involved in the contract (i.e., the buyer and the auditor). In the event that any adverse environmental conditions are discovered on the subject property, such contractual language is an attempt to place as much of the liability for informing appropriate authorities on the potential buyer and the current owner. Most state agencies indicate that any information showing evidence of environmental contamination is not protected by an attorney/client privilege arrangement. In fact, depending on the particular state, there may be provisions that require reporting of data to the appropriate agencies, regardless of who discovered the contamination and under what conditions the data were collected. However, most environmental attorneys tend to disagree. The essential problem with this issue stems from the fact that the use of the attorney/client privilege defense to protect data is not a well-litigated area of the law; therefore, very little case law exists from which to draw opinions and positions (most cases have settled prior to trial). Ethically, the concept of *due diligence* might compel some parties to notify the appropriate agencies after becoming knowledgeable of evidence indicating site contamination. For example, an independent auditor might be hired by a potential buyer to assess a site prior to purchase and discovers, during the Phase 2 audit, that the site is grossly contaminated. Even though the potential buyer might withdraw from the transaction, both the auditor and the buyer now have knowledge of environmental contamination. Although the language of the Comprehensive Environmental Response, Compensation, and Liability Act (CERCLA), or "Superfund," does not specifically compel these parties to properly advise the agency having jurisdiction over the site, the issue of due diligence must again be considered. (Reference Chapter 10 for further discussion of CERCLA liabilities.) Other environmental legislation, such as the Clean Air Act, the Resource Conservation and Recovery Act, and the Clean Water Act, contains provisions that require data reporting under certain conditions and that allow the EPA to request and receive any relevant information, including audit reports, if deemed necessary. However, unless they are notified of a possible problem or are aware of the auditing activity, the chances of a request from the EPA for audit data are somewhat remote.

Phase 3

Progression in the Phase 3 portion of the audit, where special cleanup and remediation services are provided at a premium cost, may not always be necessary or required. Actions performed in Phase 3 are highly dependent upon the results of the Phase 2 assessment. For example, results of the sampling performed during Phase 2 may indicate no or relatively minor/negligible environmental contamination that may possibly be cleaned up at minimum expense and effort. If this is true, then Phase 3 is usually not necessary. However, if Phase 2 resulted in the discovery of quite substantial environmental liability, Phase 3 usually offers cleanup and abatement services to render the subject site free of any contamination. Obviously, depending upon the extent of the problem, Phase 3 could be an extremely expensive endeavor. The usual recommendation in such cases is to find another site if possible and to immediately suspend any property transfer negotiations with existing owners.

The Audit Team

The three phases are usually conducted in sequence and, depending upon the makeup and size of the audit team, it is generally preferable to assign members of the team specific topics for review.

In order to promote a quicker review, all records should be kept in a central location. If this is not possible, facility management should assemble them prior to the commencement of the audit. Typically, the audit team will utilize some form of standardized checklist as a guide when reviewing the records. The review should include records that are not purely regulatory, such as pollution control equipment maintenance and any spill response procedures. It should be noted that property transfers of *undeveloped* land would generally call for records review, usually during Phase 1. Developed areas, such as shopping centers containing auto repair and maintenance, print shops, or dry cleaners, should definitely have their records examined.

Interviews

During Phase 1 of the audit, interviews of key facility management personnel and those at the regulatory agencies may be recommended or required, depending upon the nature of the site being assessed. Agency people may help give the auditors an idea of the facility management philosophy on regulatory compliance. Management includes not only environmental and regulatory compliance managers, but also first-line supervisors, maintenance and operations managers, and the facility (plant) manager. Checklists may again be used to direct the questioning, but the interview should not be confined to only checklist items. Owners of adjacent properties might also be interviewed to determine the extent of their environmental compliance history.

These interviews may help the audit team to:

1. Understand the facility operations, operating philosophies, and attitude toward regulatory issues;
2. Uncover areas of noncompliance and past practices that may have impact on the subject facility or property; and

3. Determine levels of understanding of standard operating procedures, their operational theory, and their regulatory compliance responsibilities.

For property transfer audits, interviews with past employees or owners may also help locate areas where possible contamination exists.

Site Inspection

Again, checklists may help to expedite this stage of the audit. The site inspection focuses not only on the operation of pollution control equipment, but also on a search for obvious noncompliance areas, such as non-permitted points of discharge, illegal disposal practices, and visible air emissions.

A detailed site inspection should include photographs and samples. Samples may be collected from soil, surface water, groundwater (if wells exist), and both indoor and outdoor air. The inspection will include a search for signs of contamination, including discolored soils and surface water and abandoned and/or leaking drums. The inspection may include a review of equipment plans and specifications for proper construction. It also should include the notation of site topographic, hydrologic, vegetation, and any wetlands characteristics.

An environmental audit of property, such as a shopping center or automobile maintenance/salvage facility for transfer, might include air and water sampling, as well as inspecting for obvious areas of disposal, both current and past.

The Audit Report

Upon completion of any audit, a detailed report should be developed addressing at least the following items:

1. Audit findings (primarily of noncompliance, but also should include a discussion of the general philosophy of the organization and management strategies);
2. Recommended actions (for bringing the facility or property into compliance); and
3. Follow-up on recommended actions to ensure implementation, if feasible.

For property transfer audits, the report should provide an indication of the likelihood of contamination and indicate any future areas of concern.

Purpose of an Environmental Audit

The variety of reasons that an environmental audit may be performed are even more numerous than the types of audits themselves. For example, a common objective of an environmental compliance self-audit (either per-formed internally or contracted to an unbiased professional consulting firm) is to provide a meaningful and realistic evaluation of a facility's basic regulatory compliance status prior to an inspection by some state or federal agency. Such an inspection will also provide excellent training for facility personnel who may be anticipating an actual regulatory compliance inspec-tion and demonstrate to management specific personnel performance short-comings and/or areas where additional commitment of resources may be required. Audits often help identify methods to reduce or minimize the level of waste produced by a given process or operation. Frequent and periodic environmental process evaluations can also assist in determining if possible substitutions can be made to replace hazardous materials with those that impose less of a threat to health and/or the environment. The collective information generated by each audit routine will provide excellent input to an environmental compliance database, which can then be used to track compliance efforts and demonstrate due diligence. Basically, an effective auditing program can provide a means to identify and solve existing environmental compliance problems, avoid potential problems, and antic-ipate the need for future actions necessary to ensure continued problem avoidance.

It is probably accurate to summarize that the exact purpose of an environ-mental audit will be contingent upon the specific needs, requirements, and current compliance status of the particular organization or facility being audited. For this reason, it is possible to discuss this aspect of environmental auditing only in a general sense, with no intent to formally define a precise purpose for performing an audit.

BASIC ELEMENTS OF AN INTERNAL ENVIRONMENTAL AUDITING PROGRAM

In attempting to develop an internal environmental auditing program, a variety of variables must be considered. These include, but are not limited to, factors such as the establishment of a clear set of goals and objectives for the program, budget provisions and/or restrictions, geographical location of facilities to be audited, types of audits to be performed, desired frequency and schedule of the audits, staffing requirements, coverage (what laws and regulations will be covered by the auditing program?), follow-up procedures, and so on. However, certain essential elements of an effective environmental auditing program should be addressed during its development to ensure program success. Basically, these are as follows:

- Full upper management commitment to the program must be obtained from the onset. This commitment not only includes support of the *idea* of a environmental auditing program, but it must also demonstrate its intentions to ensure that proper follow-up actions are fulfilled following any given audit. A policy letter, signed by the top management representative, is one method of demonstrating such commitment.
- The organizational element responsible for the auditing function must be independent from those areas that will be subjected to an audit. It hardly makes sense for an internal organization guilty of noncompliance to audit themselves. An audit program will not be successful if objectivity can not be maintained.
- A clear definition of the program objectives must be established to ensure that affected organization personnel at all levels are aware of the intended goals of such a program. It is important to provide this information early in the program's development so that potentially affected personnel will not attempt to draw their own conclusions regarding the reason and purpose for the implementation of this new program.
- All personnel designated as *environmental auditors* should receive substantial training and possess the required level of knowledge, discipline, and skill required to accomplish the established objectives of the audit. Because of the rapid pace and frequent development of important changes to the various environmental laws, it is essential that those responsible for audit program implementation maintain their competency through continued training and education.
- In order for the program to establish and maintain credibility as an effective tool, it must be applied consistently and uniformly to the greatest extent possible. Therefore, explicit, written auditing procedures and checklists should be established and used to ensure program success. This includes consistency in the development and presentation of reports and other appropriate written records.
- There should be an occasional quality control audit of the environmental auditing program itself. This process will help assure that audit objectivity is maintained and audit goals are being fulfilled. A periodic review of the reliability and integrity of the auditing program will also assist in the further improvement of the program itself by assuring the continued accuracy and thoroughness of the audits being performed.

By addressing at least the above listed elements during the development of an environmental auditing program, the organization will have established the basic foundations to ensure its success. Once the procedures for performing environmental audits are evaluated in relation to the goals and objectives established for program development, the program can then be documented as company policy.

LIABILITY CONCERNS

An obvious and understandable concern related to conducting environmental compliance audits is the confidentiality of the data and the potential for a company's own findings to be used against them by a regulatory agency or even members of the press or the public in general. Since environmental audits may identify significant violations to regulatory requirements or risks to the public health, these concerns are not without justification. However, since one of the primary goals of the audit is to identify exactly those areas of noncompliance that could possibly result in litigation or a public relations disaster, fear over the unauthorized release of potentially incriminating information should not be allowed to interfere with the accomplishment of environmental compliance goals.

The EPA recognizes the potential dilemma over this issue. While it does have authority to request certain records, it frequently will not exercise this authority. This decision is based on the assumption that routine requests for auditing records could adversely affect the auditing process in the long run, since many companies may elect not to perform audits in an effort to keep from having to provide them to the EPA upon request. Also, the EPA understands that organizations must perform self-audits with the assurance of some level of privacy. Otherwise, the objectivity of the auditing process will surely suffer. Therefore, the EPA has not stated intentions of altering its philosophy on the requesting of company auditing records. The EPA evaluates the need for such requests on a case-by-case basis, taking into account the honest and genuine efforts of a particular company to avoid and/or promptly correct compliance violations. A well-established and documented internal auditing program may demonstrate an organization's due diligence and good faith in attempting to comply with applicable regulatory requirements.

Depending upon a particular organization's situation, there may be justification for protecting an audit report from disclosure under the rules of attorney-client privilege. However, use of this protection method to ensure confidentiality of audit reports requires careful consideration, and competent legal counsel should be obtained. There are also ethical considerations and the concept of due diligence in doing what is right that must be taken into account.

PERFORMING AN ENVIRONMENTAL AUDIT

In the performance of an environmental audit, there are four basic steps in the process that, depending upon specific program requirements, may vary in nature and degree from that which is described here. However, with few exceptions, most environmental audit activities will tend to follow this simple progression through to the completion of the auditing process. This is true whether the audit is to be performed internally (e.g., a self-check), by an outside organization (e.g., a private consultant), or by an agency (e.g., EPA, state agency). These basic auditing activities can be categorized into four main areas or groups and defined as follows:

1. Preaudit
2. On-site
3. Postaudit
4. The audit report

For the purpose of simplification, these steps will be discussed here with regard to an *external* audit (i.e., an outside agency or firm conducting an on-site audit). However, those that wish to utilize the audit process for an *internal* examination can also follow the basic guidelines outlined below for each of these four.

Preaudit

Prior to the initiation of an audit, certain key activities should occur, even before commencement of the actual audit process. For example, it is essential that those personnel that will be responsible for either conducting the audit or assisting in its performance ensure that proper planning be accomplished to help guarantee that the audit will be properly focused and its objectives established and properly addressed. These personnel should also review any established or existing company auditing plans and procedures. For particularly large-scale auditing operations, the preaudit plan should be well written to include all resource requirements as well as identification of specific personnel support functions that will be necessary to accomplish the audit.

When an external agency (private, state, or federal) is to conduct a routine environmental audit of a facility, prenotification of the pending visit is typically made by telephone within a few days or weeks of the proposed audit date. Written follow-up notification is then sent to the appropriate facility representatives. In the follow-up letter, the specific authority to conduct such an audit, as well as the intended purpose of the audit and areas to be visited, should be described. In most cases, the notification letter will also identify the types of information that will be required during the audit. Such information may include specific plant or facility information, previous audit records and documentation, current pollution and/or waste control programs, and so on. Therefore, during the preaudit period, a comprehensive review of any and all information pertaining to a facility and its environmental compliance history should be performed.

On-Site

For the facility, the audit begins with the actual site visit. However, before the auditor arrives, he or she will have also prepared for the site examination by reviewing historical files, previous inspection and/or audit reports, and any other general or specific information available concerning the facility. This may include information regarding the types of known wastes and pollutants generated at the subject plant, as well as specific work practices and processes that regularly occur there. Once at the site, the auditor will then be able to recognize deficiencies, having first established a clear understanding of the facility's past performance. Therefore, it is essential that those designated company personnel participating in the on-site audit be prepared to immediately answer any questions concerning the applicability of specific regulatory requirements and provide recommendations to achieve compliance where none may currently exist.

It is extremely important to document everything that occurs during the audit, especially since the auditor will no doubt be doing the same thing. Auditors tend to utilize photographs for a variety of reasons during the performance of an audit. Photographs help clarify worded explanations; they graphically show the extent of an out-of-compliance condition; they help the auditor remember specifics during the report writing phase of the auditing process; they add incomparable detail to a report; and they positively demonstrate the actual conditions that existed during the on-site visit. Company officials should therefore be prepared to take photographs identical to those obtained by the auditor at the exact time of the audit. These will not only assist in understanding the meaning of specific citations or questions that may come later, but they will also document exactly what the auditor saw during the site visit. Additionally, these photographs may later be used in the event of some disagreement with an auditor's allegations of noncompliance.

An audit team should arrive at a facility during normal business hours and should provide proper identification to the appropriate company or facility representatives. Auditors should always follow company rules and policies pertaining to security, confidentiality of information, and any other restrictions required by the specific facility being audited.

There will be an opening conference between the company representatives and the audit team, at which time the proper credentials are presented, the scope of the audit is outlined, and the specific areas to be visited are identified. It is important to verify that these items are the same as those mentioned in the notification letter. If something has changed, the company has the right to inquire as to the reasons for any changes and the effect on the purpose of the audit caused by these changes. Any further restrictions on the auditing process, such as policies against photographs in certain areas, should be discussed during the opening conference and not during the actual audit.

Depending upon the specific scope of an audit, the auditors will usually perform a detailed review of company records and documents pertaining to waste management and pollution control. This paper audit includes an examination of facility background information, self-audit checklists and schedules, and evidence of the facility's history of recognizing and correcting deficiencies. Auditors may request copies of records and documents that they feel will assist them during the report writing phase. In the case of confidential information, the company should provide only information that is determined absolutely essential in order for the auditors to meet their stated audit objectives.

After the paper audit, the next step is to perform a walking tour of the designated areas and physically inspect the facilities under question. During this review, company officials should be especially on guard to provide quick and accurate answers to any questions the auditors may choose to ask. Therefore, the importance of assigning knowledgeable and articulate personnel to accompany the audit team can not be overemphasized. A person who is not well versed in all aspects of a facility's operation could provide the wrong answer to critical inquiries and create an unnecessary question in the auditor's mind regarding the true state of compliance activities in a given facility. The inspection will typically include observing company processes and equipment in action. The auditor will also wish to examine any equipment and/or monitoring devices currently installed in the facility (e.g., scrubbers, incinerators, wastewater treatment equipment), as well as maintenance and repair records associated with such equipment.

Auditors will generally wish to conduct interviews with staff members and other company personnel to determine the extent and understanding of a company's environmental policies and procedures. In fact, depending upon the scope of the audit, interviewing can be the single most important aspect of the environmental audit. However, as useful as the interview may be to an auditor, certain ground rules established by the EPA should be followed to ensure that the maximum benefit is obtained from this process. Auditors should never interrupt personnel who are busy performing assigned duties. The desire for interviews should be established during the opening conference, and, if possible, a schedule should be established that designates certain times during the day when interviews will be possible. Auditors will generally wish to conduct interviews in the work areas, where those being questioned will generally feel more comfortable and relaxed. Also, human nature often dictates that people being questioned will provide the answers they assume the auditor would most like to hear. Because of this potential, auditors are usually trained to ask open-ended questions that require some degree of explanation rather than those that may be answered with a simple *yes* or *no* response.

At the end of the walk-around inspection of the facility, there should be a closing conference or debriefing. Here the auditors should provide information on any imminent problems or concerns discovered during the audit. They should identify specific noncompliance issues and any required documents or records that they were not able to examine. The closing conference is also an opportunity for the company to clarify any findings that are not clearly stated or understood.

Postaudit

After the auditors have left the premises, there are still some activities related to the audit process that should occur to ensure proper management of data generated during the audit. Facility personnel should take immediate actions to confirm any of the alleged findings that the auditors may have disclosed during the closing conference. Necessary corrective steps should be implemented as soon as possible, and the results of these actions should be properly documented in company environmental records. This will not only address those situations in need of attention; it will also reflect well in terms of due diligence and good faith in compliance during any subsequent or future audits.

Another important portion of any audit is a review of company record-keeping practices and policies. Postaudit activities should therefore include steps to ensure accurate and detailed management of all data and information (checklists, photographs, observation remarks/comments, and other related documentation) that may have been generated during, or as a direct result of, the environmental audit.

The Audit Report

The last step in the audit process involves the preparation and submission of an audit report. The exact contents of the report may vary, depending upon the specific scope and stated objectives of the audit. However, as a minimum, the report should contain the basic information discussed below. It is important to the audit process that the report be submitted as soon as possible after the completion of the on-site visit. If too much time has passed, the impact that any findings and/or recommendations may have on the environmental practice of the subject facility may be lessened due to other more pressing problems that typically occur from day to day in the dynamic environment associated with many functioning business operations. Any adverse environmental conditions will only get worse if too much time passes between discovery and remediation.

The types and styles of reports that may be written subsequent to an environmental audit can differ for a variety of reasons. This is based on the fact that no mandated protocol currently exists that specifically governs the report writing process. Hence, the final appearance of a completed report may differ dramatically from those submitted previously, depending upon the agency or organization completing the report. Basically, the content of the audit report should include the following data as a minimum, which may be divided into three primary areas:

1. Front or background information.
2. Evaluation of findings and compliance/deficiency reporting.
3. Follow-up or abatement action requirements.

Front or Background Information
This section of the report will include introductory statements that focus primarily upon the purpose, scope, and objective of the audit. For example, if the audit was the result of a complaint or conducted for the purpose of determining liabilities in property transfer or acquisition transactions, then it should be stated as such in the front or introductory information. Also, the introductory paragraphs should state what the audit concentrated on (e.g., compliance with the Clean Air Act, the Clean Water Act, the Resource Conservation and Recovery Act, or any combination of the many EPA statutes).

There should also be a summary of the entire report provided in this section that provides a synopsis of all the data contained in the detail of the report. This abstract will enable the reader/reviewer to quickly grasp the essential and important aspects of the audit, without having to first dissect and wade through the main body of the report itself.

Basic but essential information, such as a description of the facility or location that was subjected to the audit should be included in this section. Exact facility name(s), locations/addresses, and contact telephone numbers are samples of the data usually recorded here. Also, a brief explanation of the facility's function or purpose (i.e., the business in which it is engaged) may be provided to establish an understanding of the operations and/or processes that were subjected to the audit. A map of the facility or location (in the event of an audited parcel of land) showing exact geographical data as well as the facility's proximity to other structures and/or topographical concerns (bodies of water, swamps, water tables, undeveloped land areas, etc.) should be included. Again, the level of detail provided will be contingent upon the scope and purpose of the audit.

The date or dates that the audit occurred should be documented here to establish the exact point in time that the audit took place. It is important to recall at this point that an audit is only a "snap-shot" of a facility's compliance status at the time the audit occurred; therefore, it may not be a true picture of a facility's actual state of compliance. For example, the facility may have been involved in a unique process or operation coincidental to the time of the audit, which may have had either a negative or positive impact on the results of the audit and, subsequently, failed to provide a true representation of the facility's compliance efforts during more normal operating conditions.

The name(s) of the individual(s) who performed the audit, the members of the audit team (if applicable), and the method by which each may be contacted in the event of some future clarification requirement should be listed in the introductory section of the report. Also, those individuals that will act as official points of contact for the audited facility should be provided to ensure that proper channels of communication are clearly understood. In some instances, the names and functions of any personnel who were interviewed during the environmental audit might also be listed here to document their participation in the audit process and to ensure that proper follow-up can occur with the right individuals, if necessary.

Finally, an extremely detailed and comprehensive report will inevitably make use of numerous unique terms, acronyms, and abbreviations that may not be entirely familiar to all those who will review the report. Therefore, a section providing explanations/definitions for terms, phrases, and abbreviations might be included in the front section of an audit report.

Evaluation of Findings and Compliance/Deficiency Reporting

This section will provide the details of the audit and specifically list the results of the audit's findings. Although the audit is usually designed to uncover or determine areas of noncompliance (i.e., deficiencies), it is not uncommon to also see reference to a particular facility's efforts that are in complete compliance with applicable regulatory requirements. However, because more action is obviously required in response to noted/cited deficiencies, this section of the report will concentrate heavily on this area of a facility's environmental program.

When a violation or compliance deficiency has been cited, it is important to realize that the auditor must evaluate each area based upon the severity or potential severity of the violation before determining the degree of the deficiency. As an example, drums found leaking or in poorly maintained condition would obviously be a more serious deficiency than an improperly completed waste manifest form, although both are violations of regulatory requirements. To help standardize the approach to noncompliance citations, the EPA has established the following system. Violations can be divided into two categories: procedural and regulatory. A *regulatory deficiency* exists when a facility is not in compliance with a specific federal, state, or local agency statute, whereas a *procedural deficiency* occurs when a facility is not in compliance with its own corporate or company policies. It should be noted that, when company policies merely incorporate the requirements of some external regulatory agency, the deficiency will be categorized as a regulatory deficiency. Once categorized, the deficiency can then be determined as either significant, major, or minor.

A *significant deficiency* is one that poses or is likely to pose an immediate and direct threat to human health, safety, the environment, or facility operations. Because of the serious potential of a significant deficiency, immediate action is required to correct the problem. Examples of significant deficiencies include, but are certainly not limited to, failure to properly ensure that a hazardous waste has been disposed of in compliance with regulatory requirements, failure to report a release of hazardous materials into the environment when required to do so by specific regulatory mandates, or operating a *treatment, storage, or disposal facility (TSDF)* without a permit to do so.

A *major deficiency* exists when conditions may pose a threat to human health, safety, or the environment. Such problems require prompt but not necessarily immediate action to eliminate such potential. Examples may include the failure to apply for appropriate permits (air, water, etc.) for a newly constructed emissions source, or failure to properly perform required inspections of waste accumulation points.

A *minor deficiency* occurs when there is evidence of occasional or temporary instances of noncompliance; these are usually administrative in nature. Examples may include using an incorrect abbreviation for the quantity of hazardous waste on a waste manifest form or submitting a permit renewal application several days after the previous one had expired.

Follow-up or Abatement Action Requirements

The final section of the report will typically contain important information on follow-up activities, such as additional site visits necessary to ensure that appropriate corrective actions have been implemented. Also, when previous audits have been conducted, the follow-up actions will evaluate the facility's responsiveness to compliance requirements. An action plan can be developed by the facility and amended as required to demonstrate that specific corrective actions and/or policy modifications have been implemented to comply with those abatement actions identified in the report.

SUMMARY

Environmental audits are performed for a variety of reasons, the most common of which is to evaluate the existing level of a facility's compliance with applicable regulatory and or company policies, regulations, and requirements. Audits may be conducted by external regulatory agencies, such as the EPA and/or state or local environmental compliance representatives. They may also be accomplished by independent private consultants or internal company officials in an attempt to "self-check" the status of existing environmental compliance policies.

There are a variety of environmental audits that may be performed at a given location, depending upon the scope and objective of the agency or individual conducting the evaluation, as well as the focus of the intended audit. For example, those that are designed to determine specific compliance status are often referred to as *environmental compliance audits*. When a program evaluation of an existing facility is desired with the specific intention of identifying environmental risks associated with current environmental policy, an *environmental liabilities audit* or *risk assessment audit* may be performed. In certain instances, as in the case of a real estate transaction, such audits are often referred to as a *property transfer audit* or *site assessment audit*. Whatever the type of audit, for whatever reason, environmental audits can be a valuable tool to the user in determining the current level of a particular program's compliance status.

In general, the actual audit process may be divided into four basic areas of activity: *preaudit, on-site, postaudit,* and preparation and submittal of the *audit report*. Each of these can be further evaluated as separate actions within the overall auditing function.

In many cases, audits performed by internal organizations or independent private consultants on large-scale operations may be divided into *phases* that permit the auditor to conduct the evaluation in planned stages. This method, commonly referred to as the *three-phase audit*, allows specific controls on the effort to be performed during each phase and, subsequently, on the costs involved in extensive assessments. Three-phase audits will often utilize *audit teams*, especially when performed on relatively large operations.

Whatever the purpose or reason for a particular audit, full support from upper management is essential to ensure a strong demonstration of commitment to environmental program requirements. Without proper involvement of upper-level officials, the auditing process will no doubt uncover program weakness areas that permeate the entire organization.

II

Major Environmental Regulations

INTRODUCTION TO PART II

Having established a basis for understanding the historical development of environmental compliance and the role of the U.S. Environmental Protection Agency (EPA) in the rule-making and enforcement process in Part I of this *Basic Guide to Environmental Compliance,* the chapters in Part II will focus on some of the major environmental regulations themselves. It is not possible to provide a complete, up-to-date reference manual describing these extremely complex and ever-changing statutes. However, each of the major environmental laws can and will be discussed in terms of purpose, intent, and enforcement strategies. The various levels of fines and penalties associated with noncompliance will be discussed as well.

In this regard, Part II will provide a basic overview of the major regulations that have helped shape U.S. environmental policy. Starting with Chapter 5 and the National Environmental Policy Act, which was signed into law in January 1970, Part II will focus on important legislative actions in chronological order through 1990. During this 20-year period, regulations concerned with preserving and protecting our nation's air and water resources, as well as those aimed at controlling the disposition of waste by-products and the cleanup of those sites where waste disposal went uncontrolled, were signed into law, thereby greatly enhancing the responsibility of enforcement agencies.

While the individual chapters in Part II will only briefly discuss each of these major milestones in U.S. environmental policy, it should be noted that many more meaningful and quite substantial regulations can and should be expected as we move towards the end of this century and into the next. At a time in our nation's history when the popular political platform is to adamantly and publicly oppose those agendas where overregulation is visibly obvious, there is no indication that this posturing will affect the environmental arena. In fact, with worldwide attention focused upon such issues as the ozone layer, acid rain, and rain forest degradation, it is probably safe to assume that environmental regulatory activities in the United States will steadily increase as our nation becomes more and more environmentally conscious.

Part II will therefore provide a fundamental understanding of the major laws that have governed our national environmental policy to date so that the reader can be better prepared for what lies ahead. Finally, to further demonstrate the practical application of these many laws, each chapter in Part II will present a brief summary of a real-world case study involving the specific act discussed in the respective chapter. Through review of these case briefs, the reader should gain a clearer understanding and appreciation for the enforcement of environmental policies in the United States.

5

National Environmental Policy Act

INTRODUCTION

The *National Environmental Policy Act*, or *"NEPA,"* was signed into law on 1 January 1970. Although its focus is to impose environmental regulations on federal agencies only, it is still considered by some to have been our basic *national charter*, mandating the protection and preservation of the environment. While ensuring compliance with the requirements of NEPA is limited to those professionals working for *federal agencies*, it is important for the novice to understand the basic objectives of this legislation, since it set the stage for what was to follow in the enactment of environmental law in this country.

Primarily, NEPA establishes national policy, sets obtainable goals, and provides a means for implementing and enforcing environmental policy. Once again, it is emphasized that the Act's *action-forcing* provisions are aimed at federal agencies and are intended to ensure that these agencies act in accordance with the letter (i.e., the written word mandating specific requirements) as well as the spirit (i.e., a true desire to act responsibly in terms of environmental protection and preservation) of the law. To accomplish this, NEPA provides regulations designed to inform federal agencies of the appropriate actions that are necessary to comply with the goals and objectives of the Act. Because the focus of NEPA is on the conduct of federal agencies, it will not typically pose a great deal of compliance problems for private sector enterprises. This chapter will therefore provide only a brief explanation of NEPA and the basic elements of compliance. The intent here is to impart a fundamental understanding of this first major legislative action concerning environmental quality in the United States.

As discussed in Chapter 1, the level of environmental awareness increased steadily among the American people after World War II, especially during the 1950s and 1960s. By the end of 1969, national attention on environmental protection had become such a visible, emotional, and highly controversial issue that Congress recognized the need for some type of firm legislative action. NEPA was enacted in response to this growing concern over environmental harm, which apparently resulted from population growth, high-density urbanization, dramatic industrial expansion, exploitation of natural resources, and the new and expanding technological advances that were characteristic of the post-WWII period. In fact, the language contained in the legislative history of NEPA makes reference to these rising concerns and indicates the belief that the most dangerous of all man's enemies in terms of survival is his own undirected (and uncontrolled) technology.

The enactment of NEPA in 1970 was the very first attempt at national environmental policy in this country. In the Spring of 1970 the first annual *Earth Day* took place in the United States to focus greater national attention on the fragile environment in which we live. With the creation of the EPA by the end of that same year, the United States was firmly positioned for the many environmental regulations that would soon follow.

PURPOSE AND OBJECTIVES

NEPA, as originally enacted, has a *two-fold purpose* designed to ensure that federal agencies act in the most environmentally responsible manner as possible under a given set of circumstances. Specifically, NEPA attempts to:

1. Inject environmental considerations into the federal agency decision-making process; and
2. Inform the public that a federal agency has considered environmental concerns in its decision making.

In order to accomplish its stated purpose, NEPA has established a basic policy in Section 101 of the Act. In doing so, NEPA articulated for the first time both a comprehensive national environmental policy and a method by which federal agency proposals could be measured and evaluated in terms of environmental needs, goals, and priorities. Consider the strong language contained in Section 101, the likes of which had never been used in any other national policy-making legislation:

> The Federal Government shall use all practical means and measures to create and maintain conditions under which man and nature can exist in productive harmony, and fulfill the social, economic, and other requirements of present and future generations of Americans [NEPA 101(a)].

The significance of this verbiage is emphasized further by the fact that, prior to NEPA, federal agencies adamantly professed that they had neither the duty nor the authority to consider environmental factors in their decision making. With the stroke of a pen, however, this attitude was permanently changed when NEPA was signed into law.

These basic goals and objectives of NEPA must be achieved through the use of federal plans, functions, programs, and resources. These objectives include the assurance of "safe, healthful, productive, and esthetically and culturally pleasuring surroundings for all Americans while attaining the wide range of beneficial uses of the environment without degradation, risk to health or safety, or other undesirable and unintended consequences."

In simpler terms, NEPA requires federal agencies to ensure the preservation of existing environmental conditions and resources while, at the same time, taking full advantage of those resources for the betterment of American society. Because these objectives seem to be contradictory to one another, it might be easier to understand why it takes so long for federal agencies to act on pending issues when the environment is perceived to be in jeopardy.

ESSENTIAL ELEMENTS OF NEPA

NEPA makes *environmental protection* a mandated requirement of every federal agency and department. Under NEPA, all federal agencies must consider environmental issues in the same manner as they consider other matters within their jurisdiction and they are *compelled* to take the value of environmental matters into account. However, it is important to note that there are no provisions in the Act that specify or dictate certain outcomes of a NEPA evaluation. NEPA *does not* attempt to mandate specific results of federal agency decision making. It merely prescribes the process necessary to properly consider environmental issues in that decision making. For example, if adverse environmental effects of a proposed action have been adequately identified and evaluated, there is nothing in NEPA that would prevent the agency from deciding that other considerations outweigh the potential costs to the environment. Airports have been constructed in remote locations even after a NEPA evaluation showed a potential threat to wildlife in the subject areas. Although other existing statutes may impose specific restrictions and substantive obligations on federal agencies for unwise decisions, NEPA prohibits only uninformed agency actions and requires that an agency strongly consider the environmental consequences of any major federal action *before* initiating such action.

In short, these requirements can be summarized into four general areas. All federal agencies must meet the following requirements, to the fullest extent possible:

1. Utilize a systematic, interdisciplinary approach in all planning and decision making when the results of such decisions may affect the environment. It is a NEPA requirement, and therefore a mandate, that federal agencies *must* consider the potential environmental effect of proposed federal agency projects.

2. Identify and develop methods and procedures to ensure that presently unquantified amenities and values may be given appropriate consideration in decision making along with economic and technical considerations. Essentially, this provision permits agencies to evaluate environmental issues and concerns in tandem with other variables that may affect the decision making process, such as cost savings and potential technological benefits that could result from the initiation of a proposed project.

3. Include an *Environmental Impact Statement ("EIS")* in every recommendation or report on proposals for legislation and other major federal actions that significantly affect the quality of the environment. Perhaps one of the more important aspects of NEPA, the EIS is the mechanism that allows for the evaluation of a proposed project's potential harm to environmental quality. Because the Act pertains strictly to federal agencies, it should be noted that under no circumstances may a private person prepare an EIS (although they may supply information that will eventually be used in the EIS preparation process). NEPA requires the EIS to address in detail the environmental impact of the proposed action; the adverse environmental effects (if any) that cannot be avoided should the proposal be implemented; alternatives to the proposed action; the relationship between short-term and long-term uses and effects on man's environment resulting from the proposed action; and irreversible and irretrievable commitments of resources that would be involved in the proposed action, if implemented.

4. Agencies must study, develop, and describe appropriate alternatives to proposed courses of action in an effort to minimize potential impacts to the environment. It is important to note that an agency's duty to conduct such studies on alternatives is independent of and does not preclude the requirement for submittal of an EIS. However, the courts have ruled that the range of alternatives that must reasonably be considered decreases as the environmental impact of the proposed action becomes less and less substantial.

The Council on Environmental Quality

Section 202 of NEPA authorized the appointment of the *Council on Environmental Quality,* or *"CEQ."* Before its abolishment by President Clinton on 8 February 1993, the CEQ consisted of three members, appointed by the

President, with advice and consent from the Senate. If the mandated use of the EIS can be considered a significant aspect of NEPA, the creation of the CEQ should be considered equally significant based upon its role in influencing environmental affairs/policy in the United States. Under the Act, the CEQ provides advice to the President on federal programs and policies affecting the environment and also prepares an annual *Environmental Quality Report (EQR)* for Congress that describes the *state of the environment* in the United States and reports the status of specific initiatives during the previous year.

Prior to 1978, the CEQ only issued "guidelines," which were merely advisory and had no force of law behind them. Federal agencies could either follow these recommendations or pursue an alternate course of action. But in 1978, as a result of an executive order, CEQ issued regulations that required all federal agencies to implement NEPA. These regulations are contained in the *Code of Federal Regulations (CFR)* at Title 40, Parts 1500–1508.

As stated above, the CEQ was abolished during the early days of the Clinton Administration. Under advisement from Vice-President Gore (an outspoken environmental supporter), Clinton announced the end of the CEQ and the creation of a new office to be called the *Office on Environmental Policy (OEP)*. Congress had delegated the CEQ the responsibility of providing the nation with a comprehensive view of environmental trends and conditions. While acknowledging the contributions made by the CEQ over the years, Gore also indicated that the Council had moved further and further away from the periphery of policy making in recent years. Gore apparently felt that the CEQ was no longer acting within the mainstream of environmental concerns. The new OEP is supposed to bring environmental considerations directly to the White House for action. In short, the new OEP is responsible for coordinating environmental policy within the federal government. The level of OEP participation in the major governmental policy councils (the National Security Council, the National Economic Council, and the Domestic Policy Council) clearly establishes the OEP on a much higher, visible plane than the old CEQ. This approach, as affirmed by Vice-President Gore, will ensure that environmental considerations will be an integral part of domestic and foreign policy. Its organizational structure should also permit all agencies within the executive branch to speak with one common voice on environmental issues and concerns.

SUMMARY

The National Environmental Policy Act of 1970 set forth unprecedented requirements for the inclusion of environmental protection provisions in all actions of federal agencies that could possibly have an impact on the environment. The major elements of NEPA include the creation of the *Council on Environmental Quality (CEQ)* and the requirement for federal agencies to provide an *Environmental Impact Statement (EIS)*. Before its abolishment in early 1992 by the Clinton Administration, the CEQ issued guidelines to federal agencies on mandatory environmental requirements and reported annually to the President on the state of the environment. The OEP replaced the CEQ and is intended to bring environmental concerns into the mainstream of U.S. foreign and domestic policy making. The EIS is an instrument that details the effect of federal projects on the surrounding environment.

Although NEPA is of compliance concern only to those professionals working on behalf of federal agencies, all environmental compliance professionals should be aware of NEPA and its statutory provisions. At the time of its enactment, NEPA established an environmental regulatory climate in the United States the likes of which had not been seen before. In the increasingly complex arena of environmental compliance, the practicing professional would do well to become familiar with the basic elements of NEPA in the likely event of having to interface with federal agencies on some type of project that would involve knowledge of and compliance with the provisions of NEPA.

CASE BRIEF: NATIONAL ENVIRONMENTAL POLICY ACT
Blue Ocean Preservation Society vs. Department of Energy
U.S. District Court, District of Hawaii
No. 90-00407 DAE, 25 June 1991

Summary

This Action was brought against the defendant, the U.S. Department of Energy (DOE), for their failure to adequately prepare an *Environmental Impact Statement (EIS)* as required by the National Environmental Policy Act (NEPA), 42 U.S.C. 4332, regarding the development of geothermal energy projects in the State of Hawaii. The lawsuit sought to compel preparation of a federal EIS for the Hawaii Geothermal Energy Project and to enjoin (prohibit) any further federal participation in the Project until the EIS was completed.

Background

The Project is a cooperative venture between the federal government and the State of Hawaii to facilitate the development of geothermal power as an alternative energy source in Hawaii. It involves four distinct stages or phases of development, leading to the private construction of a 500-megawatt geothermal power plant on the slopes of the Kilauea crater, an active volcano on the Island of Hawaii. Any attempt to obtain an EIS for the first two phases of the project was deemed moot, since these phases, which involved constructing a small research and testing plant and researching the use of underwater cables to transport power to the other Islands of Hawaii, were already completed without an EIS. Phase III involved the drilling of 25 commercial-scale exploration wells throughout the Kilauea East Rift Zone in order to verify the geothermal resource. This process was to clear the way for the Phase IV construction of the power facilities. The power plant will consist of several (up to 20) separate facilities capable of producing 25 megawatts each. They will be connected by a network of roads, plumbing, and power lines throughout the area. It will also involve laying overland and underwater cables. The majority of the land-based facilities will be networked over an area encompassing more than 26,000 acres, most of which is in the Wao Kele O Puna forest Natural Area Reserve. This area contains a large contingent of rare native plants. The federal government, through the DOE, provided the majority of the funding for the project. Nearly $35 million was spent during the first two phases, and an additional $15 million (in $5 million increments) had already been appropriated at the time the lawsuit was filed.

During the Phase III portion of the Project, the defendants in this case sought injunctive action to enjoin the federal government from any further participation on this Project until they properly file the required EIS under NEPA.

Decision

Section 102(2)(C) of NEPA requires federal agencies to prepare and file an EIS before undertaking major federal action significantly affecting the quality of the human environment. In its decision, the court determined that Phase III and Phase IV constitute major federal action,

within the meaning of the statute, based on the amount of federal funding appropriated for the Project and the DOE's participation, commitment, and involvement in the Project.

The court decision was in favor of the plaintiff to permanently enjoin federal participation, defined to include any decision-making or facilitating role, by the DOE in the Project and to require the DOE to immediately commence actions to prepare and submit an EIS. In addition, the government could no longer fund the Project, process permit applications, issue permits, or participate in any interagency meetings in such a way as to further the development of the Project.

Analysis

In order to grant the summary judgment in favor of the plaintiff, the court had to determine the applicability of NEPA in this case. The deciding factors were as follows:

1. The Project was considered a major federal action;

2. The Project posed a significant threat to the human environment in the area; and

3. The time was right to compel an EIS, since the DOE was using appropriated monies to fund the Project.

In short, the court decided that the government had taken this Project as far as it possibly could without complying with NEPA. It became clear in this decision that the policies embodied in the Act will tolerate nothing short of an absolute ban on further federal participation in such activities until compliance with NEPA is obtained.

6

The Clean Air Act

INTRODUCTION

In Part I of this text, the development of our nation's increasing concern for air pollution problems and an overview of the regulations enacted in an effort to ensure clean air in this country were briefly discussed. It is a fact that the regulation of clean air became the very first area of major regulatory focus in the United States as well as in other industrial nations around the world. Anyone new to the environmental compliance profession must recognize that the enactment of regulations to control air pollution in this country has been quite a dramatic process, resulting in increasingly more complicated requirements over the years. The Clean Air Act itself has undergone numerous revisions and amendments since it was first enacted in 1967. More recently, the 1990 Clean Air Act amendments added an additional 750 pages of regulatory requirements that have proven to be a tremendous burden on industry as well as the EPA and state agencies in trying to comply with these new provisions. Since the Clean Air Act of 1990 created such new, broad, and far-reaching requirements aimed at ensuring clean air quality far into the next century, it will be prudent to discuss the basic elements of these amendments as a separate section of this chapter. Hence, this chapter will first focus briefly on clean air requirements in this country prior to the 1990 amendments, followed by an overview and discussion of the new and challenging provisions that resulted from the enactment of the new Clean Air Act in 1990. It must be understood that a complete and detailed explanation of the entire Clean Air Act is not within the scope of this *Basic Guide to Environmental Compliance*. The objective here, as with all chapters in this part, is to impart a basic understanding of these extremely complicated regulations, highlighting the historical development, essential requirements, and primary purpose of each element of the Act so that the reader may approach this area of environmental compliance with some degree of knowledge and confidence.

BACKGROUND: HISTORICAL OVERVIEW

The regulation of clean air in the United States began in earnest with the passing of the Clean Air Act in 1967. This legislation, which predates NEPA and the creation of the EPA, was somewhat limited in scope and application. Its major focus was the provision of authority to establish air quality standards for the first time in the United States. By establishing acceptable levels of air quality, these standards defined the objectives of the entire national program for clean air assurance. However, it was not until the passing of the Clean Air Act of 1970 that the requirement for achieving or maintaining these standards gained any significant momentum.

The Clean Air Act of 1970

The Clean Air Act of 1970 was much stronger and far more comprehensive than its predecessor. In fact, it established the foundation for all regulatory efforts in this area during the past 20 years and is often referred to as the first Clean Air Act (i.e., many sources neglect to even mention or discuss the 1967 Act). It established the modern *federal air pollution control program* in the United States and set into motion the intent of those air quality standards that were first established under the Clean Air Act of 1967. Specifically, the 1970 Act authorized the newly created EPA to establish *National Ambient Air Quality Standards (NAAQS),* which set the maximum concentration levels for various air pollutants. NAAQS are promulgated on a pollutant-by-pollutant basis. These standards and the statutory authority under which they are set have remained in effect throughout the many revisions of the Clean Air Act. Under Section 108 of the 1970 Act, the EPA was required to publish a list of air pollutants that may reasonably be anticipated to endanger the public health or welfare. In response to this extremely difficult task, the EPA had applied NAAQS to only seven specific pollutants, referred to as the *criteria pollutants,* as follows:

- Total suspended particulate matters (TSP), smaller than 10 micrometers (known simply as "PM10");
- Sulfur oxides;
- Nitrogen dioxide;
- Lead;
- Carbon monoxide;

- Hydrocarbons; and
- Ozone.

The EPA had also developed, as required, a *criteria document* for each of the pollutants. The Act specifically states that the air quality criteria for a given pollutant shall accurately reflect the latest scientific knowledge useful in indicating the kind and extent of all identifiable effects on public health and welfare. At the same time, the EPA was to provide to the states and pollution control agencies information on state-of-the-art pollution control techniques, including data on the cost of such emission controls.

As a result of the 1970 Act, NAAQS are divided into two areas of concern:

1. Primary NAAQS, which focus on the protection of public health based upon established air quality criteria and allowing for a significant margin of safety; and
2. Secondary NAAQS, which are concerned with the protection of additional environmental values, such as plant and animal life, property, aesthetic sensibilities, and other items of concern to the welfare of the public.

Once the EPA sets or revises NAAQS for the criteria pollutants, the states bear the responsibility for designing and implementing the strategies and plans necessary to achieve the ambient standards.

As a method of assuring that states will take the appropriate actions, the 1970 Act directed each state to adopt a *State Implementation Plan (SIP)* to achieve NAAQS for air pollutants by meeting specific emission requirements. SIPs, then, comprise the central core of the regulatory framework. Each SIP must include a comprehensive analysis of air quality in each region and strategies that will be used to achieve compliance with NAAQS. SIPs also contain legally enforceable control requirements to ensure the attainment of the specified NAAQS for a given area.

In addition to the establishment of NAAQS and the requirements for SIPs, the 1970 Act granted the EPA the authority to establish *New Source Performance Standards (NSPS)*, which detailed national emission standards for all new sources of air pollution being proposed or constructed, as well as *National Emission Standards for Hazardous Air Pollutants (NESHAPS)*. The NSPS required the EPA to publish and periodically revise a list of categories of stationary sources that cause or contribute significantly to air pollution that may endanger the public health. After devising the list, the EPA must promulgate standards of performance for these sources that apply to any air pollutant emitted from the stationary source. It should be noted that much of the control effort has been directed toward existing facilities only. However, special standards for more than 60 *categories of sources* have been promulgated, requiring new industrial plants and existing modified ones to satisfy more stringent requirements. NSPS requires the use of the best demonstrated technologies (often referred to as the *Best Available Control Technology, or BACT*) whenever major sources of pollution are to be constructed or modified. The statutory provisions and regulations under NSPS remain in effect today, without any *significant* changes resulting from the Clean Air Act revisions and amendments since 1970.

Under NESHAPS, the EPA was required to publish a list that included each hazardous air pollutant. A hazardous air pollutant is one for which no ambient air quality standard is applicable and that, in the judgment of the EPA, may cause or contribute to air pollution that may reasonably be anticipated to result in an increase in mortality or serious illness. Because the statute required these standards to protect public health with an ample margin of safety and because the scientific understanding of cancer suggests that there is no threshold below which exposure is safe, the EPA has found it extremely difficult to establish such a list. As a result, NESHAPS were promulgated for only seven substances under the Clean Air Act of 1970, as listed below:

- Asbestos;
- Benzene;
- Beryllium;
- Inorganic arsenic;
- Mercury;
- Radionuclides; and
- Vinyl chloride.

Under the 1970 Act, each state may apply to the EPA for the authority to implement and enforce both the federal NSPS and the NESHAPS programs. However, the EPA still retains primary enforcement power over each program.

The Clean Air Act Amendments of 1977

In 1977 Congress enacted additional revisions to the 1970 Act. The 1977 amendments essentially retained the structure of the 1970 Act, but added new NAAQS compliance dates and enforcement strategies. The 1977 amendments also added two significant new programs aimed at further control over the pollution emissions in this country. The first, known as the *Prevention of Significant Deterioration (PSD)* program, was designed to prevent the deterioration of air qualities in those areas where the air was already cleaner than the levels established by NAAQS. Through a new source review process, the idea was to keep these areas clean by requiring specific and stringent control technologies for new or modified sources of emission. These PSD requirements call for careful monitoring of actual air quality conditions and actually place a limit on the amount or *increment* of clean air that can be used up by industrial projects. The second, known simply as the *Nonattainment* program, was aimed at restricting the construction of new sources of emissions in those areas of the country that already do not meet the requirements of NAAQS, until progress is made toward achieving NAAQS. The 1970 Clean Air Act had established an original deadline of 15 May 1975 for meeting NAAQS requirements. However, at least two-thirds of the nation did not comply with one or more NAAQS by this date. The 1977 amendments extended the deadline for achieving compliance with primary NAAQS through the SIPs to 31 December 1982. The amendments also authorized the individual states to extend this deadline further, to 31 December 1987, if deemed necessary.

Basically, the Nonattainment program requires owners or operators of new stationary emission sources to apply for and obtain a permit *prior* to the construction of any *major* new source or modification to any existing source in an area designated as Nonattainment. The *construction permit* must ensure that the source will comply with the *Lowest Achievable Emission Rate (LAER)*. There must also be *offsets* representing emission reductions from other sources. *Offset ratios* in the past were set at a 1-to-1 minimum. LAER for a given source is the more stringent of either the strictest limit contained in the SIP for that category of source or the most stringent emission limit achieved through practice for that category of source. Another principal feature of the Nonattainment provisions of the 1977 amendments was a requirement that existing major sources of emissions must install *Reasonably Available Control Technologies (RACT)*.

After the inclusion of the 1977 amendments, the structure of the Clean Air Act was as follows:

Title I—Established the requirements for the control of *stationary emission sources,* including NAAQS, the PSD program, and the Nonattainment program. Although Title I was concerned with stationary sources, the Act did not explicitly define a *stationary source* of emissions. However, the term is used throughout the Act to regulate any building, structure, facility, or installation that emits or may emit any air pollutant. Historically, stationary sources have typically been industrial plants or factories and similar sources of emissions. Also, both the PSD and Nonattainment programs specifically apply only to major sources of emissions. Under the 1977 amendments, a *major source* was described as any stationary source facility or source of air pollutants that directly emitted or had the potential to emit 100 tons per year of any pollutant. It should be noted that this definition was modified by Title III of the 1990 CAA amendments to include smaller emitters as major sources. See discussion of the 1990 amendments later in this chapter.

Title II—Addressed *mobile source* emissions that limited tailpipe emissions from new automobiles and other vehicles, such as aircraft. The 1970 Act required a 90% reduction of auto emissions below existing levels (the net effect being requirements to reduce emissions roughly 96% to 98% from an uncontrolled car). Under the 1977 amendments, the emissions standard for oxides of nitrogen was relaxed so that new car standards now result in approximately 75% control. Emission standards have also been applied to trucks and other vehicles. Since vehicles can move from one state to another, these controls have been applied on a national rather than state-by-state basis (although California has been permitted to require more stringent controls of its own).

Title III—Contained provisions concerning general *administrative requirements, citizen suits,* and the *judicial review process.*

It should also be noted that the EPA has the authority under the Act to regulate *indirect sources* through a SIP. An indirect source is described as any facility, building, structure, installation, real property, road, or highway that attracts or may attract mobile sources of pollution. Indirect sources may include road construction projects where the level of mobile source vehicles during the actual construction period exceed that which would normally be found in that specific area.

Enforcement Authority

The EPA has relied heavily on state agencies for the enforcement of source-specific limitations imposed by the Act. Prior to the 1990 amendments, the EPA could bring enforcement actions against violators of a statute after providing 30 days prior written notice. These actions could be brought by filing a lawsuit in federal court or by issuing an *administrative order (AO)* requiring the source of the violation to come into compliance with the applicable requirements of the Act. In civil actions, the EPA could either issue an *injunction for relief* (i.e., an order seeking relief by prohibiting a person or group from carrying out noncompliant actions) or recover civil penalties of up to $25,000 per day for each violation. Although the vast majority of such actions against noncompliant sources have been civil in nature, the EPA has begun in recent years to pursue criminal penalties more aggressively as well (see Chapter 2). Anyone who knowingly violates restrictions adopted to implement the statute is potentially subject to misdemeanor criminal sanctions. Knowingly making false statements or certifications is also viewed as a criminal offense. Maximum punishment was generally a fine of $25,000 per day of each violation, or imprisonment of up to 1 year, or both.

THE CLEAN AIR ACT AMENDMENTS OF 1990

In 1981, the National Commission on Air Quality completed and submitted its findings to Congress. Legislators then began an intensive debate over the Clean Air Act and the need for further amendments and modifications to the statute. This debate lasted through several sessions of Congress, with the resulting impasse preventing any further legislative action until 1990.

The 1990 amendments to the Clean Air Act will undoubtedly have extremely profound effects on life in this country for many years to come. Not only will these amendments renew and subsequently intensify national efforts to reduce air pollution emissions, they will also have major impacts on governmental agencies and the private economy. Estimated costs to achieve compliance are projected in ranges exceeding $25 billion per year.

The new Clean Air Act is divided into seven separate Titles covering different regulatory program requirements. The amendments strengthen the authority and increase the resources of air quality control agencies at both the federal and state levels. Although the amendments were signed into law on 15 November 1990, many of these new requirements will be implemented over the next two decades or longer before they become fully effective.

Clearly, the 1990 Amendments to the Clean Air Act can be described as the most complex piece of environmental legislation to have ever been enacted by Congress in modern history.

Essential Elements

By 1990, most major urban areas in the country with heavy industrialization still continued to have periods when they exceeded the concentrations of certain air pollutants as established by NAAQS. In fact, approximately 100 such areas remain in nonattainment for ozone. Nonattainment problems also exist for carbon monoxide, particulate matter, and sulfur dioxide. Provisions of the 1990 amendments are aimed at these nonattainment problems and establish many new control requirements. These include new and tighter standards on emissions from mobile sources (motor vehicles), requirements for the use of cleaner-burning fuels, additional controls on industrial facilities, and a host of other, more stringent control measures. Many of these new provisions will be implemented through revised SIPs, while others will result directly from the new statute and additional federal regulations required under the Act.

The Titles of the New Clean Air Act

The Clean Air Act Amendments of 1990 have been interlaced into the Act's pre-amendment framework, thereby substantially revising and expanding the existing statute. The following is a listing and brief description of the seven Titles that comprise the current Clean Air Act subsequent to the 1990 amendments. Also provided is a summary of the changes or additions that have resulted from the new amendments.

Title I: Air Pollution Prevention and Control—Contains the provisions for the establishment of *Air Quality Control Regions* and *Air Quality Control Techniques*. Requirements for NAAQS, SIPs, PSD, and Nonattainment are all found within Title I. The amendments mandate new classification of nonattainment areas and the setting of deadlines to achieve attainment on the basis of the severity of present pollution levels. They describe numerous control measures that must be implemented in nonattainment areas, including tighter controls on industrial plants and facilities.

Title II: Emission Standards for Moving Sources—This Title establishes criteria for *Motor Vehicle Emission* and *Fuel Standards,* including new provisions for reformulated gasoline. *Aircraft Emission Standards* are provided, as are new requirements for *Clean Fuel Vehicles.* As part of the ozone and carbon monoxide nonattainment programs, the amendments mandate further restrictions with tougher emission standards applicable to motor vehicles. In addition, the amendments establish new requirements for petroleum companies to produce alternative fuels for motor vehicles that burn cleaner than existing grades. The auto industry itself must begin to produce vehicles capable of burning such alternative fuels for sale initially to fleet operators in nonattainment areas.

Title III: Air Toxics—Contains *Source Definitions* applicable to emissions of air toxics. Section 112 of the 1970 Clean Air Act authorized the EPA to establish special standards for hazardous air pollutants. However, as mentioned previously, such standards have actually been promulgated for only seven substances. Title III of the new Act establishes a list of *189 pollutants* to be regulated and also establishes a list of *source categories* of polluters. Title III identifies and requires companies to install *Maximum Achievable Control Technology (MACT)* requirements, *Work Practice Standards, Modification to Existing Plant* requirements, and *Schedules for Completion.* In addition to establishing the list of pollutants, the amendments also require the EPA to promulgate new control standards for most sources of such emissions. Title III also broadens the scope of coverage for *major stationary sources* of emission to include any stationary source or group of stationary sources located within a contiguous area and under common control that emits or has the potential to emit, considering controls and in the aggregate, 10 tons per year or more of any hazardous air pollutant or 25 tons per year or more of any combination of hazardous air pollutants.

Title IV: Acid Deposition Control—Title IV addresses requirements for controlling *sulfur dioxide* emissions and *nitrogen oxide* emissions (i.e., *acid rain*). An innovative *Allowances Program* is also outlined that essentially permits the collecting and trading of emission *credits* between facilities of the same owner to keep total emission rates within legal limits and to facilitate compliance with the acid rain requirements of this Title. The amendments impose new sets of requirements, primarily on coal-fired power plants, designed to cut national emissions of sulfur dioxide approximately in half. Reductions in emissions of nitrogen oxides are also mandated.

Title V: Permits—Permitting requirements and programs are defined in this Title. The *Application process, Conditions for Permitting,* and other related information can be found in Title V of the Act. The amendments call upon states to establish comprehensive new permit programs for all *significant air emission sources.* Under Title V, the operators of such facilities are required to pay *permitting fees.*

Title VI: Stratospheric Ozone Protection—Provides a listing of the substances thought to threaten the protective ozone layer. Establishes *phase-out requirements* for ozone-depleting substances. Also identifies the requirements for a *National Recycling and Emission Reduction Program,* including the servicing of *Motor Vehicle Air Conditioners.* A *Safe Alternative Policy* is mandated in Title VI, as well as a provision for *International Cooperation.* The amendments establish new requirements to restrict emissions of *chlorofluorocarbons (CFCs)* as a further step toward addressing concerns over ozone depletion and global warming.

Title VII: Enforcement—Title VII establishes all the Enforcement provisions of the new Act, including guidelines for civil and criminal fines and penalties subsequent to violations of the Act. The amendments have greatly increased enforcement authority by adding new criminal sanctions.

Specific Effects of the New Requirements

The principal features of the new amendments can be summarized based upon the changes and additions to the Titles of the Act, as identified above. The new Act is extremely complex, with cumbersome timetables for implementation of the new requirements. The information presented in these paragraphs is an attempt to simplify the changes caused by the amendments as they relate to the existing structure of the Act subsequent to the 1977 amendments. The following is a brief overview of the effects that the new Title requirements will have on each of the specific areas of concern, as indicated.

Effects of Title I Provisions
Following are the effects of the Title I provisions:

1. *Stationary sources*—The primary effect of the new regulations on industrial facilities is the further tightening of requirements for existing sources to install *RACT,* which, under the amendments, will broaden to cover smaller sources of emissions as well (e.g., those that emit less than 100 tons per year). Under the provisions of the new amendments, the EPA is required to issue new *Control Technique Guidelines (CTGs),* defining technological control for additional categories of industrial facilities. A major problem with the CTG procedure thus far has been a concern that the EPA is requiring compliance with specified CTG requirements without going through formal rule-making procedures. The obvious concern here is that industry will be required to comply with regulations that they have not had the opportunity to review through the normal rule-making process. In the end, the EPA will issue over 40 such CTGs that will impose restrictions on the operational protocol of a given facility.

2. *Effects on state implementation plans*—Under the new Act, all states with nonattainment areas must now submit a revised SIP, identifying additional control requirements sufficient enough to demonstrate that attainment will be achieved by specified deadlines. Also, the SIPs will be required to show net reductions in total emissions from baseline inventories equating to 15% by 15 November 1996 and an additional 3% each year thereafter. Such progress requirements will be the driving factor for imposing specific new controls on individual industrial facilities. In the event that attainment is not achieved on schedule, additional requirements would be triggered to add further control measures to the SIP. In severe and extreme areas, a penalty fee could be imposed annually on any major source in the amount of $5,000 per ton of emissions exceeding 80% of the actual or permitted levels. The Act does have provisions that will allow reductions of less than 15% where an area applies *new source review* and assures that all feasible controls are installed on existing sources. Another feature of the new amendments requires the EPA to promulgate *Federal Implementation Plans (FIPs)* where states have failed to submit adequate plans.

3. *Effects on nonattainment areas*— If a violation of the standard occurs anywhere within an air quality control region, then the entire region must be classified as a nonattainment area.

For example, compliance with the new ozone standards will present the most extensive and difficult compliance problems. Under the new Act, a violation of the ozone standard will have occurred for the entire region if the fourth highest reading (over a 24-hour period) during the previous 3 years exceeded the levels prescribed in the standard at any one point in that region. Currently, this fourth highest reading (listed in parts *per million,* or *ppm*) for each nonattainment area is used as a measure in the design of further controls for that region; therefore, the reading is often referred to as the *design value* for the particular region. A major element of the new Act requires the establishment of specific *pollution classifications* of ozone nonattainment areas. In order to accomplish this, the *severity* of pollution problems that may exist (as measured by their design values) are used as a basis. Deadlines for reaching attainment in these areas are then established based upon the particular severity of the pollution problems, as shown in Table 6-1. It should also be pointed out that the new Act will permit the established boundaries of a designated nonattainment area to be redefined based upon demonstrated air quality monitoring data. This is an important aspect, since the determination of

TABLE 6-1.   Ozone nonattainment classification categories. (Source: EPA, Clean Air Act of 1990)

POLLUTION CLASSIFICATION	ATTAINMENT DEADLINE	DESIGN VALUE PARTS PER MILLION (ppm)
Marginal	11-15-1993	0.121 - 0.138
Moderate	11-15-1996	0.138 - 0.160
Serious	11-15-1999	0.160 - 0.180
Severe	11-15-2005	0.180 - 0.190
	11-15-2007	0.190 - 0.280
Extreme	11-15-2010	> 0.280

the boundary of a nonattainment area will dictate the required use of control technologies for the entire area.

Under the 1977 amendments, existing *major sources* (those with the potential to emit 100 tons per year or more) were required to install RACT. Until the 1990 amendments, the ozone nonattainment concern was primarily addressed through the control of *volatile organic compounds (VOCs)*. The new Act further extends the basic RACT requirements to include the oxides of nitrogen (NO_x), along with VOCs. Also, the application of RACT is now required for *smaller sources* in the more seriously polluted areas. Table 6-2 shows the nonattainment categories in terms of *offset ratios* and *quantities* of pollution expected.

In addition to the ozone requirements briefed above, nonattainment requirements also apply to all areas that are in violation of any other ambient air quality standards. For example, the requirements for particulate matter and carbon monoxide are also of great concern. The EPA has listed 41 areas for nonattainment of carbon monoxide standards, and 70 have been identified for particulate matter.

TABLE 6-2.   RACT requirements for smaller existing nonattainment sources. (Source: EPA, Clean Air Act of 1990)

POLLUTION CLASSIFICATION	RACT REQUIREMENTS EFFECTIVE FOR SOURCES OF VOC OR NO_x EMISSIONS AT:	OFFSET RATIO
Marginal	100 Tons Per Year	1.1 : 1
Moderate	100 Tons Per Year	1.15 : 1
Serious	50 Tons Per Year	1.2 : 1
Severe	25 Tons Per Year	1.3 : 1
Extreme	10 Tons Per Year	1.5 : 1

4. *Other Title I effects*—The new amendments establish an *ozone transport region,* extending from the metropolitan Washington, DC area up the East Coast to Maine. In this corridor, ozone nonattainment problems are interconnected (i.e., emissions in one area may cause violations in another area downwind). The significance of an ozone interstate transport region is that areas within the region may be in attainment based upon their own emissions; however, due to unique wind current phenomenon, these attainment areas may become subjected to the same stringent requirements for nonattainment areas.

Effects of Title II Provisions

Following are the effects of the Title II provisions:

1. *National mobile source standards*—The new amendments under Title II will have the most significant impact on *motor vehicle manufacturing.* Cars and very light trucks must comply with much stricter tailpipe emission standards for non-methane hydrocarbons (NMHC), carbon monoxide (CO), and the oxides of nitrogen (NO_x) The exact timetable for the implementation of these requirements is established as a two-phase process known as "Tier I" and "Tier II" standards. Tier I standards for cars and very light trucks are to be phased into effect for NMHC (0.25 grams per mile) and CO (3.4 grams per mile) between 1994 and 1998, and for NO_x (0.4 grams per mile) during 1994 and 1995. The EPA will also consider setting standards for emissions of air toxics, such as benzene and formaldehyde (as minimums), under Tier I standards. If the EPA finds it necessary, technologically feasible, and cost-effective, it must set even tighter Tier II standards to become effective between 2003 and 2006. The Act suggests that the Tier II standards be half of the Tier I levels. Also, if the EPA fails to act, the amendment's *hammer provisions* specify that the Tier II standards will automatically become effective in 2003. The amendments also require the control of car emission sources other than those emanating from the tailpipe. Evaporative emissions from NMHC on board the vehicles must also be controlled. The EPA will eventually require the installation of on-board vapor recovery systems to capture fugitive emissions of fuel vapors. The Act also requires stricter standards for trucks and buses. California's tailpipe standard for light- and medium-duty trucks were made mandatory for the remaining 49 states under the new amendments. Particulate matter and NO_x standards for heavy-duty trucks are also more strictly regulated.

The amendments establish two clean-fueled vehicle programs. Both require controls that go above and beyond those required to meet the basic mobile source control requirements. Vehicles subject to regulation are car and truck fleets in serious, severe, and extreme ozone nonattainment areas, as well as certain cars to be sold under a pilot program in the state of California. It should be noted that fleets of ten or more vehicles that are capable of being centrally fueled are covered by the new standards. However, vehicles such as those used for law enforcement, emergency use, or retail rental are specifically exempt.

2. *Clean fuels*—The petroleum refining industry is also severely effected by the new amendments. Clean fuels include methanol, ethanol, mixtures of those fuels with gasoline, reformulated gasoline, natural gas, liquefied petroleum gas, and electricity. In the most severely polluted areas, gasoline must be replaced by clean fuels meeting specifications prescribed in great detail in the legislation under two separate but overlapping programs. The first requires that starting in 1995, reformulated gasoline is phased in as the only fuel sold in the nine cities with the highest ozone levels, as shown in Table 6-3. Limits are established for oxygen content, aromatic hydrocarbons, and benzene. Reformulated gasoline sold in the nation's nine *most smoggiest cities* must have a minimum 2% oxygen content. The fuel must also meet restrictions on the formation of VOCs and other hazardous air pollutants. The second program requires that oxygenated fuels (of at least 2.7% oxygen content) are sold in carbon monoxide nonattainment areas.

TABLE 6-3.   The nine most polluted cites in the United States. (Source: EPA)

AMERICA'S MOST POLLUTED CITIES

Los Angeles, California (Includes Anaheim and Riverside)

Baltimore, Maryland

Chicago, Illinois (Extends into Indiana and Wisconsin)

Houston, Texas (Includes Galveston and Brazoria)

Milwaukee, Wisconsin (Includes Racine)

Muskegon, Michigan

New York, New York (Extends into New Jersey and Connecticut)

Philadelphia, Pennsylvania (Extends into New Jersey and Delaware)

San Diego, California

3. *Other Title II effects*—The new amendments contain other extremely broad requirements pertaining to motor vehicle operations, including the total phaseout of leaded gasoline, cold temperature standards for CO emissions, and (in serious, severe, and extreme ozone nonattainment areas) secondary ("Stage II") vapor recovery controls being installed on vehicles. Also, the Act requires manufacturers to extend their warranty on catalytic converters and other emission control equipment to 8 years or 80,000 miles, while the warranty for other emission-related components of cars and light trucks are to be shortened to 2 years or 24,000 miles.

Effects of Title III Provisions
Following are the effects of Title III provisions:

1. *Air toxics*—The primary problem associated with the 1970 Act requirement for the EPA to identify and regulate hazardous air pollutants was that the old Section 112 was based upon a zero tolerance with regard to health effects of certain air toxics. It became impossible for the EPA to combine the strategy of *absolute protection* with the ever-increasing awareness of the scientific causes of cancers in humans. The major point in the study of carcinogenicity is the EPA's traditional standpoint that no safe level of exposure exists when it comes to cancer. This operating philosophy made it virtually impossible for the EPA to regulate air toxics under the 1970 Act.

   Under the new Act, the approach to the regulation of air toxics shifted from a *risk-based approach* to a *technology-based approach*. This shift was due to the fact that the old method was not effective and newer technologies were available to reduce exposure levels to within acceptable ranges. Also, in 1989 the EPA released a summary of reports submitted by industry under Section 313 of the 1986 amendments to the Superfund Act that required the very first nationwide reporting of releases of air toxics. These alarming data were extremely influential during the formulation of the 1990 amendments to the Clean Air Act.

2. *Maximum Achievable Control Technology (MACT)*—A major feature of the Act is the creation of the list of substances to be regulated. The resultant statutory list of 189 substances can be changed by the EPA, as required. Substances may be deleted from or added to the list if scientific data demonstrate that such changes are appropriate. Private citizens can also petition the EPA to consider such changes. Under the new Act, the EPA will no longer establish control requirements based upon a substance-by-substance review. Rather, the EPA has identified a list of categories of industrial facilities that emit substantial quantities of each air toxic. Now, the standards for the listed source categories require the

maximum achievable degree of reduction in emissions for those air toxics. It is important to note that the Act contains a provision that will automatically require MACT if the EPA fails to promulgate MACT standards as required. In the event that the EPA does fail to act as required by the law, sources of emission will become subject to a case-by-case application of MACT standards after the states have implemented approved permit programs. This provision has become known as the *MACT hammer*, since it forces the application of MACT one way or another. It is expected that implementation of MACT requirements will result in tighter controls over the entire production process. MACT requires evaluation of seals, fittings, valves, regulators, flanges, and all other components where a leak potential would exist should a failure of that component occur. Generally, MACT standards require emissions of 75% to 90% below previous levels.

The new Act requires that all MACT standards for all source categories be promulgated by 15 November 2000. However, an existing source may voluntarily reduce emissions without waiting for MACT standards to be promulgated. The Act provides incentive for facilities to take such initiative. For example, an existing source can qualify for a 6-year extension of MACT requirements if it can show a 90% reduction in emissions (95% for hazardous particulates) prior to the applicable deadline imposed by a specific MACT.

It should be noted here that MACT for new sources is defined as "not less than the emission control achieved in practice by the best-controlled similar source" (as determined by the EPA). This means that, in a majority of cases, MACT should be equivalent to the *Best Achievable Control Technology (BACT)* as defined by existing PSD regulations. For existing sources, MACT shall not be less than the best performing 12% of existing sources.

3. *Residual risk*—Although it was stated previously that the new Act moved from a risk-based approach to a technology-based approach in evaluating air toxics, the identification and application of risk reduction controls still exists in the language of the new Act, albeit a more insidious requirement than under the old 1970 provisions. After approximately 8 or 9 years following the establishment of a MACT standard, the amendments now require the EPA to conduct an evaluation study to determine whether the MACT standards are adequate in terms of risk to public health with an ample margin of safety.

4. *Accidental releases and the OSHA connection*—In addition to the major concern for releases of air toxics during normal operations, the Act considers methods to prevent as well as respond to accidental and/or catastrophic releases. In fact, the EPA must identify at least 100 extremely hazardous air pollutants. Included in this list of hazardous pollutants are substances such as:

- Ammonia;
- Anhydrous ammonia;
- Bromine;
- Chlorine;
- Ethylene oxide;
- Anhydrous hydrogen chloride;
- Hydrogen fluoride;
- Hydrogen sulfide;
- Hydrogen cyanide;
- Methyl chloride;
- Phosgene;
- Anhydrous sulfur dioxide;
- Sulfur trioxide;
- Methyl isocyanate;
- Toluene diisocyanate;
- Vinyl chloride.

An *accidental release* is defined as the unanticipated emission of a regulated substance or other extremely hazardous substance into ambient air from a *stationary source*. Factory owners are required to identify possible hazards and develop *risk management plans*. In fact, the Act specifically mandates another federal agency, OSHA, to promulgate rules governing the safety of employees in a workplace.

The *OSHA connection* to Title III of the CAA can be found in Section 304 of the Act. As a result of numerous, highly publicized fatal accidents involving the release of toxic pollutants, Section 304 directs the Secretary of Labor to promulgate, under the Occupational Safety and Health Administration (OSHA), a *chemical process safety standard*. The intent of the Standard is to protect employees from hazards associated with accidental releases of extremely hazardous substances used in the workplace. OSHA's response is known, in short, as the *Process Safety Management Standard* and is found in 29 CFR 1910.119. This rule, which became final in February 1992, requires applicable employers to implement at least the following actions:

- Develop written safety information.
- Perform workplace hazard analyses (also known as *Process Hazard Analyses, or PHAs)*.
- Develop methods for responding to PHA findings.
- Conduct a periodic review of the analyses and response items.
- Allow for employee participation and discussions in all aspects of the program.
- Prepare formal operating procedures.

- Perform employee safety training.
- Ensure that contractor/contract employees have training.
- Provide appropriate response training.
- Conduct and document maintenance programs.
- Perform a pre-startup review on new and modified equipment.
- Develop formalized change-over procedures.
- Investigate every major accident or near miss.

In the Standard, OSHA provides a list of over 100 such hazardous chemicals along with designated threshold limits on quantities stored in the workplace. If an employer reaches a specified quantity for a listed chemical, then that employer is subject to the provisions of the *Process Safety Management Rule*. It should be noted that additional chemicals may be added to the list if and when they are found to pose threats of serious injury or fatality if accidentally released into the workplace.

Finally, Title III requires the creation of a *Chemical Safety and Hazard Identification Board* to investigate accidental releases of extremely hazardous air pollutants and make recommendations to prevent future similar events.

Effects of Title IV Provisions

Following are the effects of the Title IV provisions:

1. *Acid rain*—The amendments established a totally new approach on how to address and control the acid rain phenomenon. Prior to 1977, little attention was focused on this problem. Since that time, studies have indicated that the accumulated emissions of sulfur dioxide and nitrogen oxides cause damage to the environment (lakes, forests, flora, etc.). It was also determined that power plants create approximately 80% of sulfur dioxide and roughly one-third the nitrogen oxide emissions in the United States. Further, these emissions may often travel for several hundred miles in the atmosphere before being deposited on the geography. Hence, the focus of Title IV provisions is on power plant emissions of these two pollutants. The Act requires a reduction of sulfur dioxide emissions by approximately 10 million tons annually. The target reduction for nitrogen oxides is 2 million tons. These reductions are to occur in phases, with the first phase beginning in 1995 and the second phase in the year 2000. The legislation actually names 111 plants that must begin their emission reductions during Phase I. In Phase II, the allowance allocation for the 111 Phase I plants will be reduced and all remaining power plants (with few exceptions) are to be subjected to the allowance requirements.

To accomplish the required reductions, a new market-based system has been developed under the provisions of Title IV. Power plants are allocated *emission allowances* that basically require these facilities to reduce their emissions to designated levels or acquire unused allowances from others who have already achieved compliance without using up all their emission allowance. For example, if a plant reduces its emissions to the point where excess allowances are created, it can *bank* them to meet future demands or for use when Phase II requirements become effective. It can also use them at another plant under common ownership, or trade them to other plants. Once reductions have been achieved during Phase II, a cap on the permissible emissions of SO_2 that limits emissions nationally to 8.9 million tons shall be established to maintain these reduced levels (i.e., the EPA will only distribute 8.9 million allowances annually).

Under the 1990 amendments, allowance may also be obtained from the EPA, either through an annual *allowance auction* or through the *direct sale* to newly built plants.

Effects of Title V Provisions

Following are the effects of the Title V provisions:

1. *Permitting procedures*—The amendments now require, with few exceptions, all significant air emissions sources to make application for and obtain permits. Prior to the 1990 amendments, SIPs were the EPA's tools for enforcing Clean Air Act provisions. Under the new Act, SIPs will continue to be used by the states as planning documents to meet air quality objectives. However, permits issued by the states under the federal air permitting program are now the primary enforcement mechanism for the EPA. To ensure consistency in its enforcement, the EPA established minimum requirements for state plans. Hence, the permits will not replace the SIPs, but will become the principal mechanism for detailing the specific requirements as they apply to individual emission sources. The permit will attempt to resolve any uncertainties as to what requirements are applicable.

2. *Sources covered by the permitting requirement*—Permits are required for any facility in the following categories:
   a. Major source;
   b. Any source subject to Title III (Air Toxics); and
   c. All sources subject to NSPS.

3. *Permit elements*—The Act establishes the minimum elements that each operating permit must contain. First, the permit must include enforceable emission limitations and standards, a schedule of compliance, record-keeping and reporting requirements, and other conditions necessary to

ensure compliance. Second, each permit must establish inspection, entry, monitoring, compliance certification, and reporting requirements so that compliance with the terms and conditions of the permit can be verified. Third, the state may issue *general permits* to cover numerous similar sources. Each emission source to be covered under a general permit is required to submit application to the state. Fourth, the Act will allow protection against enforcement actions for operating without a permit for existing sources that submit completed applications in a timely manner. This provision is referred to as the *permit shield.*

4. *Emissions source*—It is significant to mention that the permitting requirements focus primarily on the issuance of permits for specific source emissions. However, this element of Title V becomes extremely complex when attempting to determine the exact meaning of the term *source*. It does not always mean an industrial plant or facility. In fact, it can be either an entire facility that must collectively account for all emissions under its operation or, more commonly, each point within a plant where emissions are released. This double meaning causes problems when attempting to apply permitting requirements to such emission points. For large facilities, it is not inconceivable that many hundreds of individual *sources* might exist at the same time. To attempt to specify permit application requirements for each such source would obviously be a largely unworkable task. Although the amendments do authorize a single permit to cover all sources at an industrial plant, the issue is still quite complicated, since separate emission limitations are usually applicable to each individual source.

Effects of Title VI Provisions

Following are the effects of the Title VI provisions:

1. *Chlorofluorocarbons (CFCs)*—Scientific research has provided strong indications that CFCs, along with other man-made chemicals, greatly contribute to the destruction of the Earth's protective stratospheric ozone layer as well as affecting a potential global climate change. The 1990 amendments establish a plan for phasing out the production and sale of CFCs and several other *ozone level–depleting substances (OLDS)*. Controls of products that contain CFCs are also regulated and controlled. As a result, manufacturers of OLDS are required to develop effective substitutes or risk severe loss of an entire market area.

Initially, the Act required the phaseout of Class I substances, defined as CFCs, halons, and carbon tetrachloride, by the year 2000, and methyl chloroform by the year 2002. However, in 1992, President Bush called for an acceleration of these requirements to phase out production of Class I substances by 1995, with a ban on sales occurring by 1997.

Class II is primarily comprised of those substances known as *halogenated chlorofluorocarbons (HCFCs)*, which also harm the ozone level. The production of these substances shall cease in 2015. HCFCs can be used as a replacement refrigerant until the year 2020. A complete production ban will become effective in the year 2030.

2. *Other Title VI provisions*—The Act requires a system that will maximize the recapture and recycling of Class I and Class II substances. Essentially, the blatant discharge of refrigerants from household appliances, commercial refrigerators, and air conditioners is no longer permitted. Specially equipped maintenance facilities are required to perform any type of servicing task that could possibly result in a release of these substances to the atmosphere.

Also, nonessential CFC-containing consumer products, such as party streamers, noise horns, and certain cleaning fluids for electronic and photographic equipment, are banned under Title VI.

Effects of Title VII Provisions
Following are the effects of Title VII provisions:

1. *Impacts of enforcement on stationary sources*—The new amendments add many new, tough enforcement authorities, which include both civil and criminal sanctions. The most severe penalties that can be imposed under the new Act make it absolutely essential that corporations and their management comply with the requirements of the new Act. For example, nearly all *knowing violations* will be subjected to criminal prosecution. The amendments also considerably strengthen the EPA's enforcement authority regarding violations of SIPs and federally enforceable permits.

2. *Types of enforcement*—Section 113 of the Act provides for three types of enforcement actions. The first, known as *administrative enforcement*, enables the EPA to seek penalties without having to first file a civil suit in court. The second, known as *civil judicial enforcement*, remains virtually the same as it was prior to the amendments in that the EPA still has the authority to bring civil penalties against an affected source, a major emitting facility, or a major stationary source and to recover a civil penalty of not more than $25,000 per day for each violation and to request injunctions against the same. The amendments do authorize the EPA to establish a *field citation program* for minor violations. EPA officials conducting an investigation of a facility can actually write field citations on the spot and impose penalties of up to $5,000 per day for each violation. The third, known as *criminal enforcement*, now includes felonies, in-

creased fines, and longer prison terms for criminal violations. Criminal sanctions also include provisions for record-keeping fines, negligent endangerment (negligently releasing air toxics that put another person at risk of harm), and knowing endangerment (knowingly causing a release of air toxics will subject an individual to fines of up to $250,000 per day and 15 years imprisonment; businesses can be fined up to $1 million).

The amendments also contain a radically new *bounty hunter provision* that authorizes the EPA to pay a bounty of up to $10,000 to anyone who provides information that leads to a civil penalty or criminal conviction. This provision applies to current as well as past employees.

3. *Other Title VII provisions*—The EPA is now authorized under Title VII to issue *emergency orders* to protect the public welfare and the environment rather than being limited to protecting only the public health. Under the new Act, emergency orders are effective for up to 60 days without a court order, as opposed to 24 prior to the 1990 amendments.

Suits by private citizens are now authorized under the amendments. However, it should be noted that any monetary awards granted as a result of a citizen suit (with the exception of certain attorney fees) will not be awarded to the person bringing the suit. Moneys will be deposited in a special Treasury fund that will then be used for licensing and other required services.

SUMMARY

The regulation of clean air in the United States was one of the first areas of environmental concern, with some legislative actions dating back to before the creation of the EPA. As a result of numerous amendments, the majority of which occurred in 1977 and, most substantially, in 1990, the Clean Air Act is today one of the most formidable pieces of legislation of current concern to the environmental compliance professional. One reason for the complexity of the Act is that it did not only establish numerous new regulations; it also retained many of the requirements mandated by previous versions and revisions of the Act. Many of the original provisions from the 1970 Clean Air Act such as the *National Ambient Air Quality Standard (NAAQS)*, the *State Implementation Plans (SIPs)*, the *New Source Performance Standards (NSPS)*, the *National Emission Standards for Hazardous Air Pollutants (NESHAPS)*, the list of the seven *criteria pollutants*, and the concept of *Best Available Control Technology (BACT)* still exist today. The amendments of 1977 and 1990 only added many more requirements and provisions to ensure the preservation of clean air. For example, the 1977 amendments added two significant programs designed to prevent the deterioration of air qualities below the levels established by NAAQS. One, known as the *Prevention of*

Significant Deterioration (PSD) Program, came with enforceable provisions to help guarantee that those areas already cleaner than NAAQS-prescribed levels stayed that way. The second program, called *Nonattainment,* restricts those areas that are already below the levels established by NAAQS from further degradation while, at the same time, requiring compliance-tight time-lines for achieving attainment with these levels. Subsequent to the 1977 amendments, the *Lowest Achievable Emission Rate (LAER)* for a given source had to be attained, and existing sources emitting more than 100 tons per year (a *major source* under the 1977 CAA, which was changed under the 1990 amendments) were required to install *Reasonably Achievable Control Technology (RACT)* to reduce emissions to acceptable levels.

With the 1990 Clean Air Act amendments came a host of additional and extremely complicated compliance provisions. This chapter has provided a brief overview of each of the seven new Titles created by the 1990 Act. Major focus is on the areas of stationary sources, mobile sources, air toxics, acid rain, permitting, ozone depletion, and enforcement of the Act. An example of the many new additions and changes created by the new Act is the establishment of a list of 189 toxic air pollutants (to replace the original 7 from the 1970 Act) that are now subject to regulation. Also, under Title III (Air Toxics), the concept of *Maximum Achievable Control Technology (MACT)* is established. Title III of the 1990 Act also significantly narrowed the requirements for *major sources* by reducing the action level established in 1977 from a source emitting 100 tons per year of any pollutant to one that emits 10 tons per year of any single hazardous air pollutant or 25 tons per year of any combination of hazardous air pollutants. *Chlorofluorocarbons (CFCs),* which have been determined as harmful and destructive to the Earth's protective ozone layer, will eventually be phased out of production, sale, and finally existence itself as a direct result of the 1990 amendments.

The 1990 amendments are so encompassing that they have even imposed requirements on OSHA to promulgate chemical process safety rules to protect employees in the workplace. The *Process Safety Management Rule* attempts to do just that.

Those safety and health professionals new to the environmental compliance arena, as well as the seasoned practitioner, will no doubt find the complexity of the Clean Air Act and its many amendments to be intimidating, to say the least.

CASE BRIEF: CLEAN AIR ACT
WILNER WOOD PRODUCTS CO. vs. MAINE DEPARTMENT OF
ENVIRONMENTAL PROTECTION
U.S. District Court, District of Maine
No. 90-0228-B, 10 May 1991

Summary

The plaintiff brought this case against a state agency in an effort to seek relief from enforcement due to the extreme financial burden that compliance would inflict on an already bankrupt organization. The significance of this case example is the demonstration that other federal action (in this instance, that of a federal bankruptcy court) may not prevent a state agency from enforcing Clean Air Act (CAA) provisions.

Background

Wilner Wood Products Company (WWPC) owns a woodworking facility in Maine. Under state law, WWPC must possess a valid air emission license from the Department of Environmental Protection (DEP). WWPC's license expired on 3 December 1980. On 8 January 1981, WWPC applied to renew the expired license. Under Maine law, this renewal application resurrected the validity of the old license until the DEP acted on the application for renewal. For unknown reasons (i.e., not reflected in the records), the DEP did not act on the application until 1989. In September of that year, the DEP and WWPC began discussions on necessary compliance actions. They agreed that WWPC should submit a Best Practicable Treatment (BPT) analysis 4 weeks after the DEP notified WWPC of the proper format. Under Maine law, WWPC would have to demonstrate that the proposed emissions would receive BPT, that the proposed emissions would not violate applicable air emission standards, and that the proposed emissions would not violate applicable ambient air quality standards, either alone or in conjunction with other sources. Such analyses are typically quite costly, depending on the method imposed to obtain the data. The DEP notified WWPC of the proper format on 12 February 1990. This timing was not favorable to WWPC, since 3 days earlier they had filed for Chapter 11 reorganization under the Federal Bankruptcy Code. The DEP gave WWPC until 16 March 1990 to submit its BPT analysis. Because WWPC was not in the position to pay its consultant, it did not perform the BPT analysis or comply with any of the other requirements for a new license. As a result, the DEP denied WWPC's renewal application, thereby discontinuing the effectiveness of the old license.

During this same time period, the bankruptcy court issued a temporary restraining order enjoining the State of Maine and the Commissioner of Environmental Protection from denying WWPC's renewal application until WWPC's appeal of the DEP's denial was complete. Since WWPC could not afford to risk operating without a valid permit, the bankruptcy court later issued a preliminary injunction staying the state's denial of WWPC's license pending the state appeal process. As a result, the state's defendants (the DEP, et al.) appealed the ruling of the bankruptcy court.

Decision

The decision of the bankruptcy court was vacated. Title 28 U.S.C. 959 for bankruptcy specifically states that those owners of property in bankruptcy must still manage and operate according to the valid laws of the state in which the property is situated. Since the state of Maine, under its approved State Implementation Plan (SIP), was properly enforcing the provisions of the CAA, there are no compliance exceptions for debtors who would be inconvenienced or burdened by the enforcement of state laws, including environmental laws.

Analysis

In short, federal bankruptcy court may not prevent state agencies from denying an air emissions license to a company that filed for bankruptcy, even if denial threatened to harm that company irreparably, because: 1) The debtor company must comply with state environmental laws, regardless of the burden of compliance; 2) Under SIP, state law requires a company to have a valid air emissions license; and 3) The bankruptcy court's general authority to issue stays did not extend to proceedings by a state agency to enforce its air pollution control laws.

This case demonstrates the extent of authority that states have when enforcing federal regulations such as the CAA.

7

The Clean Water Act

INTRODUCTION

Today's *Clean Water Act (CWA)* was initially established in 1972 with the enactment of the Federal Water Pollution Control Act (FWPCA) Amendments. Since that time, the CWA has been subjected to two *major* amendments: the Clean Water Act Amendments of 1977 and the Water Quality Control Act of 1987. The focus of the Act is primarily aimed at controlling the discharge of pollutants into navigable waters. Table 7-1 shows the major provisions of the Section Titles of the CWA. It is noted that, as of this writing, the CWA was being considered by Congress once again for a third round of amendments.

As a minimum, the practicing environmental professional must be familiar with the basic provisions of the CWA to ensure compliance with the law as well as the avoidance of water pollution discharges, which would prove extremely costly. Costs associated with water pollution include both real-dollar expenditures required for the cleanup of polluted waterways (reference the Exxon Valdez episode, whose cleanup costs reached into the billions of dollars) and the indirect costs that arise in the months and years following such pollution due to potentially irreparable damage to the environment, wildlife, and populations that rely on clean waterways for food, navigation, and basic survival.

The Clean Water Act and its amendments are a serious attempt to control, through federal regulations, the amount of polluting discharges that enter the rivers, lakes, streams, wetlands, or other navigable waterways that have any connection to or impact on interstate waters or commerce in the United States.

TABLE 7-1   The major sections of the Clean Water Act. (Source: EPA Clean
Water Act)

THE CLEAN WATER ACT	
SECTION NUMBER	MAJOR PROVISIONS
201	CONSTRUCTION GRANTS
208	AREA WIDE PLANNING
304	WATER QUALITY STANDARDS
307	INDUSTRIAL PRETREATMENT
311	OIL AND HAZARDOUS WASTES
401	NPDES PERMITTING
402	STORM WATER PERMITTING
404	FILL MATERIAL PERMITTING
405	SLUDGE MANAGEMENT

POLLUTION CATEGORIES UNDER
THE CWA

There are two fundamental categories of water pollution under the CWA: *point source* and *nonpoint source* emanations. It is noted that most regulatory activity has been directed at point source pollution; therefore, this category shall be primarily discussed in this chapter.

A *point source* discharge is defined in the Act as any discernible, confined, and discrete conveyance, including but not limited to any pipe, ditch, channel, tunnel, conduit, well, discrete fissure, container, rolling stock, concentrated animal feeding operation, or vessel or other floating craft from which pollutants are or may be discharged. However, the current language of the Act is clear that the term "point source" *will not* apply to agricultural stormwater discharges and return flows from irrigated agriculture. Under the point source category, there are further descriptive breakdowns of the major types of point source discharges that are regulated under the Act. A *direct discharge* point source is one that directly discharges into the waters of the United States. Those dischargers that fit this subcategory of point source must ensure that their effluent meets precise numerical limitations for various

pollutants, or they must install certain control technologies. Direct dischargers must be permitted under the CWA in order to legally proceed with such
discharges. The second type of point source is the *indirect discharge*, which is
one that discharges into *Publicly Owned Treatment Works (POTW)* facilities.
These types of dischargers are subject to specific pretreatment requirements
that are meant to ensure that the POTW will not exceed the discharge
limitations established under its operating permit. The Act defines a third
type of point source as *vessels* that spill oil or hazardous substances directly
into the navigable waterways. This includes *vessel sewage*. Finally, the Act
specifically classifies *dredged or fill materials* as a type of point source
pollution.

The second major discharge category, *nonpoint source discharges*, is defined simply as discharges into navigable water from a source other than the
end of a pipe.

BACKGROUND: HISTORICAL OVERVIEW

Prior to the 1972 amendments to the FWPCA, the prescribed regulatory
system for controlling water pollution consisted almost entirely of state-de-
veloped ambient water quality standards. This meant that the specific standards for a given waterway were dependent upon the discretion and use
requirements of the individual states. Enforcement was not consistent from
state to state and, in fact, was seldom an issue as long as discharges remained
below the specified level for that particular state.

The 1972 Amendments and the 1977 Clean Water
Act Amendments

The 1972 amendments to the FWPCA established a new system of regulations, permits, and enforcement strategies whose collective objective was the
assurance of swimmable and fishable waters. Under the 1972 provisions,
water quality requirements were to be supplemented by current technology-
based *effluent limitations standards* (i.e., the *end-of-pipe standard*), applied at
the point of discharge, for all industrial point sources, except for *Publicly
Owned Treatment Works (POTW)*. The amendments required the use of the
Best Practicable Control Technology (BPT), which were currently available
to control discharges by 1977, and the *Best Available Technology (BAT)*,
economically achievable by 1983. POTWs were required to adopt secondary
treatment methods by 1977 and the best practical waste treatment methods
over the life of the plant by 1983. Any new sources were required to meet the
established 1983 BAT requirements. Separate limits would be developed for
toxics, as required. Also, all dischargers were to be regulated by a new

comprehensive permitting process known as the National Pollution Discharge Elimination System.

Permitting Requirements

The *National Pollution Discharge Elimination System (NPDES)* permitting program was established to ensure proper authorization to discharge pollutants and is obtained from the EPA or an authorized state agency prior to discharging. In effect, the NPDES permit became what some have referred to as a *license to pollute*. Basically, the NPDES program applies to discharges of pollutants by persons from point sources into navigable waters. It is important to understand that the term *persons,* as it is used in the CWA, means any individual, corporation, partnership, association, state, municipality, commission, political subdivision, or interstate body. Basically, under the CWA, *persons* is any entity that can or will discharge pollutants.

As required by both Section 301 and Section 402 of the CWA, the discharge of pollutants is prohibited unless authorized by an NPDES permit. The NPDES program is applicable to all surface waterways, regardless of their flow or their capacity for navigation. For example, even wetlands that are either natural or man-made are covered by the NPDES permit program. The major elements of the NPDES permitting program are reflected in Figure 7-1.

The primary focus of the NPDES permit program centers first on the use of *effluent limitations standards* designed to restrict quantities, rates, concentrations, and so on, of pollutant discharges, and second on the establishment of compliance schedules for achieving these required restrictions. Effluent limitations standards are not self-implementing, which means they become effective and enforceable only when incorporated into a specific permit. The Act specifies three categories of industrial pollutant discharges that must be controlled by technology-based effluent limitations. The effluent limitations standard applicable in a given case would then be contingent on the specific type of pollutant being regulated and the nature of the point source from which the discharge originates. The three categories of pollutants for industrial discharges are *toxic pollutants, conventional pollutants,* and *nonconventional pollutants.*

Toxic pollutants are those that, after discharge and upon human exposure, will cause death, disease, behavioral abnormalities, poisoning, and so forth. These pollutants are subject to effluent limitations based upon BAT standards (see discussion on BAT standards below). A unique consideration for toxic pollutants, relative to the other types of discharges, is found in Section 307 of the Act, which identifies *Health-Based Effluent Limitations* that give the EPA the authority to establish more stringent requirements for the discharge of toxic pollutants. In considering such limitations, the EPA is

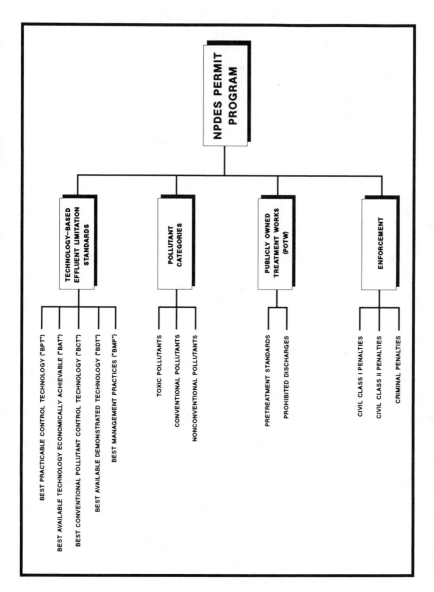

FIGURE 7-1. Major elements of the NPDES Permitting Program.

97

required to take into account various factors, such as the toxicity of a specific pollutant, its persistence and degradability once it is released into the environment, usual or potential presence in any waters of the organisms that would be affected by the toxic pollutant, the overall importance of the affected organism(s) (i.e., algae as opposed to game fish), and the nature and extent to which effective control is possible under other applicable regulations. The EPA has established these special health-based standards for toxic pollutants such as aldrin/dieldrin, DDT, endrin, toxaphene, benzidine, and polychlorinated biphenyls (PCBs).

Conventional pollutants are those that are well understood by the scientific community. These may be in the form of organic waste, sediment, bacteria and viruses, nutrients, oil and grease, suspended solids, fecal coliform, and factors affecting pH (acid or alkaline) or temperature, or may include *biological oxygen demanding (BOD)* materials. BOD is a measure of the amount of oxygen consumed in the biological processes that break down organic matter in water. Therefore, the greater the BOD in water, the greater the degree of pollution.

Nonconventional pollutants are those that are not classified or listed in the statutes as toxic or conventional. Their pollution capabilities may not be clearly or accurately defined or understood by the scientific community. Examples of nonconventional pollutants include ammonia, chlorine, and iron.

Technology-based Effluent Limitation Standards

The CWA contains requirements for the use of certain technology-based treatment requirements that establish the *minimum level of control* that must be imposed in a permit. Some of these, such as BPT and BAT, have already been briefly mentioned in this chapter. These treatment standards were promulgated by the EPA for all categories of pollutants and have been required since March 1989. The following is a brief explanation of the various technology-based treatment standards currently established by the CWA:

1. *Best Practicable Control Technology (BPT)*—The CWA specifies that, at the very least, BPT standards shall apply to all existing sources. However, the Act also requires these technologies to be replaced in most cases by the next highest available technology when it is economically achievable (i.e., "BAT"). In determining BPT standards, factors to be considered include the age of the existing equipment and plant facilities, the process used to produce the pollutants, the engineering requirements necessary to apply the control standards, and the total cost to implement the standards relative to the benefits that are expected after implementation

is complete. Initially, all sources in existence at the time of the 1972 amendments were to have implemented BPT standards by 1977.

2. *Best Available Technology Economically Achievable (BATEA or, simply, BAT)*—Section 304 of the CWA establishes the criteria to be used in establishing BAT effluent limitations. Specifically, to determine BAT standards the EPA considers the age of the equipment, the production process used at the facility, the complexity and feasibility of the engineering factors associated with the controlling technology, necessary changes in processes required to implement the technology, the cost of achieving the reduction in the effluent, and the identification of any non–water quality impacts. All sources that were required under the 1972 amendments to achieve BPT standards by 1977 must have been upgraded to BCT by 1983. One major difference between BPT and BAT, aside from the level of detail in considering implementation of the standards, is that there is currently no requirement to demonstrate a balance between the costs of implementing the control standards relative to the benefits expected as a result of those standards. Pollutants that are subject to BAT technology standards include toxics, nontoxics, nonconventional pollutants, and those that introduce thermal (heat) discharges into the effluent. *Variances* to the BAT standards are allowed, based upon factors such as effectively demonstrating that the economic impact associated with implementing the standards on an individual are greater relative to the expected environmental impact. Also, a variance is permissible if a thermal discharger can show that a BAT standard is too stringent and/or operationally restrictive.

3. *Best Conventional Pollutant Control Technology (BCT)*—This standard is much less restrictive than that required for BAT above. However, the CWA does specify that BCT be at least as stringent as the BPT limits established for the 1977 deadline. The primary factor considered in determining BCT standards is an evaluation of the costs associated with attaining a discharge reduction in relation to the anticipated benefits that will result from that reduction. Unlike BAT, BCT applies to conventional pollutants, such as BOD materials, total suspended solids (TSS), fecal coliform bacteria, and oil and grease.

4. *Best Available Demonstrated Technology (BADT, or BDT)*—Section 306 of the CWA requires the establishment of federal standards of performance for *new sources* that must be met within 90 days of the commencement of operations subject to permitting. These standards must demonstrate the highest possible degree of effluent reduction that, as determined by the EPA, are achievable by using the best available control technology, processes, operating methods, or other alternatives. In fact, unlike other technology-based effluent limitation standards, this Section specifically requires the elimination of pollutant discharge in new sources wherever

practical. Under BADT standards, a new source is one that has been constructed *after* the publication of proposed performance regulations (if that source would be subjected to such regulations). Unique to BADT is its *grandfathering provision* for any source that has been constructed to meet current BADT standards. If this is the case, the new source will not be subjected to any additional, more stringent standards of performance for as much as 10 years into the future. Since there is currently no statutory provisions for variances under BADT standards, new sources that can qualify under the grandfathering provision would do well to consider such "protection" from the imposition of further restrictive standards.

5. *Best Management Practices (BMP)*—The three major conditions for using these standards are to control specific toxic and hazardous pollutants, to supplement the other effluent standards as described above, or to control discharges from other ancillary industrial activities not specifically controlled by other standards. BMP may also be used when numerical controls for effluent reduction required under other standards are not particularly feasible. Hence, requirements for BMP standards can either be incorporated directly into a permit (either on a category or subcategory level) or on a case-by-case review basis.

Discharges into POTW Facilities.

Industries that discharge into publicly owned treatment works (POTW) facilities (i.e., indirect dischargers, as described earlier in this chapter) are subjected to *pretreatment standards,* as established by the EPA. Pretreatment standards are applicable to any pollutants that would either interfere with or would be incompatible with the proper operation of the POTW if they should pass through the facility untreated. Under the provisions of Section 307 of the Act, the EPA has established *general* pretreatment standards applicable to new and existing sources of pollutants as well as *specific* pretreatment standards for specific industry categories. According to the CWA, pretreatment means the reduction of the amount of pollutants, the elimination of pollutants altogether, or the alteration of the nature of pollutant properties in wastewater prior to or in lieu of discharge into a POTW. As a minimum, pretreatment standards must be applied whenever any of the following types of discharges are anticipated (i.e., *prohibited discharges*):

1. Any pollutant that will create a fire or explosive hazard if introduced untreated into a POTW. If there is a potential for accumulation of such a pollutant in the wastewater being discharged to a POTW, then its discharge is prohibited unless pretreatment occurs.
2. Any pollutants that will cause corrosive structural damage to the POTW facility or any of its equipment.

3. Discharges with a pH level below 5.0 are prohibited unless the POTW is specifically designed to accept a lower level pH.
4. Solid or viscous pollutants in such amounts that their discharge would cause obstruction in the normal flow and thereby interfere with the operation of the POTW facility.
5. Any pollutant present in a discharge at a flow rate or concentration level that will interfere with the normal operation of the POTW.
6. Heat present in amounts that will inhibit the required biological activity in the POTW, resulting in interference of the operation of the POTW. In no case shall heated discharges be allowed in quantities that will cause the temperature in the POTW to exceed 40C.

Enforcement of NPDES Permits

The Act specifically provides the EPA with extensive enforcement authority to ensure compliance with the requirements established in an NPDES permit. This authority includes the power to issue administrative compliance orders, to assess administrative penalties, to file suits for injunctive relief, to levy criminal penalties for willful or negligent violations, and to seek judicially imposed civil penalties against violators. Also, the Act provides EPA with the exclusive *right of pre-emption* over the states which allows for federal intervention to intervene in place of the state's enforcement of the Act where widespread violations of the NPDES program within the state are occurring. Citizen suits are also authorized under the CWA. The citizen bringing suit must have a standing interest in the violative condition and may be reimbursed for reasonable attorney's fees and expert witness costs.

Currently, the Act establishes two classes of civil penalties for violation of the NPDES permit program. For *Class I* penalties, the EPA must provide written notice of the violation and an opportunity for the violator to participate in an informal hearing within 30 days of their receipt of the written notice. *Class I* penalties may not exceed $10,000 per violation, up to a maximum penalty of $25,000. *Class II* penalties are much more severe. Such penalties may not exceed $10,000 per day for each day of the violation, up to a maximum penalty of $125,000. Class II penalties may not be assessed or collected prior to a formal notice to the violator and an opportunity for the violator to attend a formal record hearing. Before any Class I or Class II penalties are assessed, the EPA must provide notification to the public and allow ample opportunity for their comments to be received. In some cases, the public may also be allowed an opportunity to participate in any hearings pertaining to a proposed assessment. This aspect is important because the EPA's failure to allow for public notice and participation may be cause to dismiss any assessment if a person who was entitled to such participation files a petition within 30 days after the issuance of the administrative order.

In assessing civil penalties, the Act specifically states that the EPA must consider factors such as the nature, circumstances, extent and gravity of the violation, degree of culpability, economic benefit or savings resulting from the violative condition, and *such matters as justice may require* (i.e., anything else that the EPA can evaluate).

For assessment of criminal penalties, the Act establishes the following criteria:

1. Penalties for negligent violations are punishable by a fine that could range between $2,500 and $25,000 per day of violation, or by up to 1 year in prison, or both.
2. Penalties of up to $50,000 per day of violation, or imprisonment of up to 2 years, or both can be imposed against second offenders.
3. Those that are found to have intentionally violated the Act can be subjected to fines between $5,000 and $50,000 per day of violation, or up to 3 years in prison, or both. Those that intentionally violate the Act as second offenders can be punished by a fine of up to $100,000, imprisonment for up to 6 years, or both.
4. Knowingly placing another person in imminent danger of death or serious bodily injury carries penalties that include fines up to $250,000, or imprisonment up to 15 years, or both. In addition, any corporation guilty of this offense can be fined up to $1 million. These penalties will double for second offenders of this violation.
5. Any person (including responsible corporate officers) making a false statement could be subjected to a maximum $10,000 fine, imprisonment for 2 years, or both. A second time will result in fines up to $20,000 per day, imprisonment for 4 years, or both.

The Water Quality Act of 1987

A major objective of the 1987 amendments to the CWA was to change the NPDES-permitting program from being a tool used to implement the various technology-based controls to being more focused on controls that concentrate on achieving and then maintaining the water quality standards established by the individual states. In fact, the 1987 Water Quality Act focuses on state actions, responsibilities, authority, and restrictions. All the states were required to establish water quality standards by 1972 under the FWPCA. Unless these standards proved inconsistent with the objectives of the CWA, they are still in existence today. However, when a conflict between state and federal requirements does exist, either the state must make the appropriate revisions or the EPA will mandate the required changes.

Under the 1987 Act, the states are required to conduct a review of their respective standards at least every 3 years. Their review must also evaluate *toxic pollutants*, and, when necessary, the states must take action to adopt new criteria in consideration of any water guidelines that have been established for those pollutants. If such revisions to existing standards or new standards are deemed necessary, the states must submit their planned revisions or additions to the federal EPA. They must include sufficient supportive information, based upon specific *water quality criteria* and *designated water use* (e.g., public water, supply, recreation, agriculture), to justify their changes.

The water quality criteria used as a determining factor when considering changes to existing plans are also developed by the states based upon the designated use of each body of water or watershed. After determining the use designations, the states then evaluate concentration limits of pollutants as necessary to support each type of designated use. As a means of ensuring some level of consistency between the states, the EPA has established minimum criteria for 137 specific pollutants in a publication known as the *Quality Criteria for Water* (more commonly referred to as the *Gold Book*). These criteria are based upon identifiable effects of each pollutant on the public health and welfare, aquatic life, and recreation. The states are the primary force in setting water quality standards and, therefore, still maintain some degree of flexibility in developing their individual criteria. However, it is noted that this flexibility allows the states to establish requirements *more stringent* than those mandated by the Gold Book criteria.

Once water quality standards have been established for each body of water based upon its designated use and these criteria have been submitted to the federal EPA for review, states must attain compliance with these standards unless a revision to the standards has been permitted by the EPA. Normally, a revision or alteration of a standard is only allowed if the cumulative effect of revising the concentration limits will ultimately result in attainment or if the designated use of the unattained water body has been removed.

After a state has achieved attainment with an established water quality standard, any future revision requests for that standard will be subjected to the *antidegradation policy*. This policy was established in an effort to maintain and protect existing in-stream uses and existing high-quality waters. Pursuant to this policy, any request to downgrade an existing standard will not be authorized unless the state can first demonstrate that a designated use is currently unattained and that achieving attainment is not considered feasible or practical due to one of three specific conditions:

- Natural background or conditioning of the subject area will not permit attainment with a specific designated use.
- There exists irretrievable man-induced conditions that would either prevent or make attainment impractical.

- Achievement of the attainment with a designated use requirement would impose more stringent controls than BAT limits and would undoubtedly result in substantial adverse economic and social impact.

Another aspect of the 1987 Act required the states to identify any body of water within its jurisdiction where existing standard effluent limitations, as established under previous revisions to the CWA, are not adequate to ensure attainment with water quality standards. Once these waters have been identified, the states must then *rank* each, establish a level of priority based upon designated use and specific pollution considerations, and develop new standards aimed at achieving attainment or maintaining water quality standards. To fully address this issue, the 1987 amendments introduced a new Section 319 to the CWA that established a national policy calling for the control of nonpoint sources of pollution. Under the provisions of Section 319, states are required to submit a report to the EPA that identifies bodies of water where water quality standards are not attained and cannot be attained unless additional controls are placed on nonpoint pollution sources. This *nonpoint source management program* requires the state to further identify any specific individual source when that source contributes significantly to nonpoint pollution of any waters that do not meet established quality standards. The Act makes available to the state or combination of adjacent states (if applicable) $400 million over a 4-year period to implement nonpoint source management programs.

The Regulation of Stormwater and Combined Sewer Overflows

Under Section 402 of the 1987 amendments, industrial and municipal discharges of stormwater are regulated. Permits are required for stormwater runoff, except for mining operations or oil and gas exploration, production, processing, or treatment operations that are not contaminated by contact with any overburden, raw material, intermediate products, finished product, by-product, or waste product located on the site of such operations. States must establish specific stormwater management programs that include applicable performance standards, guidelines, management practices, and treatment regulations as appropriate.

Ultimately, the regulation of stormwater runoff requires industrial dischargers to comply with traditional technology and established water quality–based guidelines. Additionally, municipalities must take efforts to reduce municipal discharges of pollutants to the maximum extent possible. The Act further stipulates that any municipal stormwater permits must require the municipality to effectively prohibit non-stormwater discharges from entering storm drainage systems.

Depending upon the individual state requirements of the authority having jurisdiction, control of stormwater runoff may not only include implementing positive controls such as containment. Further stipulations might also require a detailed chemical analysis and sampling before release of the runoff will be allowed. Permissible levels for elements such as pH, total suspended solids, lead containment, and oil and grease, might be established by a state. If the sampled runoff does not comply with the water quality specifications, treatment may then be required before release of the water into grade will be permitted.

The Regulation of Sewer Sludge Disposal

The 1987 amendments directed the EPA to identify the toxic pollutants that are found in sewer sludges that may have an adverse effect on public health, the environment, or both. Acceptable practices for managing sewer sludge that contains toxic pollutants are also established by the EPA pursuant to Section 405 of the 1987 amendments. Requirements for the regulation of sewer sludge are normally incorporated into the NDPES permit for POTW operations, even when sludge disposal is not into waters of the United States. In fact, the focus of EPA regulatory efforts in this arena concentrates primarily on POTWs that incinerate sludge, have a major pretreatment program established, or have known sludge disposal problems.

Other Elements of the Clean Water Act

The CWA also establishes requirements designed to control and prevent spills of oil and hazardous substances. Essentially, the Act has provisions that focus upon spill prevention, spill reporting, spill cleanup, and imposing liability for the costs of cleanup. The Act prohibits the discharge of *harmful quantities* of oil and designated hazardous substances to waters of the United States. A harmful quantity of oil and hazardous substances is defined as that which may be harmful to the public health or welfare and includes harm to fish, shellfish, wildlife, public and private property, shorelines, and beaches. The EPA further defines a hazardous quantity of oil as an amount that either violates applicable water quality standards or that causes a surface film or sheen or a discoloration of the water or adjoining shoreline. The regulations require the development of *spill prevention, control, and countermeasure (SPCC)* plans by on-shore as well as off-shore non–transportation-related facilities that could reasonably be expected to discharge harmful quantities of oil.

Dredge and fill materials are also regulated by the CWA. Permits are required if these materials will be discharged into *navigable waters.* The EPA has delegated responsibility for regulation and permitting of dredging and filling activities to the Army Corp of Engineers (the Corp). However, the EPA retains the authority to overrule or restrict Corp decisions if the EPA determines that a specific project will have unacceptable adverse affects on municipal water supplies, shellfish beds and fishery areas, wildlife, or recreational areas. Also, while the states may administer these programs for waters other than those susceptible to use in interstate or foreign commerce and adjacent wetlands, the EPA must still approve these programs, while the Corp retains responsibility for issuing permits and ensuring that state programs are adequate. Any application for a dredge and fill permit must be certified by the state in which the discharge would originate. The state must certify that the discharge will comply with all applicable effluent limitations or water quality standards. If, for whatever reason, a state can not or will not make such certification, the EPA is required to do so. For information purposes, the EPA has established that dredge material is that which has been excavated or dredged from navigable waters. Fill material is used primarily for replacing an aquatic area with dry land or for changing the bottom elevation of a body of water.

SUMMARY

The primary focus of the *Clean Water Act (CWA)* is to control the discharge of pollutants into navigable waters. In order to establish regulatory requirements, the CWA first divides water pollution into two major categories or classifications of *point source* and *nonpoint source* discharges. With the exception of agricultural stormwater flows and those from irrigated agriculture, point sources emanate from a source such as a pipe, ditch, or tunnel, and discharge either *directly* or *indirectly* into the waterway. A nonpoint source is defined simply as one that discharges from a source *other than* the end of a pipe or other type of point source.

The CWA established a complex permitting program known as the *national pollution discharge elimination system,* or *NPDES.* In short, the NPDES permit allows for discharge of pollutants into waterways, providing that certain explicit conditions and provisions are complied with. These restrictions are based upon the use of *effluent limitation standards.* Specifically, water quality requirements are to be supplemented by these technology-based effluent limitations standards. Such standards provide requirements for technologies necessary to ensure adequate control over discharges. These technologies, which are intended to ensure the minimum level of control, focus upon the categories of *toxic pollutants, conventional pollutants,* and *nonconventional pollutants.* The NPDES program also applies to discharges into as well as discharges out of *Publicly Owned Treatment Works (POTWs).*

Enforcement provisions under the CWA allow extremely stringent and severe penalties and fines in both the civil and criminal categories. In the civil arena, penalties for violation of CWA requirements are divided onto *Class I* penalties and *Class II* penalties, the latter being the more severe. A criminal violation could result in strong monetary fines and/or lengthy prison terms, depending upon the nature and degree of the violation.

In 1987, the CWA was again amended in an attempt to further focus the objective of the Act on the water quality efforts of the individual states. The EPA established criteria for 137 toxic pollutants and required the states to meet requirements at least as stringent as these criteria. *Stormwater runoff* control and regulation as well as the regulation of *sewer sludge disposal* are also contained in the 1987 amendments.

The price of noncompliance with applicable provisions of the CWA is too great—both in terms of direct monetary cost as well as the indirect costs that result from harm or damage to our nation's waterways. As a minimum, the practicing environmental compliance professional must have a basic understanding of the many requirements contained in the CWA. This chapter outlined the fundamental elements of this important environmental legislation.

CASE BRIEF: CLEAN WATER ACT
UNITED STATES vs. RUTANA
U.S. Court of Appeals
No. 90-3343, 08 May 1991

Summary

The defendant in this criminal case was charged in circuit court with the knowing discharge of pollutants into a public sewer system in violation of the Clean Water Act (CWA), 33 U.S.C 1251, provisions. He was subsequently fined $90,000 on 18 counts ($5,000 each count) and sentenced to 5 years probation and 1,000 hours of community service. The United States appealed these decisions, stating that the circuit court improperly adjusted the fine and sentencing downward based upon considerations not directly related to the facts of the case.

Background

John Rutana was a part-owner and chief executive officer of a now-bankrupt corporation known as Finishing Corporation of America (FCA). In late 1985, FCA began operating a metal finishing plant in Campbell, Ohio. The plant was located directly across the street from Campbell's wastewater treatment plant (CWWTP). FCA's plant was constructed with a plastic discharge pipe, which was intended to transport sulfuric and nitric acids. This pipe led into a city sewer line, which in turn fed into CWWTP. The CWWTP facility discharges into the Mahoning River, a source of drinking water for a number of communities. During late 1986 and early 1987, CWWTP began experiencing problems associated with chemical wastewater discharges coming from FCA. CWWTP notified Rutana of these problems, which included two massive bacteria kills at

CWWTP. In addition, the Ohio Environmental Protection Agency sent a letter to FCA that contained a copy of the federal regulations pertaining to chemical wastewater discharges. Rutana claimed to have implemented a mixing plan to neutralize the acid and alkaline discharges. For approximately 1 year thereafter, no additional problems were documented involving the FCA plant.

The ineffectiveness of Rutana's plan became apparent in March 1988 when CWWTP again experienced problems with FCA's wastewater. A federal investigation was then initiated. Despite repeated attempts by the City of Campbell and the Ohio EPA to get FCA to stop the discharges, and despite Rutana's obvious awareness of the problem, at least 18 separate instances of illegal discharges were documented during 1988. Two of these resulted in injury to a CWWTP employee who was burned while trying to obtain a sample of FCA waste coming into CWWTP. After federal agents threatened to obtain an injunction to prevent further discharges, Rutana voluntarily agreed to close the FCA plant, although at least one additional illegal discharge occurred in December 1988, after the plant was supposedly closed.

Decision

Rutana was indicted by a grand jury on 18 counts of knowingly discharging pollutants and causing pollutants to be discharged that caused corrosive structural damage and that had a pH of less than 5.0 into a public sewer system and, thereby, into the Campbell, Ohio, Waste Water Treatment Plant in violation of national pretreatment standards. He was also indicted on two counts of knowing endangerment of CWWTP employees and on two counts of making false statements in a matter within the jurisdiction of the EPA. The company itself, its general manager, and even a minor shareholder in FCA were also indicted on similar counts.

In a plea bargain, Rutana pleaded guilty to all 18 counts of violation of the CWA and all other charges were dismissed. The other defendants entered into similar plea bargain arrangements. Under the CWA, the maximum penalty that could have been imposed on Rutana for each violation was three years in prison and a $50,000 per day fine. The presentence report calculated that the sentencing guidelines indicated a term of 27 to 33 months, based upon an offense level of 18 and a criminal history Category I (Rutana had no prior offenses). However, at the sentencing hearing held 2 March 1990, the district court judge, citing the case as unusual, departed downward from the level 18 established in the presentence report to a level of 6, sentencing Rutana to just 5 years probation combined with 1,000 hours of community service. In addition, the court imposed a fine of $90,000. The government then filed an appeal.

The appeal was based on the fact that the district judge adjusted the sentence downward because Rutana owned another business that employed some 26 people. If he were sentenced to prison, these innocent people would lose their employment. The appeal claimed that these circumstances were not unusual enough to satisfy the requirements for a downward adjustment of penalties and sentences. The appeals court ruled in favor of the U.S. government and ordered the case back to the district court for resentencing.

Analysis

In this extremely complex case, the owner of the chemical plant was knowingly violating wastewater pretreatment standards. These actions could have resulted in fines in excess of $1 million and a prison term of up to 3 years. However, the judge in the district court evaluated unrelated circumstantial factors and allowed a plea bargain arrangement to reduce the penalties downward. The appeals court determined that the federal district court must resentence the individual because: 1) The court considered the individual's ownership of a second business in deciding not to sentence him to serve a prison term; 2) The federal sentencing guidelines did not permit the court to consider the effect of incarceration on the individual's business ventures; and 3) To the extent that other factors would have supported a sentence reduction, the court again failed to properly articulate those factors during sentencing. The district court was also ordered to reconsider the $90,000 fine imposed because it was not clear whether or not the judge improperly thought that the provision of the Act allowing a $5,000 fine per violation was mandatory.

In short, criminal violations under the CWA could result in substantial fines and penalties. The U.S. government is determined to ensure, to the maximum extent possible, that such violators receive the toughest penalties allowable under the law. In fact, the significance of this case brief is not in the court's final decision over Rutana's criminal activities, but in the fact that the U.S. government is willing to pursue, through judicial appeal, the maximum prosecution possible in such cases.

8

Resource Conservation and Recovery Act

INTRODUCTION

With the possible exception of the Clean Air Act Amendments of 1990, there is perhaps no other existing environmental legislation that has caused more consternation and dismay for American industry than the *Resource Conservation and Recovery Act (RCRA)*. Normally pronounced *rick-rah*, this landmark legislation was enacted by Congress in 1976 as an amendment to the *Solid Waste Disposal Act (SWDA)*. RCRA, which was amended in 1980 with the Solid Waste Disposal Act Amendments and again in 1984 under the *Hazardous and Solid Waste Act (HSWA),* has become the essence of national policy concerning the methods of managing hazardous waste.

The stated objective of Congress in promulgating RCRA was to develop comprehensive and integrated legislation aimed at protecting the environment from mismanagement. In order to accomplish this, RCRA is intended to establish the necessary framework for the management of hazardous wastes from the moment it is generated (i.e., its creation) up to the time it is either neutralized, destroyed, or otherwise disposed of properly. This approach has often been referred to as the *cradle-to-grave* concept of waste management. The overriding element of concern in 1976 was to positively address the then unregulated disposal of discarded materials and hazardous wastes onto land areas. Since that time, RCRA has become an extremely complex and cumbersome Act that, as of this writing, was again being considered for yet additional amendments. By most accounts, the RCRA of tomorrow will probably increase the level of complexity even further and present greater compliance challenges for the practicing environmental professional as well as the nation as a whole.

This chapter will briefly explain the purpose and intent of RCRA, as summarized above, and provide basic information on the current compliance requirements contained in the Act. Due to the complex and diverse regulatory framework of RCRA, the EPA has developed a *three-tiered* system to administer RCRA requirements. These rules impose varying degrees of restrictions on the different types of waste-related activities. Since wastes are not subject to these regulations until they are in fact *generated,* this chapter will focus primarily on this first tier. The second tier, regulations on *transporters,* and the third tier, regulations for the *treatment, storage, and disposal* of wastes will also be discussed, but only briefly. The reader should note that the management of hazardous wastes, as mandated by RCRA and the many separate pieces of legislation that it has spawned, is only one area of concern to the environmental compliance professional. However, it is *the* one area that can also pose severe problems in attempting to comply with mandated waste management requirements. Therefore, it is highly recommended that additional training and education be sought and obtained on RCRA compliance requirements if readers find themselves involved with this aspect of environmental regulation. Appendix A of this text provides a listing and brief description of recommended sources for additional education. Many more sources exist that are too numerous to mention here. However, based upon the severe problems associated with misinterpretation of RCRA requirements, it is highly recommended that the reader first verify the quality of any proposed training seminar or materials before investing time and resources.

BACKGROUND: HISTORICAL OVERVIEW

Despite serious efforts, the original Act contained some serious shortcomings. Most analysts will agree that the legislation had little effect on promoting the concept of conservation and the importance of waste management. The language in the 1976 law was vague in many areas, which almost immediately created much confusion among industry and subsequently led to regulatory loopholes.

RCRA sets forth three basic goals to ensure a successful hazardous waste management program. First, a description of the wastes to be managed and an identification of those persons responsible for the disposition of those wastes must be established. Second, a system for positively tracking the location of all hazardous wastes, from their point of generation to their ultimate disposal, must be put into place. Third, the program must promote proper waste management practices that ensure the protection of human health and the environment. Essentially, RCRA can be viewed as a type of licensing and waste tracking program. The Act provides for regulatory control over five areas of concern in the management of hazardous waste. Specifically, RCRA regulates the *generation, storage, transportation, treatment,* and *disposal* of hazardous waste. While the scope and intent of RCRA remained relatively unchanged through the 1980 amendments, Congress finally attempted to refine this legislation once and for all on 8 November 1984, with the enactment of the Hazardous and Solid Waste Amendments (HSWA).

The 1984 Amendments to Hazardous and Solid Waste Act

With 72 major provisions contained in the 1984 amendments to HSWA, the amendments are considered to have changed RCRA into the most far-reaching environmental legislation in the United States. It still remains such today, although some may argue that the Clean Air Act of 1990 may snatch this ominous distinction away from RCRA. Regardless of which act is more rigorous, it is a fact that RCRA presents a serious challenge to the practicing environmental compliance professional.

The amendments of 1984 directed the EPA to perform a microscopic review of the existing RCRA requirements and ensure that every possible loophole was removed once and for all. For their part, Congress took positive steps not to reproduce in the new Act the same ambiguous and vague statutory language contained in the previous legislation. The new law specifically instructs the EPA when to finalize rule making and what requirements must be contained in the new rules. In addition, the new amendments contained *hammer provisions*, which require the EPA to issue new rules by statutory (hammer) deadlines. If the EPA can not meet a particular deadline, then the hammer provision requires very stringent Congressionally mandated regulations to become effective.

The RCRA regulations are contained in Title 40 of the U.S. Code of Federal Regulations (CFR), beginning at Part 260. Figure 8-1 shows the current breakdown of 40 CFR, with the individual Part titles provided for reference purposes.

In short, the 1984 amendments included regulations aimed at controlling leaking *underground storage tanks (USTs)*, improving the management of wastes from *small quantity generators*, phasing out land disposal of untreated hazardous waste *(Land-Ban)*, identifying additional hazardous wastes not previously regulated, requirements for *waste minimization*, and establishing specific controls on the burning and blending of hazardous waste as fuels.

In order to determine if a waste is to be regulated under RCRA, one must first decide whether a waste is in fact hazardous. At face value, this should seem a relatively easy task. However, evidence of the complexity of RCRA can be seen in its definition of a hazardous waste.

Hazardous Waste Determination

According to RCRA, a waste is hazardous if it is a *solid waste* that is either *ignitable, corrosive, reactive,* or *toxic.* Figure 8-2 is a graphic representation

40 CFR PART NUMBER	REGULATIONS PERTAINING TO	APPLICABLE RCRA SECTION
124	Public Participation	3005
260	General Requirements, Definitions, Petitions	1004, 3007
261	Identification and Listing of Hazardous Waste	3001
262	Generators of Hazardous Waste	3002, 3017
263	Transporters of Hazardous Waste	3003
264	Permitted Hazardous Waste TSD Facilities	3004
265	Interim Status Hazardous Waste TSD Facilities	3004
266	Specific Hazardous Waste Facilities	3004, 3014
267	New Interim Status Land Disposal Facilities	3004, 3020
268	Land Disposal Restrictions	3004
270	EPA Administered Permit Programs	3005
271	State Hazardous Waste Program Requirements	3006

FIGURE 8-1. Correlation between RCRA regulation sections and 40 CFR requirements. (Source: EPA)

of the interrelationships between these primary elements of the waste determination process. RCRA's definition of a hazardous waste seems to provide relatively simple instruction on the methods used to determine the hazardous and, therefore, regulated nature of a particular waste. However, exploring each of these waste determination methods will reveal varying degrees of complexity that provide clear indications of the difficulties the EPA faced in meeting its Congressional mandate to remove the loopholes from the Act.

The use of the term *solid* in the determination of regulated waste is perhaps the most confusing element of this EPA equation. Webster defines *solid* as resisting change of shape, having the parts firmly cohering; distinguished from liquid and gaseous; hard, compact; full of matter, not hollow; and so on (Webster 1990). Despite this conventional and generally accepted understanding, the EPA chose to use the term *solid waste* to identify anything that has reached the end of its useful life and is to be discarded. Hence, according to RCRA, solid waste includes solid, liquid, and even contained gaseous materials as well as garbage, sludge, and refuse. To further complicate the issue, the definition also pertains to materials that are being burned or incinerated; those that are being stored, accumulated, or treated prior to or instead of waste disposal, burning or incineration; and industrial and mining by-products that may sometimes be discarded.

Once it has been determined that a material meets any of the requirements specified for solid wastes (and it probably will), it will only be subjected to regulation under RCRA if it is also determined to be *hazardous*. In other words, while all wastes may be solid, they may not all be hazardous and, if they are not hazardous, then they are generally not regulated (see Solid Waste Exclusions below). To be labeled as a hazardous waste, the material must meet the criteria for *either* ignitability, corrosivity, reactivity, or toxicity. If a chemical can be characterized in any of these categories, it is referred to as a *characteristic waste*.

To be considered hazardous due to *ignitability*, the waste can be a liquid, a non-liquid, a compressed gas, or an oxidizing substance. For liquids, the determination is a function of the material's *flash point*. The flash point is that temperature at which the material will provide a sufficient quantity of vapors to ignite in the presence of an ignition source. Under RCRA, a liquid with a flash point below 60°C (140°F) is considered ignitable and is, therefore, a hazardous waste. This determination might provide some degree of confusion for the practicing safety and health professional familiar with the Occupational Safety and Health Administration (OSHA) definition of a flammable liquid. Under OSHA criteria, a liquid with a flash point below 100°F is considered flammable. The reader is cautioned not to confuse the OSHA requirements for flammable liquids with those specified under RCRA for ignitable liquids. With a non-liquid waste, the determination is based on the

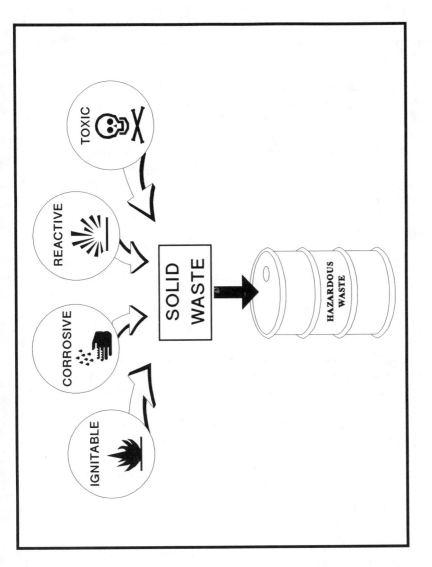

FIGURE 8-2. Basic elements of characteristic hazardous wastes under RCRA.

115

material's ability to cause a fire under standard pressure and temperature either by friction, absorption of moisture, or spontaneous chemical change. Also, if a non-liquid material is such that it would burn vigorously and persistently once ignited as to create a hazard, then it shall be determined ignitable and a hazardous waste. Any compressed gas with a pressure of more than 40 psi (pounds per square inch) at 70°F or 140 psi at 130°F is considered ignitable if any of the following conditions also exist:

1. At standard atmospheric pressure and ambient temperature, a mixture of 13% or less by volume with air forms a flammable mixture, or the flammable range with air is greater than 12%, regardless of the lower limit.
2. Using specified flame projection apparatus, the flame projects more than 18 inches beyond the ignition source with fully opened valve, or the flame flashes back and burns at the valve or any valve opening.
3. Using specified drum apparatus, there is any significant propagation of flame away from the ignition source.
4. Using specified closed drum apparatus, there is any explosion of the vapor-air mixture in the drum.

Finally, any waste that is an oxidizing substance (i.e., one that readily yields oxygen to propagate combustion) shall also be considered an ignitable hazardous waste. Examples of oxidizers include chlorine, inorganic peroxides, and nitrates.

A material is hazardous if it is *corrosive*. According to RCRA, corrosive wastes can be either aqueous or non-aqueous. Aqueous wastes are corrosive if the pH is 2.0 or less (an acid) or 12.5 or greater (a base). If an aqueous or non-aqueous waste will corrode steel at a rate of 1/4 inch per year under specified testing protocol, then the waste meets the characteristic requirements for corrosivity and is considered hazardous.

A *reactive waste* is one that meets any of the following criteria, as specified by RCRA:

1. It is normally unstable and will readily undergo violent change without detonation.
2. When mixed with water, the waste reacts violently, forms potentially explosive mixtures, or emits toxic fumes in dangerous quantities.
3. It contains cyanide or sulfide, which, when exposed to pH conditions between 2 and 12.5, emits toxic fumes in dangerous quantities.
4. It is capable of detonation or will react explosively when subjected to a strong initiating source or when heated under confining conditions.
5. It is readily capable of detonation or explosive decomposition or reaction at standard temperature and pressure.

6. It meets the criteria for a Class A, Class B, or forbidden explosive, as defined by the U.S. Department of Transportation (DOT) in 49 CFR Part 173.

Unlike other waste categories discussed in this chapter, there is no prescribed test method to determine reactivity, due to the potentially dangerous consequences that could result from such testing.

To determine whether or not a waste is *toxic*, it must be subjected to the EPA's *Toxicity Characteristic Leaching Procedure (TCLP)*. This procedure is used to test for the presence of specific metals and organic and inorganic chemicals in a waste for their potential to leak, or leach, out of an unlined container at a disposal site and effectively contaminate the groundwater supply to toxic levels. The regulations provide a list of these contaminants, known as the *D List*, which provides the maximum level of concentration of certain toxic contaminants for use when applying the TCLP characteristic test. Under this requirement, a waste with a leachate containing any one of these D-listed substances at a level exceeding pre-established regulatory thresholds will be considered a hazardous waste due to toxicity and, therefore, subject to RCRA regulation. If the TCLP test demonstrates that the chemical constituents in the leachate are below the regulatory levels found on the D list, then the waste will automatically be removed from the list.

The *mixture rule* is also used to determine the hazardous nature of a waste product. Although the EPA has specifically excluded numerous chemical mixtures from this rule, it is still generally true that any mixture of a listed hazardous waste (see below) with another nonhazardous waste will render the entire volume of the waste product hazardous and subject to regulation. The intent is to prevent the potential for disposal of regulated wastes by mixing them with other materials that can normally be freely discarded.

Listed Wastes under RCRA
In an effort to facilitate the waste determination process, the EPA has developed a listing of several hundred substances. These *listed wastes* are provided by name in Title 40 of the Code of Federal Regulations (CFR) at Part 261. If a solid waste consists of one of these listed chemicals, then it is a hazardous waste under RCRA.

The Toxic Lists
There are essentially two lists for *toxic wastes* that provide the generic names of commercial chemicals and chemical intermediates. If a chemical appears on either list, then it will be regulated as hazardous when it is discarded. The first list is known as the *P List* and contains chemicals classified as *acutely toxic*. P-listed wastes are more closely regulated with special requirements

than other listed wastes. The second list is known as the *U List*, which contains toxic chemicals that are not considered acutely hazardous. Regardless of the list on which they appear, each of these substances are regulated once the decision has been made to discard them. The particular condition of the chemical at the moment it is discarded is of no concern in the waste determination process. Hence, it makes no difference if the discarded material is a finished product suitable for resale but is to be discarded as *surplus* or for some other reason; or if it is an *off-specification* product discarded because of commercial unsuitability or shelf-life expiration; or if it is a *residue* of some container liner to be discarded as a normal event; or even if it is contaminated soil or other debris generated during a *spill cleanup*. The key element to remember is that a P-listed or U-listed chemical becomes hazardous and regulated the moment a decision is made to discard that chemical.

The Specific and Nonspecific Source Lists
The regulation lists a number of industrial processes that are the source of waste products considered to be hazardous. The waste products of these many processes include:

- A large variety of waste solvents;
- Metal finishing sludge and baths;
- Certain cyanide heat-treating sludge;
- Inorganic pigment sludge;
- Wastes generated in the manufacture of petroleum products;
- Some chemicals and pesticides;
- Preservatives used to treat wood;
- Lead;
- Iron;
- Steel;
- Explosives; and
- Veterinary pharmaceuticals.

There are two lists provided in the regulations to address such wastes. The first, known as the *K List*, describes numerous specific industrial processes whose wastes are considered hazardous. These listed wastes are considered *specific source* wastes because they have been classified according to the specific industry in which they are produced. The second list, called the *F List*, provides generic descriptions of several types of *waste streams* that are commonly found in industrial processes, but are *nonspecific* to any one source. For example, spent halogenated and non-halogenated solvents are F-listed wastes. While solvent wastes are common to a variety of industrial processes, the source of their generation may not be specific to any one process. RCRA defines a spent solvent as that which no longer meets the specifications for which it was originally intended. The regulating of spent solvents provides another example of how the 1984 amendments made RCRA much stronger than previous legislation would allow. Prior to 1984, the spent solvent list applied only to technical-grade or pure-form industrial solvents. However, because it is generally true that many solvents used in industry are in fact *mixtures* of either listed solvents or a combination of listed and unlisted solvents (or non-solvent additives), RCRA was amended to include the regulation of solvent mixtures as well. If a mixture contains more than 10 percent, by volume, of an F-listed spent solvent, then the waste shall be considered hazardous. Wastes found on both the F list and the K list are also coded to indicate which hazardous characteristics they will exhibit. Most are coded, at the very least, as toxic ("T"). Other codes used in the regulation are as follows:

Ignitable waste (I)
Corrosive waste (C)
Reactive waste (R)
Toxicity characteristic waste (E)
Acute hazardous waste (H)

The Master List of Hazardous Constituents
The EPA has provided a list consisting of several hundred generic chemical names. Each of these substances are either toxic, carcinogenic, teratogenic, or mutagenic, or are a constituent of a class or group of chemicals that display these characteristics. It is important to note that the Hazardous Constituent List is *non-regulatory* in nature and serves as a source of information only. It simply indicates that a chemical constituent has been determined hazardous by the EPA and therefore meets the basic requirements for listing as a hazardous waste.

Solid Waste Exclusions
Although Congress intended RCRA to include as a solid waste virtually anything that might be thrown away, certain specific wastes have been excluded from the regulatory requirements. Exclusions under RCRA are allowed either because a material is already regulated or because its hazardous nature has been determined insignificant. Wastes currently excluded from RCRA regulation include:

1. Domestic sewage that passes through a public sewer into a Publicly Owned Treatment Works (POTW) facility for treatment (reference Chapter 7 for further discussion on POTWs) is not considered solid waste.
2. Industrial wastewater from point-source discharges that are regulated under the Clean Water Act (CWA) and are permitted under the Na-

tional Pollutant Discharge Elimination System (NPDES). However, wastewater resultant from the waste treatment process is subject to RCRA regulation, as are the sludges that are collected, stored, or treated before being discharged (reference Chapter 7).

3. Wastewater resultant from irrigation return flows is not regulated under RCRA.

4. Nuclear materials, as defined by the Atomic Energy Act, are not subject to regulation under RCRA.

5. Waste material resultant from certain mining procedures that are not removed during the extraction process are not considered solid wastes and are therefore excluded from RCRA requirements.

6. Reclaimed materials, such as pulping liquors and spent sulfuric acid, are excluded if such materials are to be reused in the original process or to produce new virgin materials. However, in the case of sulfuric acid, if the waste is being accumulated strictly for recycling and resale, it will be subjected to RCRA regulations (see section titled "Recycling Wastes for Reuse," below).

7. A large number of pulping solid wastes are excluded from RCRA. These include, but are not limited to, wastes such as regular household trash, garbage, and septic tank wastes from homes, hotels, and motels; natural fertilizer wastes; fossil fuel–burning wastes collected by pollution control equipment; energy and mineral recovery wastes from energy exploration and mining; wastes resultant from cement production processes; some wood waste products that fail the TCLP test, but are used by the generator as intended; certain chromium wastes that fail the TCLP test, but solely due to the presence of trivalent chromium; and any sample of solid waste, water, soil, or air that is being transported for testing purposes.

8. Wastes generated in storage and transport tanks, pipelines, or other vessels not normally used for waste storage or treatment are excluded.

9. Empty containers have a special exclusion provision, since no container can ever really be totally empty. Compressed gas cylinders are considered empty if they are at atmospheric pressure (roughly 15 psi).

10. Certain *mixtures* of waste products are excluded from RCRA regulation. In some cases, mixing a hazardous waste with other wastes might not render the entire mixture hazardous due to the dilution process. Therefore, the regulations only require waste mixtures to be considered hazardous if the subsequent mixture exhibits one or more of the characteristics of ignitability, corrosivity, reactivity, or toxicity. It should be noted that this exclusion does not include any of the process wastes from specific (K List) and nonspecific (F List) sources that are labeled as toxic.

11. Waste pesticides disposed of during a farming process are not subject to RCRA regulation if these pesticides were purchased by an individual

farmer for his or her own use and properly disposed of by that farmer on his or her own land.

12. Wastewater mixtures containing certain specific spent solvents are not considered hazardous unless the quantities of such solvents exceed the levels established in the regulations. Also, RCRA does not consider heat exchanger sludge from petroleum refining to be hazardous waste. Wastewater containing very small amounts of discarded commercial chemical products is excluded if the waste results from spills occurring during normal processing operations. There is also an exclusion for laboratory wastewater if the annualized average flow does not exceed 1 percent of the total wastewater flow from the laboratory.

RCRA is specific with its mixture exclusions in an effort to ensure that mixing of wastes is not being performed as a type of treatment process. For example, if the only reason mixing is done is to neutralize a hazardous waste, the EPA might consider this a treatment process that requires permitting. Caution is also warranted when considering exclusions for wastewater mixtures. While these mixtures may be excluded from the regulatory provisions for hazardous waste under RCRA, they are still subject to the requirements of the Clean Water Act.

Recycling Wastes for Reuse
The issue of regulating recycled wastes is extremely complicated and well beyond the scope of this text. However, RCRA basically dictates that recycled material will be subject to regulation if the material is a solid waste when recycled. This determination is not as simple as it may appear. The state of the recycled material may be dependent upon the hazardous characteristics of the *secondary material* as well as the recycling process to be used. RCRA defines hazardous secondary materials as spent materials, sludges, by-products, commercial chemical products, and scrap metal.

According to the EPA, recycling activities include any of the following four groups of activities:

1. Use constituting disposal (direct placement of wastes onto land).
2. Burning (for energy recovery, or using wastes to produce a fuel).
3. Reclamation (regeneration or recovery of wastes).
4. Speculative accumulation (collecting wastes for recycling, with no immediate market for the recycled materials or accumulating wastes without recycling at least 75% within 1 year's time).

Table 8-1 shows which of these materials are considered solid wastes if they are to be recycled. Because recycling is supposed to produce useful products

TABLE 8-1   Secondary materials solid waste determination matrix. (Source: EPA, RCRA)

SECONDARY MATERIALS
SOLID WASTE DETERMINATION

TYPE OF MATERIAL	INTENDED USE			
	Use Constituting Disposal	Energy Recovery/Fuel	Reclaimation	Speculative Accumulation
Spent Materials	■	■	■	■
Sludge	■	■	■	■
Sludge Exhibiting Characteristic of Hazardous Waste	■	■		■
By-Products	■	■	■	■
By-Products Exhibiting Characteristic of Hazardous Waste	■	■		■
Commercial Chemical Products	■	■		
Scrap Metal	■	■	■	■

that do not meet the definition of wastes, RCRA is not applicable. It should be noted, however, that any waste products that may result from the recycling process will be subject to regulation if these products are to be disposed of.

Used Oil Burned for Energy Recovery

Used oil burned for energy recovery and any fuel produced from used oil by processing, blending, or other treatment is subject to RCRA regulation if it is determined to be a hazardous waste because it contains any of the characteristics or listed wastes or it has been generated by a small-quantity generator (see section titled "Small-quantity Hazardous Waste Generators," below). RCRA has divided used oil fuel into categories known as *specification used oil*, *off-specification used oil*, *oily waste*, and *hazardous waste fuel*. A *specification used oil* is any that does not exceed the limits for constituents and contaminants established in Table 8-2. Conversely, an *off-specification used oil* is any that does exceed the limits specified in Table 8-2. An *oily waste* is not defined as a used oil, since it normally has never been used. Oily wastes, such as those resultant from oil spills and cleaning processes, are not regulated unless they

TABLE 8-2   Requirements for "specification used oil."

CONSTITUENT OR PROPERTY	FINAL ALLOWABLE LEVEL
ARSENIC	5 PPM MAXIMUM
CADMIUM	2 PPM MAXIMUM
CHROMIUM	10 PPM MAXIMUM
LEAD	100 PPM MAXIMUM
TOTAL HALOGENS	4,000 PPM MAXIMUM
FLASH POINT	100°F MINIMUM

have been contaminated or mixed with used oils and/or determined to be a hazardous waste. When a small-quantity generator mixes used oil fuel with a hazardous waste, it is referred to as a *hazardous waste fuel.*

Requirements for Generators of Hazardous Waste

The regulations are quite specific, with requirements imposed on those persons that generate or participate in the generation of solid wastes that are hazardous. According to RCRA, a *generator* is any person, by site, whose act or process produces hazardous waste or whose actions first cause a waste to become subjected to regulation. Under RCRA, the EPA regards a *person* as an individual, trust, firm, joint stock company, federal agency, corporation, partnership, association, state, municipality, political subdivision of a state, or an interstate body. Hence, being a generator is not contingent upon the nature or type of waste-producing entity, but rather on the actions of that entity with regard to its processes that produce a hazardous waste.

Any person producing waste must first verify if the waste to be produced is subjected to any of the solid waste exclusions allowed under RCRA. If the waste is not excluded from the requirements, the generator must then determine if it is a listed waste. If necessary, that person must also make the proper hazardous waste determination for characteristic wastes, as described earlier in this chapter.

Once the generator determines whether a particular waste is excluded or is, in fact, subject to the requirements of RCRA, an *EPA identification number* must be obtained. In addition to acquiring the appropriate permit, a generator can not treat, store, dispose of, transport, or contract for transport hazardous waste without having obtained an identification number from the EPA. Likewise, the generator must verify that any transporter or waste *treatment, storage, or disposal facility (TSD or TSDF)* have also obtained an EPA identification number for those activities.

The principal element of the hazardous waste regulations concerned with the transport of wastes for off-site treatment, storage, or disposal is the *Uniform Hazardous Waste Manifest* (EPA Form 8700-22) and, if necessary, its continuation sheet (EPA Form 8700-22A). The manifest is a multi-copy document used as the primary tracking record for a waste and will accompany that waste until its final disposition. Copies are then returned to the generator with the completed disposition documented on the form. The generator must retain these copies for at least 3 years. The manifest (Figures 8-3 and 8-4) must designate one facility that is approved to handle the type of waste and, if desired, one alternate facility. The law specifically requires the generator to hand sign the manifest and to obtain hand-written signatures of the initial transporter of the waste.

Waste packaging and labeling requirements specified by the Department of Transportation (DOT) are incorporated into the law by reference. The generator must therefore be familiar with the requirements listed in 49 CFR Parts 172, 173, 178, and 179 as well. The Hazardous Waste label shown as Figure 8-5 is currently approved for use under these regulations.

The law allows generators to accumulate hazardous wastes on their site for up to 90 days, without having to obtain a permit. However, this allowance is permitted as long as the waste is placed in approved containers or tanks. The date that each accumulation period began must be clearly marked and visible for inspection on each container label. The *accumulation start date* is that date when the first drop of waste has been put into the container (except at *satellite accumulation sites*, described below). Each container must be clearly marked with the words "HAZARDOUS WASTE" in addition to its required labeling. Any generator who accumulates waste for longer than a 90-day period automatically becomes a storage facility and will be subjected to the additional stringent requirements imposed on such facilities. (Note: The EPA will grant extensions up to 30 days due to unforeseen, temporary, and uncontrollable circumstances.)

UNIFORM HAZARDOUS WASTE MANIFEST	1 Generator's US EPA ID No	Manifest Document No	2 Page 1 of	Information in the shaded areas is not required by Federal law
3 Generator's Name and Mailing Address			A. State Manifest Document Number	
			B. State Generator's ID	
4 Generator's Phone ( )				
5 Transporter 1 Company Name	6 US EPA ID Number		C. State Transporter's ID	
			D. Transporter's Phone	
7 Transporter 2 Company Name	8 US EPA ID Number		E. State Transporter's ID	
			F. Transporter's Phone	
9 Designated Facility Name and Site Address	10 US EPA ID Number		G. State Facility's ID	
			H. Facility's Phone	

11 US DOT Description (Including Proper Shipping Name, Hazard Class, and ID Number)	12 Containers No / Type	13 Total Quantity	14 Unit Wt/Vol	I. Waste No.
a				
b				
c				
d				

J. Additional Descriptions for Materials Listed Above	K. Handling Codes for Wastes Listed Above

15 Special Handling Instructions and Additional Information

16 GENERATOR'S CERTIFICATION: I hereby declare that the contents of this consignment are fully and accurately described above by proper shipping name and are classified, packed, marked, and labeled, and are in all respects in proper condition for transport by highway according to applicable international and national government regulations.

If I am a large quantity generator, I certify that I have a program in place to reduce the volume and toxicity of waste generated to the degree I have determined to be economically practicable and that I have selected the practicable method of treatment, storage, or disposal currently available to me which minimizes the present and future threat to human health and the environment, OR, if I am a small quantity generator, I have made a good faith effort to minimize my waste generation and select the best waste management method that is available to me and that I can afford.

Printed/Typed Name	Signature	Month Day Year

17 Transporter 1 Acknowledgement of Receipt of Materials		
Printed/Typed Name	Signature	Month Day Year

18 Transporter 2 Acknowledgement of Receipt of Materials		
Printed/Typed Name	Signature	Month Day Year

19 Discrepancy Indication Space

20 Facility Owner or Operator Certification of receipt of hazardous materials covered by this manifest except as noted in Item 19		
Printed/Typed Name	Signature	Month Day Year

FIGURE 8-3.   Uniform Hazardous Waste Manifest form. (Source: EPA)

Figure 8-6 shows the factors that influence a 90-day hazardous waste accumulation site.

Generators may accumulate without a permit up to 55 gallons of a single *waste stream* or up to 1 quart of an acute hazardous waste in containers at or near their point of generation where the waste initially accumulates. A waste stream is that waste or set of wastes that are produced as a result of a specific

UNIFORM HAZARDOUS WASTE MANIFEST *(Continuation Sheet)*	21 Generator's US EPA ID No		Manifest Document No	22 Page	Information in the shaded areas is not required by Federal law		
23 Generator's Name				L. State Manifest Document Number			
				M. State Generator's ID			
24 Transporter ____ Company Name		25 US EPA ID Number		N. State Transporter's ID			
				O. Transporter's Phone			
26 Transporter ____ Company Name		27 US EPA ID Number		P. State Transporter's ID			
				Q. Transporter's Phone			

28 US DOT Description *(Including Proper Shipping Name, Hazard Class, and ID Number)*	29 Containers		30 Total Quantity	31 Unit Wt/Vol	R. Waste No.
	No	Type			
a					
b					
c					
d					
e					
f					
g					
h					
i					

S. Additional Descriptions for Materials Listed Above	T. Handling Codes for Wastes Listed Above

32 Special Handling Instructions and Additional Information

33 Transporter ____ Acknowledgement of Receipt of Materials		Date
Printed/Typed Name	Signature	Month Day Year
34 Transporter ____ Acknowledgement of Receipt of Materials		
Printed/Typed Name	Signature	Month Day Year
35 Discrepancy Indication Space		

FIGURE 8-4.   Uniform Hazardous Waste Manifest form continuation sheet. (Source: DOT, EPA)

process. The hazardous nature of a waste stream has usually been identified and established based upon an analysis of the generating process. This accumulation site, referred to as a *satellite accumulation site,* must be under the direct control of the operator of the process that generated the waste, and no other waste from any other process can be entered into the container. Once a container at a satellite site reaches the 55-gallon mark (1 quart for

HAZARDOUS WASTE

FEDERAL LAW PROHIBITS IMPROPER DISPOSAL

IF FOUND, CONTACT THE NEAREST POLICE, OR PUBLIC SAFETY AUTHORITY, OR THE U.S. ENVIRONMENTAL PROTECTION AGENCY

GENERATOR INFORMATION:

NAME _____

ADDRESS _____ PHONE _____

CITY _____ STATE _____ ZIP _____

EPA   /MANIFEST
ID NO./ DOCUMENT NO. _____/_____

ACCUMULATION   EPA
START DATE _____ WASTE NO. _____

D.O.T. PROPER SHIPPING NAME AND UN OR NA NO. WITH PREFIX

HANDLE WITH CARE!

FIGURE 8-5.   Facsimile of DOT-accepted hazardous waste container label. (Source: DOT, EPA)

acute hazardous wastes), the date shall be entered on its label, which begins the 90-day clock, and it must be removed from the area and transferred to an approved 90-day site within a 72-hour period. If this is not accomplished, then the satellite site automatically becomes a 90-day site and is subject to additional requirements (such as documented weekly inspections, posting of emergency information, fire protection on site, and spill control equipment). Figure 8-7 shows the factors that influence a satellite accumulation site.

Any generator that ships any hazardous wastes off-site to a TSD facility within the United States must submit a report to their Regional Administrator (see Chapter 2) by March 1 of each even number year. This *biennial report* must cover the activities of the generator during the previous year, including their EPA identification number as well as that of any transporters and that of the off-site TSD facility used. The report shall list descriptions and quantities of each hazardous waste shipped off site and a description of the efforts

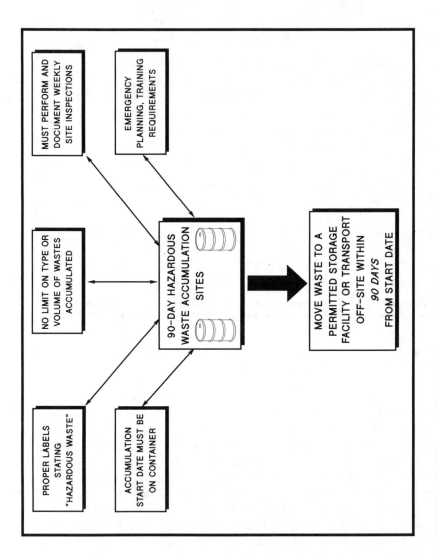

FIGURE 8-6. Elements affecting 90-day accumulation sites.

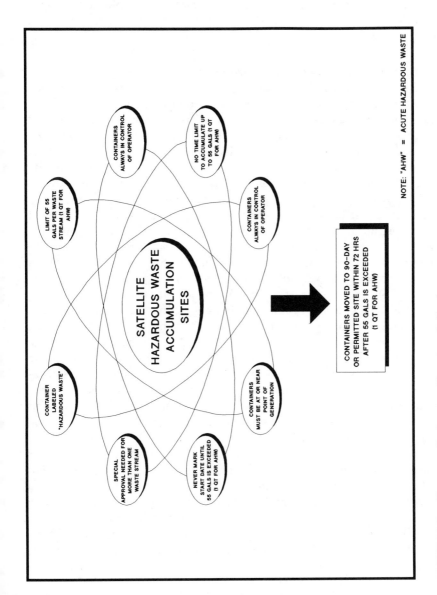

FIGURE 8-7. Elements affecting a satellite accumulation site.

129

undertaken during the previous year to minimize the volume and toxicity of the wastes being generated. The report must contain a signed certification by the generator.

Small-quantity Hazardous Waste Generators

The discussion thus far has focused on the requirements imposed upon generators of hazardous wastes. These generators are sometimes referred to as *large-quantity generators* in an effort to differentiate them from those that are responsible for the generation of wastes in amounts less than 1,000 kilograms per month. To ensure fair and reasonable application of the RCRA regulations on firms whose waste activities pose little relative threat or risk to the environment, the EPA has made a distinction for generators based upon the quantity of wastes generated over a specific period of time. Companies generating between 100 and 1,000 kilograms of hazardous waste per month (i.e., up to five 55-gallon drums), or a total of 1 kilogram of acute hazardous waste (P-listed wastes) per month, or generating less than 100 kilograms of hazardous waste and 1 kilogram of acute hazardous waste per month are referred to as *small-quantity generators (SQGs)*.

Those SQGs generating less than 100 kilograms of hazardous waste during any month are known as *conditionally exempt* small-quantity generators. These need only comply with the basic requirements for identification and disposal of wastes. A conditionally exempt SQG may either treat or dispose of acute hazardous waste in an on-site facility or ensure delivery to an off-site treatment location. Conditionally exempt SQGs will remain such as long as wastes are not accumulated in excess of 100 kilograms per month. However, if a conditionally exempt SQG should accumulate more than 1,000 kilograms of hazardous wastes *at any time,* then the full regulations for generators will become effective for that SQG.

The SQG must still comply with many of the regulatory requirements imposed upon regular generators. Specifically, the statutes require the SQG to notify the EPA of their generating activities, obtain an EPA identification number, use the approved multi-copy manifest form when transporting wastes off of their premises and maintain the form for not less than 3 years, consider waste minimization strategies, and comply with applicable Department of Transportation (DOT) requirements. If SQGs treat or dispose of their wastes on their own property, then they must also comply with the requirements for treatment, storage, and disposal facilities. The major relief for those generators that qualify as an SQG concerns storage requirements. According to RCRA, an SQG can store hazardous waste on site for periods up to 180 days or, if the waste must be transported more than 200 miles for disposal, they may remain in storage on site for up to 270 days without a permit.

It should also be noted that many of the states have their own requirements for SQGs that may be more stringent than the federally mandated exemptions. The reader should check with their appropriate state agencies for clarification (reference Appendix 3 of this text).

Emergency Requirements

Generators that accumulate wastes on site must develop, maintain, and update a detailed written *contingency plan* to deal with emergencies such as fires, explosions, and spills or other types of unplanned discharges of wastes. Specific procedures for dealing with such emergencies must be established in the plan. It must identify the type and location of emergency equipment that is to be used when facility personnel respond to emergency situations. The plan must also identify by name, address, and telephone number each person that is qualified to be an emergency response coordinator. Arrangements with any local emergency response authorities must be made in advance and detailed in the plan. If there are areas within the facility where evacuation could become necessary, these procedures must also be included in the written plan. Once approved by the appropriate managing element of the organization, the plan must be kept on file at the facility and a copy furnished to local authorities, such as fire, rescue, and hazardous material/emergency response teams. The plan must be updated whenever changes in the facility operations occur that might render existing provisions inadequate.

The contingency plan must identify at least one competent person to act as *emergency coordinator*. This person must have the ability and be of recognized authority to coordinate all the emergency response activities detailed in the plan. Because of the responsibilities associated with this position, the emergency coordinator must be highly trained and completely familiar with all the requirements of the contingency plan as well as the location of wastes in the facility and all operations that could lead to emergency response actions. In the event of an emergency, the designated emergency coordinator must:

1. Ensure that all alarms and other internal emergency notification and communication systems are properly activated to alert the affected personnel of the emergency.
2. Notify local authorities and emergency response agencies if their assistance will be required.
3. Identify the source, character, and amount of any released materials, and determine the extent of the affected area.
4. Evaluate possible hazards to health and the environment that could result from the emergency situation, taking into consideration both direct effects (e.g., soil contamination reaching groundwater supplies) and indirect effects (e.g., water runoff from fire-fighting activities).

5. If it is determined that a health or environmental threat could result outside of the facility boundaries that could necessitate an evacuation of citizens, the coordinator must immediately notify their appropriate state and local authorities. (Note: Regardless of any possible evacuation, the EPA's National Response Center should still be notified at 800-424-8802, 24 hours a day.)

6. Ensure that all necessary precautions are taken to contain the accident, such as plant shutdown and appropriate monitoring of equipment, and actions necessary to prevent the occurrence of future similar events.

7. Arrange for cleanup of any spilled materials and for the treatment, storage, and disposal of all contaminated by-products resultant from the emergency.

8. Take steps to ensure that incompatible materials are not introduced into the affected area until cleanup procedures are completed.

9. Keep a written record of the actions taken in response to the emergency to ensure an accurate and complete account of the emergency response activities. (NOTE: This responsibility is not required but highly recommended.)

The operator of a facility who has experienced any type of emergency situation that required activation of their contingency plan must file a written report with their EPA Regional Administrator within 15 days of such emergency. The report must detail the circumstances of the emergency, an assessment of the actual as well as potential effects on health and the environment, and an estimation of the quantities and status of contaminated materials recovered from the scene of the emergency.

Requirements for Containers and Tanks

The regulations establish numerous requirements, with provisions for each type of container or tank that will be used to hold hazardous waste products. In short, the standards require that each container be made of the *right materials* (i.e., materials compatible with the waste to be contained), with sufficient integrity to prevent leakage. If leaks do occur, then the container must be drained and removed from service. RCRA *container management* requirements specify spill prevention techniques, such as ensuring that a container remains closed except when wastes are to be added or removed. RCRA requires weekly inspections of containers at accumulation sites to document the condition and integrity of each container.

The 1984 amendments attacked the problem of *underground storage tanks (USTs)*, which have presented a serious concern for many years to the United States. Literally hundreds of thousands of USTs were known to be in existence. The concern arose as a result of an inability to determine if or when these tanks leaked. The EPA decided that the only way to ensure rapid detection of leaks from existing as well as new USTs was to require *secondary containment* (e.g., liners, vaults, double-walled tanks) of the entire system that is capable of holding 100% of the actual volume of the largest tank within its boundaries. Provisions for monitoring the area between the primary and secondary containment systems are also required. This technique, known as *interstitial monitoring,* can be an extremely expensive endeavor over the long term. As a result, many owners of existing USTs have opted, where possible, to invest in the one-time expense of having their USTs removed and replaced with above-ground tanks. (Note: Tanks that remain more than 10% below the surrounding grade are still considered USTs, by definition.) When such actions are not feasible, the EPA does allow the use of alternative monitoring and leak detection techniques that are at least as stringent as the interstitial technique, subject to their review and approval. It should be noted that sump tanks that are installed to catch fugitive leaks or spills are considered secondary containment systems and would not require any additional containment. Installation of secondary containment systems and monitoring equipment on new or existing USTs must be certified by an independent professional engineer as meeting the requirements established by the EPA for these systems. The engineer must also ensure that the design and installation of a new tank and/or secondary containment system are structurally sound. By 1995, all existing USTs must meet the secondary containment and monitoring requirements of RCRA.

Training Requirements Under RCRA

RCRA has established specific training requirements for personnel at facilities that store hazardous waste on site. It is important to note that the regulations do not, on the surface, require such training for generators who accumulate wastes at a 90-day accumulation site. However, a deeper analysis of the regulation will show that those generators who accumulate waste on site must, in fact, comply with the training requirements for *interim status* (i.e., those awaiting approval) TSD facilities, which do require such training. This is just one example of the many confusing aspects of the RCRA regulations. It reinforces the fact that the environmental compliance professional must be exhaustively thorough in reviewing the applicability of specific regulations. The training requirements are aimed at those personnel who are employed at TSD facilities as well as generators who accumulate waste on site as authorized under applicable RCRA regulations.

Basically, employees should be trained to perform their duties in compliance with the applicable regulations. This obviously means that the training must include a review of these regulations. Employees must also be familiar with the appropriate emergency response actions and their part in the emergency response process.

Employers are also required under the law to document their *training compliance* and to maintain appropriate *records* of their training activities. New employees can not work in unsupervised waste management positions before receiving the required training. These requirements also stipulate that the employer maintain a specific *job title* for each position in the organization that requires hazardous waste management functions along with the name of each employee in those positions. A *written job description* that includes the basic duties and the required skills, education, and qualifications for each of the hazardous waste management positions must also be maintained by the employer. Finally, a written description of the *type and amount of training* that the employer will provide to each person in a waste management position must be maintained.

Training records for *existing personnel* must be maintained for as long as the facility remains in operation. The employer must maintain copies of training records of *former employees* for a period of 3 years from the employee's last day of work. If employees are *transferred* from one facility to another within the same company, their training records must also be transferred to the new company facility.

Enforcement

RCRA provides for enforcement of its requirements and also establishes penalties for noncompliance. Basically, depending upon the specific circumstances, the EPA can enforce RCRA through the issuance of *administrative orders* and/or *compliance orders*, or through the imposition of *civil actions* and/or *criminal suits*, with varying degrees of *fine* and *penalty* associated with each.

Administrative Orders

If the EPA receives information indicating that hazardous waste may be present at a facility and there is a potential for release that will present a substantial threat of harm to human health or the environment, then the EPA may issue an administrative order to require certain actions from the owner or operator of that hazardous waste facility. These actions may include the monitoring, testing, and analysis of the facility, with a required report sent to the EPA. Such administrative orders might also be issued to a current or past owner of a facility who can not demonstrate actual knowledge of the presence of hazardous waste and its potential release from that facility. In issuing an administrative order, the EPA must list the information and facts that led it to believe that a threat to human health or the environment exists at the subject facility. Upon receipt, the recipient has a total of 30 days to submit back to the EPA its proposed work plan for accomplishing the requirements outlined in the administrative order. The recipient is also permitted the opportunity to confer with the EPA Administrator who will be reviewing their work proposal. If the recipient does not present a plan for accomplishing the requirements of the administrative order or if their proposed plan is not acceptable to the EPA, then the EPA can conduct its own monitoring, testing, and analysis in connection with the threatened release of hazardous waste. Failure or refusal to comply with the requirements of an administrative order could result in a civil action to require compliance and a civil penalty of up to $5,000 for each day the recipient refuses or fails to comply.

Compliance Orders

The EPA can issue an order assessing civil penalties for any past or current violation and require compliance with RCRA if it obtains information that any person has violated or is in violation of the RCRA hazardous waste requirements. In the compliance order, the EPA must specify the exact nature of the violative condition(s). If the recipient does not request a public hearing to challenge the order within 30 days after its receipt, the order becomes final. A compliance order may also revoke or suspend any permits previously issued by the EPA and may assess a monetary penalty of up to $25,000 per day for each of the noncompliant conditions. In addition, if the violator fails to take corrective action within the time period specified in the compliance order, then the EPA can assess an additional $25,000 civil penalty for each day the violator continues to remain noncompliant.

Civil Actions: RCRA includes provisions which allow the EPA to commence civil action in the United States District Court in the district in which the violation occurred. EPA may initiate such actions to seek appropriate relief which may include the judicial enforcement of the applicable RCRA requirements, a temporary or permanent injunction, and/or monetary penalties.

Criminal Suits

The EPA may also seek appropriate criminal penalties against any person who knowingly violates specific RCRA requirements. Violations that can be subject to criminal action include the transport or consignment for transport of any hazardous waste to a facility that does not have a permit as required under RCRA; the treatment, storage, or disposal of any hazardous waste without a permit, or knowingly operating in violation of that permit; the omission or falsification of any RCRA-required records; the transport of hazardous wastes without a manifest; and the export of hazardous waste without the consent of the receiving country. Upon conviction, the person found in criminal violation will be subject to a fine of up to $50,000 for each day of the violation or imprisonment for 2 to 5 years. If it is a conviction for a second violation, the fines and prison sentence could be doubled. If the violator knowingly placed another person in imminent danger of death or serious bodily injury, that person may be subjected to a fine of up to $250,000 and/or imprisonment for up to 15 years. (Note: If such a violator is an organization, it will be fined up to $1,000,000.)

In addition to the above described actions, RCRA also allows the EPA to bring suit in the appropriate federal district court against any person who has contributed to the management of hazardous waste (i.e., the handling, storage, treatment, transportation, or disposal) in such a way as to present an *imminent hazard* and substantial danger to health and the environment.

One final area of action available under RCRA is its provision for *citizen suits*. RCRA permits any person to bring a civil action against any other person, including the EPA itself, a state agency, or private person, for violations of RCRA requirements. The citizen must, however, provide the EPA, the local agency of the state in which the alleged violation occurred, and any alleged violators with notice 60 days prior to filing their impending citizen suit. If the person bringing the suit alleges that the violation may present an imminent and substantial endangerment to health or the environment, then notice 90 days prior to the filing of the suit is required.

Delegation of Authority to the States
The Act contains provisions for the federal standards established by RCRA for the management of hazardous wastes to be implemented on the state level. In fact, the EPA has promulgated regulations concerning the authorization of hazardous waste programs by the individual states. For states to obtain such authorization, their programs must be consistent with and equivalent in scope and intent as federally mandated requirements. The states must also provide for adequate enforcement of RCRA requirements.

Land Disposal Restrictions
The 1984 amendments also focused on minimizing or eliminating the land disposal of hazardous waste (sometimes referred to as *Land-Ban*), with specific restrictions on such activities at landfills and surface impoundments. For example, the requirements prohibit the placement of bulk or non-containerized liquid hazardous waste in landfills. In fact, RCRA even prohibits the placement of nonhazardous liquids into landfills unless no other method of disposal is reasonably available and the placement of the liquid will not present a contamination hazard to underground drinking water supplies. Also prohibited is the land disposal of a group of liquid hazardous wastes containing concentrations of certain hazardous metals (the *California List*). Finally, the EPA has developed an extensive list of restrictions on the land disposal of all other *listed* and *characteristic wastes*.

Special Rules for Hazardous Wastes

RCRA contains a number of special rules to address certain unique circumstances involving the generation of hazardous wastes under specific conditions. One such rule, the *mixture rule,* was briefly discussed earlier in this chapter. In addition to this rule, anyone new to the environmental compliance profession will certainly encounter at least the following two common rules:

The Derived From Rule—This rule stipulates that waste generated from the treatment, storage, or disposal of hazardous waste is itself a hazardous waste, unless it does not exhibit any of the hazardous characteristics or it is not a listed waste.

The Residue Rule—Also known as the "One-inch Rule," it states that any residue left in empty containers will not be regulated under RCRA, provided that all hazardous wastes are removed from the container using the practice commonly employed to remove materials from that type of container and that no more than 1 inch of residue remains.

Other Elements of RCRA

The Act contains numerous other provisions that focus on requirements for items such as groundwater monitoring, procedures for the closure of storage facilities, and underground injection requirements. A detailed discussion of each of these topics is beyond the scope of this *Basic Guide.* However, Appendix A provides sources of additional information and training and should be consulted if such advanced knowledge is desired in any of these subject areas.

FUTURE TRENDS FOR RCRA

As of this writing, RCRA is past due for reauthorization. It is probably a safe assumption that any new RCRA could only be more stringent than previous or present versions. Companies have learned that proper and effective hazardous waste management makes good business sense. This attitude must prevail through RCRA reauthorization, or many businesses probably will not survive. No one can be sure what elements of RCRA will be most affected by any new Congressional actions or mandates associated with reauthorization. However, it is expected that the new law will further broaden the agency's powers to force companies that violate the standards to comply immediately with the law or face even stronger and tougher penalties. Congress is also expected to require a waste minimization program for generators, rather than simply recommend them.

SUMMARY

The *Resource Conservation and Recovery Act (RCRA)* of 1976, along with applicable amendments and revisions in subsequent years, established a system for regulating and managing hazardous wastes from the *cradle to grave.* In its broad and extremely complex regulatory framework, the Act provides the EPA with the authority to regulate virtually every aspect associated with the *generation, transportation, treatment, storage,* and *disposal* of hazardous wastes.

Although the original Act attempted to provide for meaningful regulation in these areas, its language was vague; subsequently, numerous loopholes existed. A major goal of the *1984 amendments* was to plug these many loopholes with tighter and more stringent regulatory controls. In its present form, RCRA is perhaps one of the most formidable pieces of environmental legislation that today's compliance professional must deal with on a daily basis. The extent of the Act's complexity is evident even in its definition of a hazardous waste, which requires first that the waste be solid. Despite conventional wisdom and scientifically valid definitions, the term *solid* (according to RCRA) means just about any form of matter imaginable.

RCRA also establishes additional considerations to ensure proper *waste determination.* It identifies waste characteristics, such as *ignitability, corrosivity, reactivity,* and *toxicity.* Under the toxicity determination, the EPA has developed a list of chemical compounds that must be tested for in a procedure known as the *Toxicity Characteristic Leaching Procedure (TCLP).* If any of the chemicals on this list (known as the *D List)* can leach into the soil and contaminate groundwater, these wastes meet the characteristic requirements for toxicity. These *characteristic wastes* are regulated as hazardous wastes if they are also considered solid wastes.

In an effort to facilitate the waste determination process, the EPA has provided several lists of regulated wastes. These *listed wastes* are subject to regulation, as are the characteristic wastes. The lists include *toxic wastes* (the *U List)* and *acutely toxic wastes* (the *P List); wastes from specific sources* (the *K List)* and *nonspecific sources* (the *F List).* The *master list of hazardous constituents* is also provided as a non-regulatory list for information purposes only and contains several hundred chemicals known to be toxic, carcinogenic, teratogenic, or mutagenic.

Congress realized that many wastes that meet the RCRA definition of a solid hazardous waste might not present a serious threat to human health or the environment, or its concentration level in the overall waste is insignificant, or its discharge may be already regulated under some other law such as the Clean Water Act. Therefore, RCRA allows for certain specific solid waste *exclusions.* There are also numerous provisions to exclude certain waste *reclamation* activities, and the Act provides for the specific regulation of *recycled* materials. There is a great deal of attention on *used oil burned for energy recovery* purposes, and regulations focus on *specification used oil, off-specification used oil, oily waste,* and *hazardous waste fuel.*

This chapter focused on the requirements placed on *generators* of hazardous waste, with particular emphasis on *small-quantity generators (SQGs).* There was also discussion concerning *record-keeping* requirements, the *Uniform Hazardous Waste Manifest, training provisions, emergency response plans,* and *enforcement* procedures. A brief description of some of the basic requirements related to those regulations that pertain to *treatment, storage, and disposal (TSD)* facilities was provided. Particularly, generators of hazardous wastes are allowed to accumulate waste on their premises at either *satellite accumulation sites* or *90-day accumulation sites,* without having to obtain a TSD permit. A major element of the 1984 amendments concerned the problems associated with leaks from *underground storage tanks (USTs).* RCRA provides regulations to ensure that *secondary containment systems* and *monitoring devices* are installed on existing USTs and that all new USTs can not be put into place until properly certified as meeting the stringent construction and integrity requirements. RCRA also establishes numerous restrictions and prohibitions on the land disposal of certain types of hazardous wastes *(Land-Ban).*

By all accounts, RCRA imposes a serious compliance problem for today's environmental professional as well as for industry itself. With its reauthorization, past due as of this writing, RCRA promises even tougher and more stringent regulatory controls on the management of hazardous wastes as our nation moves into the 21st century and beyond.

CASE BRIEF: RESOURCE CONSERVATION AND RECOVERY ACT
HAZARDOUS WASTE TREATMENT COUNCIL
vs.
ENVIRONMENTAL PROTECTION AGENCY
U.S. Court of Appeals, District of Columbia Circuit
No. 90-1443, 26 July 1991

Summary

This case involves a petition to the EPA for review of the State of North Carolina's Hazardous Waste Regulations based on a claim that the state's requirements were inconsistent with federal RCRA regulations, 42 U.S.C. 6926.

North Carolina has enacted a statute that requires a thousand-fold dilution of discharges from commercial hazardous waste treatment facilities into surface waters located upstream of public drinking water intakes. The request for review was denied by the EPA, and the petitioner then filed an appeal.

Background

RCRA provides a comprehensive federal program for the management of hazardous waste, but permits the individual states to administer their own program, with authorization of the EPA. However, the Act specifically states that the agency may not approve a state program if, among other things, that program is not equivalent to the federal program or if such program does not provide adequate enforcement of compliance with the Act's requirements. If a state falls into one of these categories, the EPA must notify the state of their deficiency and, if not corrected within 90 days, the EPA is required to withdraw authorization of the state program. The petitioner claims that North Carolina's program is inconsistent with federal requirements and, therefore, the EPA should withdraw the state's authorization.

In its refusal to act on the request, the EPA emphasized that RCRA also specifies that a state may impose requirements that are more stringent than those established by EPA regulations. During the appeal, the petitioner reasoned again that state programs must be consistent with federal regulations and, further, that any aspect of a state program that unreasonably restricts, impedes, or operates as a ban on the free movement across the state border of hazardous waste or to other states for treatment, storage, or disposal at authorized facilities shall be deemed inconsistent and, therefore, grounds for withdrawal. On these grounds, the appeal sought review and withdrawal of North Carolina's authorization of its state program.

Decision

The administrative law judge determined that withdrawal of the state's approval was not warranted. This determination was based on several factors, the most important of which concluded that the state's requirements did not unreasonably restrict or operate as a ban on the free movement of hazardous waste across North Carolina's borders. Because the EPA is charged with the administration of RCRA, the court deferred to the agency's interpretation whenever the statute is silent or ambiguous with respect to a specific issue. As long as such interpretation is reasonable and consistent with the statutory purpose of RCRA, the court will hold the interpretation. The court concluded that the EPA properly declined to withdraw authorization of North Carolina's program and denied the petition for review.

Analysis

The EPA was not required to withdraw its approval of a state hazardous waste treatment program under RCRA after a state adopted more stringent requirements than that specified in the federal statutes because: 1) The EPA found that withdrawal was required only if the state law banned particular waste treatment technology within the state; and 2) The EPA reasonably determined that the state requirement did not render the state RCRA program inconsistent with the federal program.

In short, while it is true that RCRA requires consistency between state and federal programs, it does not mandate uniformity. In fact, the statute expressly gives the states the authority to impose site-selection standards that are more stringent than those imposed by the federal authority. This case clearly demonstrates that the Act provides extensive authority for state regulation of hazardous waste treatment programs.

9

Toxic Substances Control Act

INTRODUCTION

The *Toxic Substances Control Act (TSCA)*, normally pronounced *TOS-KA,* was enacted in 1976 as the eventual response to a 1970 CEQ (Council on Environmental Quality—see Chapter 5) report entitled "Toxic Substances." Basically, the CEQ focused on an identified need to enact regulations aimed at toxic chemicals, with special emphasis on metal or metallic compounds and synthetic organic chemicals, present in the air, water, soil, consumer products, and food, that might endanger human health and the environment. TSCA attempts to address much of these concerns (food and food products are not currently regulated by TSCA).

The Act is divided into two titles:

Title I, "Control of Toxic Substances," is extremely broad in scope and establishes 30 distinct Sections that contain much of the regulatory compliance requirements facing most of industry today.

Title II, "Asbestos Hazardous Emergency Response," is rather limited in scope and deals primarily with asbestos in schools.

The major objective of TSCA is to ensure that the EPA obtains detailed information on the production and use of chemical substances or mixtures, as well as the health and environmental effects associated with such production or use. Since much of the requirements necessary to achieve this objective are outlined in Title I, this *Basic Guide* will focus primarily on TSCA Title I provisions.

TSCA also provides the necessary authority for the EPA to issue regulations on the manufacture, processing, distribution (in commerce), use, and disposal of chemical substances or mixtures. Along with this authority, however, comes an obligation for the EPA to seriously consider any economic and social impacts created by any such regulatory actions under TSCA. The applicability of TSCA is extremely broad, encompassing virtually every aspect of the toxic chemical industry that could possibly affect commerce. In fact, TSCA not only imposes regulatory controls over imports of chemical substances, but also regulates exports as well.

Although industry's efforts at TSCA compliance have taken somewhat of a back seat over the years to other environmental regulations, such as RCRA and CAA, TSCA imposes stringent regulatory controls on chemical substances and mixtures, accompanied by very serious fines and penalties for noncompliance. The practicing environmental compliance professional would do well to become familiar with the basic requirements of this law. TSCA has been referred to by some as the *sleeping giant* of the environmental regulations. The price of ignorance and noncompliance under TSCA could result in penalties and fines so severe that some businesses simply might not survive.

BASIC REQUIREMENTS UNDER TSCA, TITLE I

TSCA defines a *chemical substance* as any organic or inorganic substance of a particular molecular identity. This includes any combination of such substances that occur in whole or in part, either as a result of a chemical reaction or that occur in nature. Chemical substances also include any element or uncombined radical. This definition excludes mixtures, pesticides (when their manufacture, processing, and distribution in commerce is for use as a pesticide), tobacco or tobacco products, and any source material or special nuclear materials. Also specifically excluded are food, food additives, and drugs and cosmetics (when their manufacture, processing, and distribution in commerce are intended for use as such items). Items that are subject to tax under the Internal Revenue Code, such as firearms, are also excluded from TSCA provisions.

The other target of TSCA regulations, *mixtures,* is defined as any combination of two or more chemical substances if the combination does not occur in nature and is not, in whole or in part, the result of a chemical reaction. However, the law specifically mentions that the term *mixture* does not apply to those combinations that are comprised from *new chemical substances.* A new chemical substance is any chemical substance that is not included on the *TSCA Inventory* of existing chemical substances, which was compiled at the time of TSCA promulgation in 1976. Essentially, regulators compiled a list of virtually every chemical substance manufactured, processed, distributed in commerce, used, and disposed of in 1976. This list of roughly 66,000 chemicals became the TSCA Inventory List of existing chemicals. Henceforth, any chemical substance that does not appear on that list or its subsequent revisions is considered a new chemical substance subject to the *Premanufacture Notice* requirements (see section titled "Permanufacture Notice," below) . The Inventory does not pretend to identify all chemical substances currently in U.S. commerce, as some substances are not subject to TSCA and because new chemical substances are continually in the process of being added to the inventory. Over 4,500 of the substances on the Inventory List are claimed as *confidential* by the manufacturer, processor, or distributor. These chemicals are assigned generic names only. Should a chemical substance not be found on the Inventory's public database, a potential importer or manufacturer intending to manufacture or import the substance for *commercial purposes* must request the EPA to search the *Master Inventory File* to determine if the substance is among those listed as confidential. If the substance has never been added to the inventory, then, regardless of its actual age, it is considered a new chemical substance.

Special Definitions Under TSCA

According to TSCA, the term *manufacture* means to import into the customs territory of the United States or to produce or manufacture a chemical substance. It must be understood that a substance is considered to have been manufactured even if its production was not intentional (e.g., chemical by-products, accidental production of a new chemical substance as the result of unforeseen or unintentional incidents involving chemical substances).

TSCA also focuses its regulatory standards on those chemical substances that have been processed. Under TSCA, *process* is defined as the preparation of a chemical substance or mixture, after its manufacture, for distribution in commerce. Such processing can result in the chemical substance either remaining in the same form as it was received or being changed in some way from the form or physical state in which it was received.

Another aspect of consideration is the *distribution into commerce* of chemical substances. TSCA intends this to mean either the introduction, holding, or selling of a substance, mixture, or article into commerce.

For the purpose of TSCA, an *article* is a manufactured item that is formed to a specific size and shape during manufacture and whose end use function is dependent in whole or in part on that specific size and shape. Those features of the article that impact commerce must not change in chemical composition during the article's end use. (Note: TSCA does not consider fluids and particles as articles, regardless of their respective shape or size.) A *health and safety study* is defined by TSCA as any study of any effect of a chemical substance or mixture on health and/or the environment, including underlying epidemiological studies, studies of occupational exposure, and toxicological, clinical, and ecological studies of a chemical substance or mixture.

Finally, a key to a chemical substance's applicability to TSCA is its effect on commerce. *Commerce* is defined as trade, traffic, transportation, or other commerce between a place in a state and any other place outside a state or actions that might affect such trade, traffic, or commerce.

Testing of Chemical Substances or Mixtures

TSCA gave the EPA the authority to require testing of any chemical substance or mixture subject to TSCA if the EPA can determine that the substance or mixture may present an unreasonable risk of injury to health or the environment and that testing is required to develop needed data. In making a decision to require testing, the EPA must evaluate risk by considering both the hazard posed by the substance and the effects of exposure to the substance. The EPA can also require testing of mixtures if the effects of exposure can not be otherwise ascertained because there is insufficient information and experience to predict their effects on health and the environment.

In making its determination of whether testing shall be required, the EPA must only show that the manufacture, distribution in commerce, processing, use, or disposal of a chemical substance or mixture *may* either:

1. Pose an unreasonable risk of injury to health or the environment.
2. A substantial quantity of a chemical substance or mixture is produced and may enter the environment in substantial quantities.
3. There is or may be a significant human exposure to such substances or mixtures.

Testing of widely used substances is often funded by industry trade organizations, manufacturers, and importers. Less widely used substances are usually tested by the manufacturers or importers themselves or by contract with a laboratory. In some cases, processors may be required to pay for testing. Allocation of testing costs among responsible firms is typically worked out by industry and, if required, the EPA.

Interagency Testing Committee

Whenever new chemical substances or mixtures are to be introduced into commerce, the EPA must establish testing criteria to determine the effect that these materials may have on health and the environment. To facilitate this process, TSCA established a committee to make recommendations to the EPA regarding chemical substances and mixtures to which the EPA should give priority when promulgating new testing rules. This *priority list* is then published in the Federal Register. This *Interagency Testing Committee (ITC)*, which is comprised of members from numerous agencies, issues priority designations for such substances that are considered to be suspect human carcinogens, mutagens, or teratogens. The ITC must make new recommendations (if appropriate) and update existing ones on a semi-annual basis, and the EPA must respond to the designation of each chemical within a year of its listing by the ITC. The EPA's response will either be to initiate the required rule-making procedures to address the ITC-designated chemicals or to demonstrate why such rule making is not required.

Priority listing of a chemical substance or mixture by the ITC requires automatic reporting under TSCA's *Preliminary Assessment Information Rule (PAIR)* and the TSCA *Health and Safety Data Reporting Rule.* PAIR requires manufacturers to submit production and exposure data on priority list chemicals within 90 days of the publication in the Federal Register of those chemicals. Likewise, under the Health and Safety Data Reporting Rule, manufacturers, processors, and importers must submit health and safety studies within 90 days of the chemical's publication in the Federal Register. Priority designation is usually followed by the promulgation of a test rule.

Once a rule is promulgated, any manufacturer, processor, or importer subject to it must either submit a letter of their intent to comply with the rule and conduct the testing or seek an exemption from the EPA. The EPA will grant exemptions from a test rule if it can be demonstrated that the applicant's substance is equivalent to a chemical substance for which data has already or will soon be submitted. The person requesting such an exemption must sign an agreement to reimburse those that actually generate the test data.

Premanufacture Notice

TSCA also allows the EPA to regulate the introduction of new chemical substances into the United States by requiring a manufacturer or importer of that chemical substance to file a *Premanufacture Notice (PMN)* at least 90 days prior to commencement of commercial production or importation. An importer is not required to file a PMN if a new chemical substance is to be imported as part of an article. A review of the PMN provides the EPA with its first opportunity to evaluate the new substance. Depending upon the results of its review, the EPA may allow commercial production of the new chemical substance without any limitations. However, it may limit or even prohibit production on the basis that insufficient evidence exists to permit a reasoned evaluation of the substance's effect on health and the environment. In some cases, the EPA can choose to extend the PMN review period for an additional 90 days, if necessary, to complete their evaluation. If the EPA has taken no restrictive actions upon expiration of the PMN review period, commercial manufacture or import of a new chemical can begin. Within 30 days of beginning manufacture or import, the manufacturer or importer must file with the EPA a *Notice of Commencement of Manufacture*. Upon their receipt of this notice, the EPA adds the new chemical to the TSCA Inventory.

It should be noted that the EPA may have concerns about a specific new chemical substance based on the information provided and might propose restrictions or controls on the chemical's use or production in U.S. commerce. In this situation, most companies will choose to negotiate a *premanufacture consent order* with the EPA that will allow production of the new chemical under restricted circumstances. Premanufacture consent orders apply only to the manufacturer or importer who had submitted the PMN and who signs the consent order and severely limits any other potential manufacturer or importer from engaging in any such actions with the same chemical substance. Therefore, after a premanufacture consent order has been adopted, the EPA can promulgate a *Significant New Use Rule (SNUR)*. The SNUR will then be applicable to all potential users, manufacturers, processors, or importers of that new chemical substance. To facilitate the quick issuance of new SNURs, the EPA promulgated the *generic SNUR* in 1989. Notice of SNURs is made through the Federal Register.

TSCA Regulation of Existing Chemicals

TSCA provides the EPA with the authority to regulate existing chemicals that present or will present an unreasonable risk of injury to human health or the environment. Polychlorinated Biphenols (PCB), asbestos, and fully halogenated chlorofluoroalkanes are currently regulated by the EPA under TSCA. The EPA can prohibit or limit the use, manufacture, processing, distribution, or disposal of a substance under TSCA regulations. They can also require warnings, record keeping, risk notification, or even the replacement of a substance. In taking such actions, TSCA requires the EPA to choose the least burdensome restriction that is deemed adequate to protect against the risk posed by the substance.

The EPA may determine that a chemical substance or mixture presents an *imminent hazard* or unreasonable risk of serious or widespread injury to health or the environment. In this event, the EPA can bring civil action in district court for seizure of the subject chemical substance.

Information Reporting

As discussed earlier, two methods that the EPA uses to obtain information is through the PAIR and the Health and Safety Data Reporting Rule, which require manufacturers to report certain information to the EPA and conduct health and safety studies on a limited number of chemicals. In addition to these methods, the EPA promulgated the *Comprehensive Assessment Information Rule (CAIR)* under TSCA Section 8. CAIR is a standardized series of questions designed to gather more detailed information about chemical usage and exposure. The first CAIR, for example, was promulgated in December 1988, and required detailed information from importers, manufacturers, and processors of 19 chemical substances.

It should be clear at this point that much of the TSCA requirements are aimed directly at manufacturers, processors, importers, and those who distribute chemical substances into commerce in the United States. Many safety, health, and environmental professionals are associated with firms that participate in such activities, while a great many more are not. Section 8 of TSCA authorizes the EPA to establish the reporting and record-keeping requirements necessary to provide them with information on which to base its regulatory actions. All safety, health, and environmental professionals should be aware of these provisions, regardless of the applicability of other TSCA requirements. Specifically, under TSCA Section 8(c), manufacturers and certain processors and users (if such use can be determined as processing) of chemical substances and mixtures must keep records of *allegations* of significant adverse reactions to health or the environment believed to have been caused by a specific substance or mixture. An 8(c) allegation may be made by any person, including an employee, union, citizen activist, plant neighbor, or another company on behalf of its employees. The allegation need not be supported by scientific or medical evidence for the purpose of TSCA, but it must establish a link between an adverse health effect and a chemical substance or mixture, a particular company's product or process, or an abnormal experience by persons or the environment.

It is important to realize that TSCA does not require the recording of *known human health effects* under Section 8(c). This means that the known effects of exposure to a substance, such as those that are typically listed in the Health Hazards Section of a Material Safety Data Sheet (MSDS), do not have to be recorded. In other words, if it is already known that exposure to volatile solvent vapors causes depression of the central nervous system, such exposure is not *new information* and no TSCA 8(c) allegation is necessary. However, if a person *alleges* that exposure to those same solvent vapors caused hair loss or some other previously unknown exposure effect for which no documentation exists, an 8(c) allegation would then be warranted. This condition does not pertain to significant environmental reactions resulting from alleged exposure, which must always be recorded (unless occurring as a result of a spill or accidental discharge that has already been reported to a federal agency).

The EPA requires the collection, recording, filing, and retaining of all 8(c) allegations. Records that pertain to employee health must be kept for a minimum of 30 years following the allegation. Other records must be retained for 5 years. Figure 9-1 shows a sample form that can be used to record TSCA 8(c) allegations.

The primary intent of TSCA under Section 8(c) is to create a historical record of significant adverse reactions and so provide a way to identify previously unknown chemical hazards. Allegation records must be maintained at a location that is central to a company's chemical operations, such as a safety, health, or environmental department, so that any discernible pattern of risk can be detected. These records are subject to EPA inspection at any time, and a centralized location will facilitate their review. The agency may also publish rules requiring persons to submit to the EPA all allegations concerning a particular chemical in support of any special studies they may wish to conduct.

Reporting of Substantial Risk Information

Any person who manufactures, imports, processes, or distributes into commerce a chemical substance and who learns that the substance presents a *substantial risk* of injury to health or the environment must immediately inform the EPA (unless that person has actual knowledge that the EPA already knows this information). The intent is to ensure that companies do not withhold crucial information from the EPA concerning the dangers associated with chemicals. It is a company's responsibility to identify substantial risk information and report it to the EPA within 15 working days after the company becomes aware of the information.

Export and Import Notification

TSCA requires any person who exports or imports or who intends to export or import a chemical substance or mixture (but not articles) to notify the EPA of their intentions. If those materials to be exported have been tested under TSCA guidelines and are shown to present an unreasonable risk to health, the EPA will inform recipient governments. TSCA's import policies are intended to protect the health and environment of the United States, while its export policies are aimed at providing information to foreign governments

TSCA SECTION 8(c) RISK ALLEGATION FORM

Allegation of Significant Adverse Reaction to Health or the Environment

Alleging Party:_____ Date of Alleged Exposure: _____

Check One: ☐ Employee   ☐ Customer   ☐ Contractor   ☐ Other

Location of Complaint: Component: _____ Facility:_____ Building:_____
Room Number: _____ Work Area:_____ Tank:_____
Other: _____

Allegation Caused By (check all that apply):

☐ Chemical   Name of Chemical: _____

☐ Operation   What Operation: _____

☐ Process   Describe Process: _____

☐ Emission   Location of Emission: _____

☐ Product/Article Describe: _____

ALLEGATION (BE SPECIFIC):

☐ HEALTH EFFECT: _____
_____
_____

Person's Age: _____ Male: ____ Female: ____ Route of Exposure:_____

☐ ENVIRONMENTAL EFFECT: _____
_____
_____

Type of Plant: _____ Type of Animal: _____

Description of Contaminated Area:_____

Other Information (concentration, mitigating factors, etc.):_____
_____
_____

I AUTHORIZE RELEASE OF THIS INFORMATION.

Date of This Report: Signature of Alleger

_____   _____ Ph.#_____

                            Name of Person Recording Information

FIGURE 9-1.   Sample TSCA 8(c) Risk Allegation Form.

regarding chemical substances and mixtures so that those governments can make decisions to protect their own citizens.

No person may bring into the United States a chemical substance or mixture if it does not comply with TSCA. Prior to bringing any chemical substance into the country, an importer must certify that the substance is either exempt from TSCA or is in compliance with TSCA. These *import certification* requirements apply to any shipment of a chemical substance, whether imported in pure bulk form or as part of a mixture. Mixtures as a whole are exempt from import certification, but their chemical constituents are not. Incidentally, there are no *de minimus* or low-volume exclusions under this section of TSCA.

When an importer has no actual knowledge of the chemical composition of an imported chemical substance or mixture, the importer must make attempts to discover the shipment's chemical constituents (e.g., by contacting the principal supplier or foreign manufacturer) in order to ensure that all imported chemical constituents comply with TSCA. If a shipment is found to be in violation of TSCA, the documented *good faith efforts* of the importer to verify compliance with TSCA may serve to avoid or reduce any civil penalties.

Enforcement

The Act provides the EPA with the authority to enforce TSCA provisions, and the agency may even confiscate substances that are found to be in violation of TSCA. TSCA specifies that it is unlawful for any person to fail or refuse to comply with any rule or order issued under TSCA. This includes using (for commercial purposes) any chemical substance or mixture that the person knew or had reason to know was in violation of TSCA. The failure or refusal to establish and maintain records, to submit reports, notices, or other required information, or to permit authorized access or copying of such records will be considered a violation of TSCA.

Violations of TSCA, as described above, are subject to civil and criminal penalties. *Civil penalties* can carry fines of up to $25,000 for each day of a violation. Civil penalties under TSCA are administratively imposed by the EPA, without the need to bring an action in a court. Knowing or willful violations of TSCA may subject the offender to *criminal fines* of up to $25,000 per day and a maximum of 1 year in prison. These criminal sanctions may be in lieu of or in addition to any civil penalties.

TSCA also contains provisions for *citizen suits.* Any person may file a suit against any violator of TSCA, including federal, state, and local agencies or authorities. This includes citizen suits against the EPA to compel performance of the Act's requirements. Suits against the EPA are brought in the U.S. District Court for Washington, D.C., or in the district court for the area where the plaintiff resides. Suits filed against other alleged violators are typically brought where the violation occurred or where the defendant resides. Plaintiffs in any such citizen action must provide the EPA and the violator with notice of intent to sue at least 60 days prior to initiating the suit. However, according to TSCA, a person who has provided the proper notice of intent to sue a violator has the right to intervene if the EPA commences a proceeding to issue an order against that violator. For example, if the EPA has failed to take the appropriate actions required for imminent hazards, then the notice period required before filing a citizen suit is reduced to only 10 days. It is important to note that TSCA contains no private right of action provisions. This means that, under TSCA, there is no expressed or implied right for any one person to seek redress for personal injury from an employer or owner/operator.

SUMMARY

This chapter provided an extremely brief overview of the *Toxic Substances Control Act (TSCA)* of 1976. Title I of TSCA provides regulatory controls of *chemical substances* and *mixtures* to ensure that any person who *manufactures, imports, processes,* or *distributes into commerce* any such chemical substance or mixture will be subjected to TSCA requirements. Because TSCA has not received much of the high-profile publicity as other environmental mandates, such as RCRA, some analysts have referred to TSCA as a *sleeping giant* among the environmental regulations.

At the heart of the regulation is the *TSCA Inventory* of existing chemical substances. Basically, any chemical substance or mixture subject to TSCA at the time of its enactment were included on this list (approximately 66,000 chemicals). Any chemical substance or mixture occurring after that has been considered a *new chemical substance.* Manufacturers, importers, processors, and those who distribute new chemical substances into commerce must first submit a *Premanufacture Notice (PMN)* to the EPA. The Agency can then require testing of these substances to determine the nature and extent of any harmful effects on health and the environment. In addition, TSCA established an *Interagency Testing Committee (ITC)* to identify chemicals that should receive priority from the EPA in terms of testing requirements. This *priority list* is aimed at those substances believed to cause cancer in humans, or that adversely affect gene development, or that cause damage to or loss of a developing human fetus. Such priority listing of a chemical automatically imposes reporting requirements under TSCA's *Preliminary Assessment Information Rule (PAIR),* the *Health and Safety Study Data Reporting Rule,* or the *Comprehensive Assessment Information Rule (CAIR).* If, based upon information received, the EPA has concerns about a new chemical substance, it may issue a *premanufacture consent order* on that specific requester. Since other chemical manufacturers or importers may wish to engage in activities involving the same chemical, the EPA often issues a *Significant New Use Rule (SNUR)*, which will impose the same restrictions on all those involved with the subject chemical. In cases where the EPA has determined that a chemical substance poses an *imminent hazard* to health or the environment, they can seek civil actions to control the substance.

TSCA also contains provisions for reporting of *risk allegations* under Section 8(c). If any person alleges that their exposure to a particular substance has caused an effect that is considered a new symptom of exposure, it must be recorded and the information maintained for a period of 30 years (for health effects) or 5 years (for other effects, such as that on the environment). Also, any person that has information to indicate that a substance will pose a *substantial risk* of injury to health or the environment is required to immediately notify the EPA.

The EPA imposes restrictions on both the *import* and *export* of chemical substances in an effort to protect the United States from importation of new chemicals and to inform foreign governments of chemical hazards prior to export. Importers must provide the EPA with an *import certification*, indicating that the chemical substances to be imported meets EPA TSCA requirements.

Violators of TSCA provisions can be subjected to either *civil* or *criminal* fines and penalties. Stiff monetary fines can accompany either type of action, with jail time included under any criminal violation. TSCA also allows for *citizen suits* against any person violating TSCA requirements.

Any safety, health, or environmental professional new to the environmental compliance arena might be drawn to other, more pressing and higher profile regulatory requirements, such as those enacted to manage hazardous waste, clean water, and clean air. However, ignorance of TSCA will be a poor excuse for a noncompliant situation under this law. In an effort to impart a basic understanding of the Act's objectives, this chapter provided the fundamentals of this highly complex legislation.

CASE BRIEF: TOXIC SUBSTANCES CONTROL ACT
CITIZENS FOR A BETTER ENVIRONMENT
vs.
ENVIRONMENTAL PROTECTION AGENCY
U.S. District Court, Northern District of Illinois
No. 85 C 8000, 28 May 1991

Summary

This case demonstrates that a citizens' petition for EPA action brought under the Toxic Substances Control Act (TSCA), 15 U.S.C. 2620, may not always be successful, especially when the plaintiff can not substantiate the charges with scientifically valid evidence. It is important to realize that the courts historically provide much discretion on behalf of citizen's groups, but not when such groups are unprepared for the case that they themselves have brought.

Background

The plaintiffs in this case, Citizens for a Better Environment (CBE), filed a citizens' petition (First Petition) on July 27, 1984, under the provisions of TSCA, seeking that a rule be issued to remedy what the plaintiffs believed was an unreasonable risk to health and to the environment in Southeastern Chicago. The EPA denied the First Petition, stating that other authorities administered by the EPA can adequately address the problems raised by the petitioners. In other words, no specific action would be taken by the EPA as a result of the petition, since an avenue for investigative action already existed within the EPA, making a petition under TSCA unnecessary. The plaintiffs did not commence a civil action in response to the EPA denial within the TSCA-specified 60-day time period. However, the following April, the petitioners filed a Second Petition, pursuant to TSCA Section 21, requesting action by the EPA to issue rules requiring the testing of chemical substances or mixtures in certain situations. The EPA again denied the petitioner's request. This time, CBE did file a civil action within the 60-day time period to seek evaluation of the Second Petition by the court.

In the Second Petition, the plaintiffs alleged a need for testing of 11 identified substances, based on an Illinois Environmental Protection Agency study that indicated that the substances were present in Southeast Chicago. These substances included coke oven emissions, benzene, chromium, arsenic, cadmium, nickel, toluene, xylene, acetone, copper, and lead. Because of the presence of multiple chemical substances, the Second Petition and the complaint against the EPA sought testing of the substances for the interactive effects. The Second Petition requested the EPA to issue a rule requiring testing that would include various tests of each of the identified substances individually as well as in combination with every other identified substance.

In denying the Second Petition, the EPA stated that no standards presently exist for the testing of multiple chemicals for their interaction and that the state of the art in this area is insufficient for prescribing the testing requested by the plaintiffs. Also, the Second Petition sought testing of the individual substances on their own, which was denied because the toxicological properties of each are already known and documented and, therefore, a regulatory decision can be made concerning them without the need for further testing.

Decision

The court essentially upheld the EPA's denial of the petition because: 1) The plaintiffs could present no proof that the provisions of TSCA were violated; 2) The EPA found that testing of multiple hazardous substances in combination was not scientifically feasible; and 3) CBE failed to show that the testing they sought was feasible.

In short, the petitioners requested the EPA to issue additional rules under TSCA where no need for such action was warranted or could be demonstrated by the plaintiff.

Analysis

TSCA contains a comprehensive scheme for regulating chemical substances that may present risks to the public and for developing information about substances when their effects on the environment are not known. The key element of law in this case is the TSCA provision that requires the EPA to identify the effects of hazardous substances on human health and the environment if those effects have not been previously discovered. Also, the studies of such effects must be scientifically feasible and valid. In the subject case, the effects of the 11 substances were individually known or identifiable by existing standards and, therefore, there was no need for additional testing or new rules under TSCA. As to the effects of the substances taken in combination, no scientifically valid and feasible methods for testing could be identified by either the EPA or the plaintiff and, therefore, the petition was denied.

It should be noted that, had the plaintiffs been able to present a scientifically valid and feasible testing procedure, the court would have ruled in their favor, under the provisions of TSCA.

10

Comprehensive Environmental Response, Compensation, and Liability Act

INTRODUCTION

The *Comprehensive Environmental Response, Compensation, and Liability Act (CERCLA)*, also known as *Superfund*, was enacted in 1980 as the eventual result of numerous highly publicized environmental disasters, such as New York's Love Canal. The intent of CERCLA, normally pronounced *SIR-KLA*, was to provide stiff regulatory requirements to address the *release of hazardous substances* from existing hazardous waste sites as well as those resulting from any future spills of hazardous substances. However, as has been the case with numerous other environmental laws discussed in this text, the original version contained numerous ambiguities and inconsistencies, making compliance with its complex requirements even more difficult. In an attempt to rectify these concerns and to address what Congress considered the EPA's somewhat dismal record of CERCLA enforcement since its enactment, CERCLA was amended in 1986 under the *Superfund Amendments and Reauthorization Act (SARA)*. Unlike basic regulatory programs, such as RCRA and other acts related to hazardous wastes, substances, and materials, CERCLA is, for the most part, *self-implementing* legislation, with guidance documents defining policy rather than rule making.

This chapter will describe the basic compliance requirements under Superfund. The compliance professional must realize that the regulatory language of the Superfund legislation makes certain parties strictly liable for response costs incurred as a result of a release or threatened release of hazardous substances from a facility and that this liability is both *joint* (shared in ownership or action) and *several* (not shared; distinct and separate). It is therefore strongly suggested that the reader who may be concerned over their particular organization's level of applicability under these rules should seek information in addition to that which can be provided here. Reference Appendix 1 for recommended sources of training on CERCLA and other environmental regulations. It should also be noted at this point that Title III of SARA also contains many new provisions dealing with emergency planning activities and community involvement. These aspects shall be discussed separately in the next chapter.

Special Definitions Under CERCLA

As has been previously mentioned, CERCLA concerns itself primarily with the *release* of *hazardous substances* into the *environment* from *facilities*, the remediation and cleanup of those releases, and the reimbursement by *potentially responsible parties (PRP)* of *response costs* resultant from such cleanup activities. While this definition may seem somewhat simplistic and easy to understand, one must examine the CERCLA meaning of these terms in order to gain a better appreciation of the far reaching complexity of the Act.

According to CERCLA, a *release* includes any spilling, leaking, pumping, pouring, emitting, emptying, discharging, injecting, escaping, leaching, dumping, or disposing of hazardous substances into the environment. SARA included in this definition the abandonment or discarding of barrels, containers, and other closed receptacles containing any hazardous substances or pollutant contaminant. While it appears as though CERCLA has included in this definition virtually every conceivable method by which a substance can reach the environment, the Act specifically excludes exposures that are regulated under separate laws. These include exposures in the workplace (OSHA regulated), auto and engine exhaust emissions (CAA regulated), by-product or special nuclear material or nuclear incident (NRC regulated), and the normal application of fertilizer (FIFRA regulated).

The second important term in the CERCLA formula is *hazardous substance*. While most safety, health, and environmental professionals understand the requirements for substances to be considered hazardous, CERCLA took no chances and includes almost every possible established definition of hazardous substance as its own. Specifically, CERCLA includes substances designated as hazardous discharges and toxic pollutants under the Clean Water Act, hazardous wastes under the Resource Conservation and Recovery Act, hazardous air pollutants identified under the Clean Air Act, and those imminently hazardous chemical substances or mixtures identified under the Toxic Substances Control Act. In case neither of these Acts include a specific material, a hazardous substance is also any that might be specifically designated as such under CERCLA, Section 102.

The *environment* is defined as waters (including navigable waters, waters of the contiguous zone, ocean waters, any other surface water, groundwater, or drinking water), land surface or subsurface, or the ambient air.

Under the Superfund Program, a *facility* has been broadly defined to include any structure, installation, equipment, landfill impoundment, storage vessel, vehicle, or any site or area where hazardous substances have been deposited or otherwise have come to be located. This means that the simple presence of hazardous substances at a site will qualify that site as a facility.

CERCLA has established that any individual or company is a *potentially responsible party (PRP)* if they are potentially responsible for or contributed to the contamination problems at a Superfund site. Whenever possible, the EPA requires a PRP, through administrative and legal actions, to clean up hazardous waste sites they have contaminated. A PRP can be an owner, an operator, a transporter, a generator, or other entity as ruled on by the courts. In fact, this definition of PRP has far-reaching ramifications. For example, the courts have determined on more than one occasion that banks and other lending institutions who provided loans to hazardous waste management organizations *participated in the management of* those organizations by providing such loans; therefore, the bank itself is viewed as a PRP. Banks acquiring land titles through foreclosures are also PRPs.

Finally, *response costs* under CERCLA include those costs associated with the cleanup, removal (including costs associated with emergency response), remedial action (costs associated with permanent remedies), and related enforcement activities.

BASIC REQUIREMENTS UNDER CERCLA

Superfund imposes specific requirements on the EPA to ensure that the objectives of the Act are fulfilled. Under the Superfund Program, the EPA must identify and list those locations or sites throughout the United States where hazardous substances or wastes either have caused or may cause damage to the environment. This list is known as the *National Priority List (NPL)* and is subject to revision as new sites are identified. In concert with the development of the NPL, EPA also defined procedures and requirements to ensure that NPL sites are properly cleaned up by the government or other responsible parties. These procedures are contained in the *National Contingency Plan (NCP),* as required by the Act.

A key provision of CERCLA was the creation of a special fund, the *Hazardous Substance Response Trust Fund,* from which reimbursement of cleanup costs could be obtained (hence the Act's nickname *Superfund*). Under SARA, the Superfund has four primary funding sources:

1. Taxes on petroleum;
2. Taxes on 42 listed chemicals, including imported substances derived from those chemicals;
3. $1.25 billion from general tax revenues; and
4. A broad-based corporate income tax on amounts exceeding $2 million of minimum taxable income.

The Superfund Program also requires the EPA to create claim procedures so that parties who have performed the costly cleanup of sites, but were not responsible for the site contamination, can seek reimbursement. CERCLA charges the EPA with the responsibility of seeking remediation of spills or abandoned hazardous sites by either forcing private parties to perform the required cleanup or by completing the cleanup themselves and seeking cost recovery from those parties responsible for the site (see definition of *potentially responsible party,* or *PRP,* above).

Aside from the EPA responsibilities briefly discussed above, CERCLA also imposes numerous compliance requirements on the owners or operators of facilities involved in the handling of hazardous substances. Many of these requirements are related to reporting and notification. Any person in charge of a facility or vessel must notify the *National Response Center (NRC)* as soon as they have knowledge of a release of any *reportable quantity (RQ)* of a hazardous substance into the environment. CERCLA defines these maximum allowable levels of release for numerous chemical substances in the Code of Federal Regulations, Title 40, Part 305. Once a release reaches a prescribed RQ amount, the NRC, as well as the Local Emergency Planning Committee (LEPC), State Emergency Response Commissions (SERC), and any other applicable state and local municipalities, must be notified. The NRC, which is located at the U.S. Coast Guard Headquarters in Washington, D.C., can be reached 24 hours per day at 1-800-424-8802 (or 1-202-246-2675). CERCLA understands that some processes may involve the *continuous release* of hazardous substances. To facilitate reporting requirements, CERCLA permits less frequent reporting under such circumstances if the owner or operator can provide notification far enough in advance to establish the continuity, quantity, and regularity of the release. Also, continuous releases must be stable in quantity and rate, such as is expected with routine, anticipated, intermittent releases that are normal to plant operations.

Any owner or operator of a facility, as well as persons who may have accepted hazardous substances for transport or selected a facility for storage, treatment, or disposal, must notify the EPA of the existence of that facility and any known or suspected release from that facility. While CERCLA intends this reporting requirement to be all-encompassing, the Act specifically excludes certain facilities regulated under RCRA, facilities with less than 55 gallons of hazardous waste, sites with only minor contamination problems that do not threaten the environment, and facilities that receive only household wastes.

Basic Elements of the National Contingency Plan (NCP)

The NCP provides methodology for the identification, assessment, and remediation of hazardous waste sites. Because the NCP is actually a rule under CERCLA, it is subject to revision and modification as necessary. Essentially, the NCP is concerned with site identification, site listing, and site cleanup. The basic elements of the NCP include the following:

1. *Site Identification*—CERCLA provides a numerical scoring system, based on a site assessment made by the EPA or a state, known as the *Hazard Ranking System (HRS)*. The HRS evaluates and prioritizes those sites located near populated areas with primary focus on the potential hazard to those populations.
2. *Site Listing*—The HRS score of a given site is then used to determine the priority of investigation, enforcement, and cleanup for that site. Sites that score the highest are placed on the *National Priority List (NPL)*. The NPL contains well over 1,200 proposed and final sites in the United States, which are often referred to as *Superfund sites* by the media.
3. *Site Cleanup*—Once a site has been identified and listed under the NCP, the Plan then prescribes the evaluation criteria, procedures, methods, and restrictions that must be considered to properly perform the site cleanup. For example, cleanup methodology must take into consideration any land disposal restrictions imposed by RCRA or by other federal or state agencies. Also, any state or federal drinking water standards must not be violated during remedial actions.

Once a site has been properly identified and listed under the NCP, removal actions should be taken immediately. If this is not possible or feasible, then the site will most likely move through the *Remedial Investigation/Feasibility Study (RI/FS)* process. During this process, the site will be assessed and evaluated to determine the extent of the contaminated conditions and to develop alternatives necessary to properly consider and select remedial actions. The first element of this process, the *remedial investigation (RI)*, involves a comprehensive evaluation of the extent of contamination in the soil, groundwater, or surface water, with specific site characteristics, such as geology and hydrology, given proper consideration. Once this field work has been accomplished, the RI phase will identify *Applicable or Relevant and Appropriate Remediation (ARAR)* standards on both the state and federal level. Under SARA, the selection of ARAR cleanup standards must be cost-effective, with proper consideration given to both the short- and long-term costs. The ARAR standards themselves must be protective of human health and the environment so that no further damage is created during the remediation process. It is desirable that the cleanup standards contain provisions for treatment procedures necessary to reduce volume, toxicity, and/or mobility of any contaminants. ARAR solutions must be permanent, and those technologies to be used must be the maximum practicable for the situation. The final element of the RI phase is the performance of a *risk assessment* to establish baseline data upon which current or potential threats to health or the environment can be compared and acceptable exposure levels can be established.

Once the RI portion of the process has been completed, the *feasibility study (FS)* can begin to determine the necessary and appropriate remedial actions required to correct the situation. In order to accomplish this, the FS will evaluate the information collected during the RI against established criteria. Once such actions have been identified, there must be a presentation of the proposed remedies to the public, with ample opportunity provided for their comment.

A third element of this process requires the documentation of the remedial action selection process, the ultimate objective of the remedy selected, and how the actions selected will achieve the desired goals. This information is recorded as a *record of decision (ROD)*, to permanently document the actions taken in each specific case.

After the RI/FS process and the ROD has been properly completed, the NCP requires *Remedial Design/Remedial Action (RD/RA)* steps to develop and design the actual remedy (RD) with the eventual implementation on the remedy through its construction (RA).

ENFORCEMENT, PENALTIES, AND LIABILITIES

The Act states that the EPA has primary CERCLA enforcement responsibilities. But, dependent upon the specific circumstances, other federal as well as individual state regulations might also apply. The EPA must involve the applicable states and local municipalities and the public whenever proposing or implementing a remedy for any Superfund site. In fact, the Act allows for significant citizen involvement, including the right to bring civil suit against the EPA for failure to perform nondiscretionary duties under CERCLA. It should be noted that there is nothing in CERCLA that provides a private right of action to citizens for recovery of cleanup costs or other claims of personal injury, other than possible attorney's fees.

The federal government is authorized under CERCLA to take action in response to the release or substantial threat of release into the environment of hazardous substances or any pollutant or contaminant that may present an imminent and substantial danger to the public health or welfare. SARA provides the EPA with wide discretion in determining whether private parties may undertake the response activity as opposed to having the federal government conduct such activities. SARA also gives the EPA subpoena powers and other strong enforcement and information-gathering methods. The EPA is empowered under SARA to enter and inspect suspect property to determine the source of any release and to initiate remedial actions if necessary. In addition, the federal government can actually acquire properties if required for remedial actions, if the state agrees to accept the property once the actions are completed. SARA significantly expanded the role of the *Agency for Toxic Substances and Disease Registry (ATSDR)* in the cleanup process. ATSDR's duties involve preparing lists and toxicological profiles of health-threatening substances found at NPL sites and conducting health assessments at those sites.

Basically, Superfund establishes liability on four classes of PRPs for certain costs and damages arising from releases or threatened releases of hazardous substances, as follows:

1. A current owner or operator of a facility or, in the case of abandonment, the most recent owner or operator of the facility is responsible for the condition of that facility under CERCLA. SARA amended this provision to exclude state and local governments as PRPs if they acquired the ownership through bankruptcy or other involuntary circumstances and did not cause or contribute to the release. SARA also provides an *innocent purchaser* defense if the purchaser can establish its due care and can meet the stringent standard that it had no reason to know that hazardous substances were in fact present or that the owner acquired the property by inheritance or bequest.
2. Those parties who owned or operated a facility at the time the hazardous substance was disposed of are considered PRPs under CERCLA, without question.
3. Any party who arranged for the disposal or treatment of a hazardous substance at another party's facility (i.e., the generator) shall be viewed as a PRP and held liable for remedial actions under CERCLA.
4. Any party who accepts a hazardous substance for transport to a selected disposal or treatment facility (i.e., the transporter) is a PRP.

The Act makes each type of PRP liable for three types of costs or damages that arise out of the remediation process, as follows:

1. The response costs of removal or remedial action incurred by the federal or state governments are reimbursable by the PRP under Superfund.
2. Response costs incurred by other parties in support of site cleanup and remediation must be reimbursed by the PRPs, as defined by CERCLA.
3. Any damages to natural resources owned and controlled by any government must be rectified by the PRP.

Civil penalties under Superfund of not more than $25,000 per violation may be assessed against PRPs who fail to provide notice of a release of hazardous substances into the environment. This penalty also applies to those who knowingly destroy, conceal, or falsify any records related to an unpermitted release. If an owner or operator of a regulated vessel fails to maintain the required financial responsibilities established under CERCLA, then the same fining structure will be applied. In addition, the $25,000 fine per violation shall be imposed if a PRP violates any settlement agreements, administrative orders, or consent decrees issued under CERCLA.

Although CERCLA allows for extensive fines and penalties, as briefly discussed above, there are also limits to liability established under the law. In addition to the innocent purchaser provision previously discussed, Superfund specifically limits liability for each release to the cost of response actions plus $50 million for any damages to natural resources. However, this limitation excludes those releases that were willful, that were caused by a violation of regulations, or where a PRP did not cooperate with established requirements. Also, if damages to any natural resources occurred as a result of a permitted release (i.e., approved by a government authority), the PRP will not normally be held liable for the damages. The statute further offers some limited defense against liabilities in the event that a release was caused by an act of God, an act of war, or a third party. The third party defense is credible if it can be established that the act or omission of a third party, other than an employee or agent of the PRP, led to the release and that the PRP exercised due care with respect to the hazardous substance that was released.

Actions to recover any costs associated with removal actions must be brought within 3 years of the completion of such actions. Claims to recover costs resulting from any remedial actions must be brought within 6 years of the completion of those actions.

SUMMARY

This chapter briefly discussed only the most basic and essential elements of the *Comprehensive Environmental Response, Compensation, and Liability*

Act (CERCLA) of 1980 and the *Superfund Amendments and Reauthorization Act (SARA)* of 1986. These Acts are primarily concerned with the *release* of *hazardous substances* into the environment by *facilities*, either occurring in the past or those that have significant potential for such releases in the future. The regulatory framework of CERCLA, which is largely *self-implementing*, is aimed at *removal* of contaminants and *remedial* actions necessary to return the contaminated resource to its original, pre-contamination state. In seeking remedies for such actions, CERCLA looks for cost reimbursement from those responsible parties as well as from any *potentially responsible parties (PRPs)* involved in the contamination of the subject site.

To determine priority in response actions for sites found to be contaminated, the EPA develops a *National Priority List (NPL),* which utilizes a *Hazard Ranking System (HRS)* to literally *score* the level of hazard associated with a specific site, thereby establishing the response priority for that site. In addition to the NPL, the EPA prescribes procedures for the proper cleanup of these sites in its *National Contingency Plan (NCP).* The NCP contains numerous provisions designed to ensure the appropriate level and degree of response for a given situation. These include the identification, listing, and cleanup actions of each contaminated site. If immediate cleanup actions are not implemented, then a *Remedial Investigation/Feasibility Study (RI/FS)* must be performed. During the RI phase, *Applicable or Relevant and Appropriate Remediation (ARAR)* standards for cleanup of the site along with a *risk assessment* must be identified. Throughout the entire RI/FS process, a *Record of Decision (ROD)* must be maintained to properly document those decisions made in support of the site remediation. After the RI/FS is complete, *Remedial Design/Remedial Action (RD/RA)* steps must be implemented to remedy the situation. Another key provision of CERCLA is the creation of a special fund known as the *Hazardous Response Trust Fund* (or *Superfund*), from which reimbursement of cleanup costs can be obtained.

Once a release into the environment of a *reportable quantity (RQ)* of hazardous substance becomes known, the *National Response Center (NRC),* run by the U.S. Coast Guard in Washington, D.C., must be notified immediately. CERCLA provides stiff penalties for those who fail to comply with its provisions. The Act provides the EPA with broad enforcement authority that includes the ability to take whatever actions necessary in response to a release and to seek reimbursement for the response costs from any PRP that can be identified. The *statute of limitations* for reimbursement is 3 years, following completion of response actions, and 6 years, following completion of any remedial actions.

Although Superfund primarily concerns itself with after-the-fact response and remedy actions associated with a release of a hazardous substance into the environment, there are numerous actions that a party can take to ensure that they do not become potentially responsible during some future CERCLA action. Such actions include conducting internal audits to evaluate the level of compliance with established regulatory requirements. Proactive organizations that identify and correct internal deficiencies and noncompliance problems can substantially reduce future response costs under CERCLA. Also, by improving waste disposal practices today, the degree of any potential CERCLA actions could be minimized or eliminated.

Those who choose, either knowingly or out of ignorance, not to comply with existing disposal regulations today might find themselves labeled a potentially responsible party and liable under some future CERCLA response action. This chapter provided only an introduction to the complexities of the Superfund Program. The reader is encouraged to seek additional information and training if they are or could possibly be involved in CERCLA activities.

CASE BRIEF: COMPREHENSIVE ENVIRONMENTAL RESPONSE, COMPENSATION, AND LIABILITIES ACT
SANFORD STREET LOCAL DEVELOPMENT
vs.
TEXTRON INC.
U.S. District Court, Western District of Michigan
No. 1:90-CV-582, 08 August 1991

Summary

This case demonstrates the far-reaching aspects of CERCLA when attempting to define its regulatory applicability to contaminated sites that have changed owners several times prior to the discovery of any contamination. The plaintiffs sought recovery of cleanup costs under the Comprehensive Environmental Response, Compensation, and Liability Act (CERCLA), 42 U.S.C. 9601-75, associated with remedial activities arising from PCB contamination in a facility that it purchased from another organization, which had purchased the site from the original owner.

Background

From the early part of this century until 1982, the defendant Textron oper-

ated a foundry commonly known as CWC Plant #1 in Muskegon Heights, Michigan. The economic downturn of the early 1980s forced Textron to close the facility with the hope that it could be opened at a later date. As a result, the plant's electrical system, including several transformers containing PCBs, remained inoperative. In early 1984, Textron decided to either sell or demolish the facility. After a failed attempt to first donate the plant to the City of Muskegon Heights, Textron sold it to a third-party defendant known as Delta Properties. Delta specialized in the refurbishment of old manufacturing sites for other uses. The property sold for $25,000, which was substantially lower than the appraised value of $200,000. All of the plant's electrical equipment, including the PCB-containing transformers, was included in the sale.

Although Delta owned the plant for approximately 10 months, its redevelopment plans never materialized due to disputes with the City of Muskegon Heights. During this period, Textron had disconnected the facility from its central power grid, and an inspection by the Michigan Department of Natural Resources found no PCB leakage from the transformers. Delta eventually sold the building in 1987 to third-party defendant Great Lakes Development Corporation for the sum of $1,000. Great Lakes also encountered problems with the city over refurbishment plans for the facility. After a portion of the old CWC Plant #1 was rezoned, Great Lakes sold the facility to the plaintiff, Sanford, in the summer of 1988 for the sum of $30,000. During a post-sale inspection in December of that same year, Sanford representatives discovered the presence of PCB-containing oils in the penthouse housing the transformers. Sanford incurred response costs and filed litigation requesting a summary judgment to recover most if not all of these costs from previous owners under the provisions of CERCLA. Textron filed a third-party complaint suggesting that, at the time of the initial sale to Delta, the purchaser was well aware of and in fact specifically accepted responsibility for the disposal of the transformers as a condition of the sale. In consideration of this promise, Textron agreed to the extremely low sale price of the property.

Decision

The court held that former owners of a facility can be liable under CERCLA for costs of cleaning up PCBs leaking from transformers on that facility. The plaintiff maintained that Textron was liable for its disposal of the transformers under Section 107(a)(3) of CERCLA. To establish such liability under this section of the Act, a plaintiff must demonstrate that the defendant was a *person* within the meaning of the statute; that the person owned or possessed hazardous substances; that the defendant, by contract, agreement, or otherwise, arranged for the disposal or treatment of those substances at the facility; that a release or threatened release of hazardous substances at the site occurred; and that response costs were incurred as a result of the release or threatened release.

The plaintiff contended that Textron *arranged for the disposal* of the transformers when it sold CWC Plant #1 to Delta in 1986. CERCLA specifies that, if the sale of a hazardous substance can be characterized as a transaction concerning the disposal of that substance, the individual making the sale may be subject to CERCLA liability. Since Textron admitted that its primary reason for selling the facility for such a low price was to quickly dispose of the transformer problem, the court agreed with the plaintiff that Textron is liable because it acted to *arrange for the disposal* of the subject transformers. Similarly, Delta also arranged for disposal when it sold the property to Great Lakes, and Great Lakes arranged for disposal when it sold the building to Sanford. Therefore, all previous owners of the facility were deemed potentially responsible parties (PRPs) under CERCLA and held liable for response costs.

Analysis

The court held that former owners of a facility can be liable under CERCLA for costs of cleaning up PCBs leaking from transformers on that facility because: 1) CERCLA liability requires a finding that a party *arranged for the dis-*

posal of hazardous wastes at that facility; and 2) evidence could support a finding that previous owners of the facility arranged for such disposal of hazardous substances when they sold the plant housing PCB-containing transformers to a third party.

In short, the court ruled in favor of the plaintiff and granted its request for summary judgment against the defendants.

The principle element of law in this case rested on the plaintiff's burden of proving that the defendants were liable for response costs under CERCLA. This burden of proof was fulfilled based on the evidence, which supported the claim that the previous owners arranged for the disposal of the transformers and, subsequently, became a PRP under the law.

11

Emergency Planning and Community Right to Know Act

INTRODUCTION

In the previous chapter, the basic elements of the *Comprehensive Environmental Response, Compensation, and Liability Act (CERCLA)* of 1980 and its 1986 amendments under the *Superfund Amendments and Reauthorization Act (SARA)* were briefly presented and discussed. Title III of SARA added new provisions that mandated actions in the area of emergency response and a community's right to know about specific and potential actions and activities involving chemical substances and releases in their neighborhood. SARA's Title III is known as the *Emergency Planning and Community Right to Know Act (EPCRA)* of 1986. While it is a fact that Title III of SARA resides in the Superfund program described in the previous chapter, the provisions of EPCRA are quite different and are therefore addressed separately here. This chapter will outline the basic elements and compliance requirements under this Act to provide the reader with the fundamental understanding necessary to determine their applicability to its regulatory mandates. Also, since EPCRA obtains the majority of its enforcement provisions from CERCLA and, in fact, most cases are brought under CERCLA, no case brief is provided at the end of this chapter.

As a result of an increasing awareness and subsequent concern by communities over the types of chemicals and hazardous commodities that may be utilized or stored in or that simply pass through their neighborhoods, SARA Title III was established in an effort to provide the public with pertinent information on hazardous chemicals in their communities. The Act requires each owner or operator of a facility at which hazardous chemicals are produced, used, or stored in specific quantities to supply information and/or Material Safety Data Sheets (MSDS) about each hazardous chemical to the state and local authorities. The public can then access this information through their state and local officials.

BASIC ELEMENTS OF SARA TITLE III

SARA Title III is divided into three major sections called Subtitles. Subtitle A, entitled *Emergency Planning and Notification,* requires the development of comprehensive local emergency response plans that are to be used in the event of a local emergency chemical release and contains reporting requirements for chemical spills. Subtitle A requirements are located in Sections 301–305 of the Act. Subtitle B, *Reporting Requirements,* imposes community right-to-know reporting requirements on owners or operators of facilities so that all reported information can be made available to the public. These provisions can be found in Sections 311–313 of EPCRA. Subtitle C contains the *General Provisions* and includes enforcement authority and other related provisions. These regulations are contained in Sections 321–324.

Subtitle A—Emergency Planning and Notification

One of the key elements of the SARA Title III legislation, emergency planning and notification requirements, is contained in the sections of this subtitle. It is important to remember that a primary objective of EPCRA was to provide a means of informing local communities of the hazards associated with chemicals being used, processed in, or transferred through their area. To effectively accomplish this objective, SARA Title III also requires certain actions on the part of the community and state authorities, the major elements of which are briefly described below.

Section 301: Establishment of State Commissions, Planning Districts, and Local Committees

Section 301 expands upon the principle of *hazard communication* established by the Occupational Safety and Health Administration (OSHA) for an employee's right to know about the hazards they will or might come in contact with in the workplace. Specifically, Section 301 establishes a federal community right-to-know program so that the public can have access to the same level of information as employees do, regarding the hazardous chemicals manufactured, used, or stored by facilities in their neighborhoods. In order to ensure an orderly and formalized transfer of such information between the facility owner/operator and the public at large, Section 301 also requires the establishment of two agencies through which the information is to be processed: The *State Emergency Response Commission (SERC)* and the *Local Emergency Planning Committee (LEPC).*

SARA requires the SERCs to oversee the state implementation of the Act's requirements, including the establishment of procedures for receiving and processing information from the facilities throughout the state. Under SARA Title III, the SERCs designate emergency planning districts to facilitate the preparation and implementation of emergency plans. Once the districts have been identified, the SERC for each state must then appoint the members of the *Local Emergency Planning Committee (LEPC)* for each emergency planning district.

The LEPC should include a representative from each of the following groups of interested parties:

- Elected officials from the local area;
- Fire, police, hospital, and other emergency personnel;
- Community groups;
- The media; and
- Owners or operators of local facilities.

The organizational structure of the LEPC must contain a Chairman, a Community Emergency Coordinator, and an Information Coordinator. Each LEPC must establish operating rules or procedures that will include provisions for public notification of the LEPC's activities, public hearings, and procedures to respond to public comments and requests for information, as well as methods that the LEPC will use to distribute the emergency plan.

Section 302: Substances and Facilities Covered and Notification Requirements

SARA Title III established a list of *extremely hazardous materials* and included the quantity of each chemical that, if present in a facility, would subject that facility to the provisions of EPCRA, Subtitle A. These pre-established amounts of chemicals are referred to as the *threshold planning quantities (TPQ)*. Under Section 302, owners or operators of facilities who have at least the TPQ for any one listed chemical or material must within 60 days after reaching that TPQ, notify their SERC that the facility is subjected to Subtitle A of SARA Title III. The facility must also provide information to their LEPC to assist in the development of an emergency response plan. Included in the information to be provided to the LEPC must be the name(s) of facility representatives who will participate in the emergency planning process. The list of extremely hazardous substances, their associated TPQs, and the notification responsibilities of the facilities are all contained in Title 40 of the Code of Federal Regulations in Part 355. The law allows the list to be revised periodically as long as the toxicity, reactivity, volatility, disbursability, combustibility, or flammability of the substance is taken into consideration and evaluated before placing a new item on the list.

Section 303: Comprehensive Emergency Response Plans

This section requires the LEPC to draft a comprehensive emergency plan for their districts to cover facilities that have present one or more of the extremely hazardous substances in an amount exceeding established TPQs. Plans, which must be revised annually, must include at least the following information:

1. A list designating the facilities in the district covered by the plan, with special emphasis on those facilities considered to be at greater risk of an emergency situation than others;
2. Identification of the transportation routes used to transport hazardous materials to or from each listed facility;
3. Designation of responsible personnel for each listed facility, as well as community representatives;
4. The procedures to be used to effect proper notification of all appropriate parties in the event of an emergency;
5. Methods used to estimate the results of any release and the areas likely to be affected by such releases;
6. Established evacuation plans to ensure the timely and effective movement of persons that could be affected by a release;
7. Training programs that will be used to familiarize responding organizations, with the actions to be taken in the event of an emergency release; and
8. Established schedules for conducting emergency exercises to test the effectiveness of the plan.

Any facility that is subject to these requirements must submit to both the SERC and their LEPC the name of each designated facility representative that will participate in the emergency planning process. Also, when any changes occur or are expected to occur within a facility that could affect the planning process, the owner or operator must notify the appropriate LEPC and the SERC.

Section 304: Emergency Notification Requirements

The reader will recall the discussion of *reportable quantities (RQs)* presented in the previous chapter under CERCLA. The owner or operator of a facility that has experienced a release of a reportable quantity of an extremely hazardous substance must notify (by telephone or radio) their state and local planning committees immediately. They must indicate to the appropriate community emergency coordinator or the LEPC, as well as the SERC, the area(s) likely to be affected by the release. This requirement applies even if a particular facility is not subject to the emergency planning requirements specified under Sections 302 and 303 above.

Except when a release will be contained within the boundaries of the facility, notification to the state and local committees must include as much of the following information that is known at the time the notification is made:

1. The name of the chemical or substance released;
2. Whether or not the substance is extremely hazardous;
3. An estimate of the quantity released;
4. The time and duration of the release;
5. The medium or media into which the release occurred (air, water, soil, etc.);
6. Any known or anticipated acute or chronic health risks and, where appropriate, advice regarding medical attention necessary for exposed individuals;
7. Proper precautions to be taken (including evacuation);
8. The name and telephone number of the facility representative to be contacted for further information.

The law requires the owner or operator to submit a written follow-up report as soon as possible after the emergency to include information regarding the specific actions taken to respond to and contain the release, any known or anticipated acute and chronic health risks associated with the release, and advice regarding medical attention necessary for exposed individuals, if applicable.

Civil penalties of up to $25,000 can be imposed for each violation of Section 304 requirements. If the violation is continuous, then a penalty of up to $25,000 per violation will be imposed for each day of the violation(s). Any second or subsequent violation of the same requirement will result in a civil penalty of up to $75,000 for each day the violation continues. *Criminal violations* will be imposed upon any person who knowingly and willfully fails to meet the notification requirements specified in Section 304, as briefly discussed above.

Subtitle B—Reporting Requirements

The second major aspect of SARA Title III involves the information reporting requirements imposed upon facility owners and operators. The important elements of these requirements are provided below.

Section 311: Material Safety Data Sheets (MSDS)
Under this section of Subtitle B, the owner or operator of any facility that is required to prepare and have an MSDS as prescribed by OSHA's Hazard

Communication Standard (29 CFR 1910.1200), must also submit the MSDS for each hazardous chemical to the LEPC, SERC, and the local fire department that would respond to their facility in the event of any emergency. SARA does allow the owner or operator to submit a list of hazardous chemicals in lieu of an MSDS if the list is grouped by hazard category (immediate health hazard, chronic health hazard, fire hazard, sudden release of pressure, or reactive hazards). The list must also include not only the chemical name of the substance, but any common or trade names and any hazardous components of the substance as described on its MSDS. Whenever new and significant information is discovered concerning a chemical for which an MSDS has already been submitted, the owner or operator must provide a new MSDS within 3 months to the LEPC and the fire department. It is important to note that the term hazardous chemical does not refer to any food, food additives, color additive, drug, or cosmetic regulated by the Food and Drug Administration. Also, any household or personnel substances, those used in laboratory research or hospitals, and any routine agricultural substance are not regulated under this section of the Act.

Violators of Section 311 requirements shall be liable for civil and administrative penalties of up to $10,000 for each violation for each day of the violation.

Section 312: Emergency and Hazardous Chemical Forms

Facilities subject to Section 311 requirements are automatically subjected to Section 312. This section requires the owner or operator of the facility to submit an annual inventory form to the SERC, the appropriate LEPC, and their local fire department. This form, known as a *Tier I* form, must be submitted by March 1 of each year to cover the inventory of the previous calendar year. Tier I forms provide estimates of the maximum amounts of hazardous chemicals in each category present at a facility at any time during the preceding calendar year. In addition, the form provides estimates of the average daily amount of hazardous chemicals in each category at the facility, and the general location of those chemicals in the facility. Figure 11-1 shows a facsimile of the Tier I form.

Upon request from the SERC, LEPC, or local fire department, the facility must submit a *Tier II* form in addition to the Tier I form. The Tier II form, as shown in Figure 11-2, provides basically the same information as that appearing on the Tier I form, with the addition of information pertaining to the storage of hazardous chemicals in the facility. SARA allows owners or operators to submit the Tier II form in lieu of the Tier I at their discretion. Since a request may be made for a Tier II form anyway, it might be suggested that it be submitted initially to avoid any subsequent requests. Once the

Page _____ of _____ pages
Form Approved OMB No. 2050-0072

Tier One

EMERGENCY AND HAZARDOUS
CHEMICAL INVENTORY

Aggregate Information by Hazard Type

FOR
OFFICIAL
USE
ONLY

ID #

Date Received

Important: Read Instructions before completing form

Reporting Period   From January 1 to December 31, 19 _____

Facility Identification

Name _____

Street Address _____

City _____ State _____ Zip _____

SIC Code ☐☐☐☐   Dun & Brad Number ☐☐ — ☐☐☐ — ☐☐☐☐

Owner/Operator

Name _____

Mail Address _____

Phone ( ) _____

Emergency Contacts

Name _____

Title _____

Phone ( ) _____

24 Hour Phone ( ) _____

Name _____

Title _____

Phone ( ) _____

24 Hour Phone ( ) _____

☐ Check if site plan is attached

	Hazard Type	Max Amounts	Average Daily Amounts	Number of Days On-Site	General Location
Physical Hazards	Fire	☐☐	☐☐	☐☐	
	Sudden Release of Pressure	☐☐	☐☐	☐☐	
	Reactivity	☐☐	☐☐	☐☐	
Health Hazards	Immediate (Acute)	☐☐	☐☐	☐☐	
	Delayed (Chronic)	☐☐	☐☐	☐☐	

Certification *(Read and sign after completing all sections)*

I certify under penalty of law that I have personally examined and am familiar with the information submitted in this and all attached documents, and that based on my inquiry of those individuals responsible for obtaining the information, I believe that the submitted information is true, accurate and complete.

Name and official title of owner/operator OR owner/operator's authorized representative

Signature _____   Date signed _____

 # Reporting Ranges

Range Value	Weight Range in Pounds From....	To.....
00	0	99
01	100	999
02	1000	9,999
03	10,000	99,999
04	100,000	999,999
05	1,000,000	9,999,999
06	10,000,000	49,999,999
07	50,000,000	99,999,999
08	100,000,000	499,999,999
09	500,000,000	999,999,999
10	1 billion	higher than 1 billion

FIGURE 11-1.   SARA Title III, Tier One reporting form. (Source: EPA, SARA, Title III)

Tier Two

EMERGENCY
AND
HAZARDOUS
CHEMICAL
INVENTORY

*Specific
Information
by Chemical*

Page _____ of _____ pages
Form Approved OMB No. 2050-0072

Facility Identification

Name
Street Address
City   State   Zip
SIC Code   Dun & Brad
                    Number

FOR
OFFICIAL   ID #
USE
ONLY   Date Received

Owner/Operator

Name
Mail Address
Phone ( )

Emergency Contacts

Name
Title
Phone ( )   24 Hour Phone ( )
Name
Title
Phone ( )   24 Hour Phone ( )

Important: Read instructions before completing form

Reporting Period From January 1 to December 31, 19 _____

Chemical Description	Physical and Health Hazards	Inventory			Storage Codes and Locations (Non-Confidential)
		Max. Daily Amount (code)	Avg. Daily Amount (code)	No. of Days On-site (days)	*Storage Locations*

Chemical Description

CAS _____   Trade Secret ☐
Chem. Name _____
Check all that apply: Pure ☐ Mix ☐ Solid ☐ Liquid ☐ Gas ☐

Physical and Health Hazards:
Fire ☐
Sudden Release of Pressure ☐
Reactivity ☐
Immediate (acute) ☐
Delayed (chronic) ☐

Storage Code

CAS _____   Trade Secret ☐
Chem. Name _____
Check all that apply: Pure ☐ Mix ☐ Solid ☐ Liquid ☐ Gas ☐

Fire ☐
Sudden Release of Pressure ☐
Reactivity ☐
Immediate (acute) ☐
Delayed (chronic) ☐

CAS _____   Trade Secret ☐
Chem. Name _____
Check all that apply: Pure ☐ Mix ☐ Solid ☐ Liquid ☐ Gas ☐

Fire ☐
Sudden Release of Pressure ☐
Reactivity ☐
Immediate (acute) ☐
Delayed (chronic) ☐

Optional Attachments *(Check one)*
☐ I have attached a site plan
☐ I have attached a list of site coordinate abbreviations

Certification *(Read and sign after completing all sections)*

I certify under penalty of law that I have personally examined and am familiar with the information submitted in this and all attached documents, and that based on my inquiry of those individuals responsible for obtaining the information, I believe that the submitted information is true, accurate and complete.

Name and official title of owner/operator OR owner/operator's authorized representative   Signature   Date Signed

FIGURE 11-2. SARA Title III, Tier Two reporting form. (Source: EPA, SARA, Title III)

required inventory forms have been filed, the local fire department can conduct on-site inspections of the facilities under their jurisdiction.

The SERC or the LEPC must make available to the public the information contained on any Tier II form for any facility. The public can have access to such information after filing a written request with the appropriate planning committee. If the SERC or LEPC does not have Tier II information available for a specific facility, it can request the facility owner to provide such information on hazardous chemicals that a facility has stored in excess of 10,000 pounds. If that facility always had less than 10,000 pounds of a hazardous chemical in storage, both the SERC and the LEPC have the authority to request Tier II information anyway, provided that the public, in its request, has demonstrated a sufficient need to know such information.

Section 313: Toxic Chemical Release Forms

Title 40 of the Code of Federal Regulations, Part 372, Subpart E provides a list of *specifically listed toxic substances.* Any facility releasing, emitting, or disposing of any of these listed substances must provide the EPA and state agencies with an annual report, each July 1, detailing the nature and circumstances of any and all such releases that occurred during the previous year. This form, the EPA *Form R,* is a six-page, four-part form that provides in exhaustive detail all information related to the release of listed toxic chemicals. The information provided on the Form R is then used by the EPA to develop their *toxic release inventory (TRI).* With regard to toxic chemicals *used* at a facility, the Form R must be filed if the facility uses more than the *reporting threshold* of 10,000 pounds during the reporting year. Any facility that *manufactures or processes* more than the reporting threshold of 25,000 pounds per year of any listed toxic chemicals must submit the required EPA Form R. A *de minimus* exemption from the threshold and release reporting requirements exists if the toxic chemicals present in mixtures are in concentrations less than 1% (0.1% for carcinogens).

The requirements of this section apply to owners or operators of facilities in the *standard industry classification (SIC)* codes 20–39 (Figure 11-3) and who have ten or more employees. While the regulation states that Section 313 applies only to those facilities that manufactured, processed, or otherwise used a listed toxic chemical, the EPA may apply these requirements to additional facilities pursuant to its rule-making authority. Also under Section 313, manufacturers who sell mixtures or trade name products containing listed toxic chemicals must inform purchasers of the presence of those chemicals so that the purchaser can comply with the Section 313 reporting requirements. This *supplier notification* must contain at least a statement that the substance contains a listed toxic chemical, the name of each toxic chemical and its associated *chemical abstract system (CAS)* number, and the

STANDARD INDUSTRY CLASSIFICATION ("SIC") CODES 20 – 39	
CODE NUMBER	CLASSIFICATION
20	Food and Kindred Products
21	Tobacco Manufacturing
22	Textile Mill Products
23	Apparel and Other Textile Products
24	Lumber and Wood Products
25	Furniture and Fixtures
26	Paper and Allied Products
27	Printing and Publishing
28	Chemicals and Allied Products
29	Petroleum and Coal Products
30	Rubber and Plastic Products
31	Leather and Leather Products
32	Stone, Clay, and Glass Products
33	Primary Metal Industries
34	Fabricated Metal Products
35	Machinery, Except Electrical
36	Electrical Equipment and Supplies
37	Transportation Equipment
38	Instruments and Related Products
39	Miscellaneous Manufacturing Products

FIGURE 11-3.   Standard Industry Classification Codes applicable to SARA, Title III.

percent by weight of each toxic chemical. If an MSDS is available, it must be attached to the supplier notification.

Subtitle C—General Provisions

This subtitle contains most of the nonspecific operating provisions of SARA Title III as well as information pertaining to trade secrets, enforcement requirements, and the civil penalties permitted under the law.

Section 321: Relationship to Other Laws
This section specifically states that SARA Title III will not preempt any state or local laws of the same nature. However, there are some restrictions on state laws. Those state laws that deal with MSDS submittal requirements that were in place before 1 August 1985 are unaffected by SARA. But those enacted (signed into law by the state governor) after 1 August 1985 must be identical to the SARA Title III requirements regarding MSDS information.

Section 322: Trade Secrets
If certain requirements are fulfilled, EPCRA will permit the withholding of specific information regarding a chemical's identity from the SERC, LEPC, and local fire department. To qualify as a *trade secret*, the formula, pattern, process, device, or other information that is used in the submitter's business provides an advantage over competitors who do not know or use this information. The withholder of such information must still provide the generic class or category of the substances (i.e., hazardous chemical, extremely hazardous substance, or toxic chemical). The person claiming a trade secret must provide *ample justification* to explain the reasons why the information is claimed to be a trade secret. During a notification of any emergency release of an extremely hazardous substance, the chemical identity information can not be withheld to protect a trade secret.

Section 325: Enforcement
The EPA may issue *administrative orders* demanding compliance with other applicable sections of the Act. As is the case with other environmental legislation, administrative orders can be enforced in the district courts.

Section 326: Civil Actions
Civil actions include citizen suits against facility owners or operators for their failure to submit a follow-up emergency notice, as required under Section 304 and MSDS under Section 311, an inventory form under Section 312 (Tier I or Tier II), or a toxic release form under Section 313 (Form R). Section 326 also provides authority for the states or local governments to seek action

against a facility owner or operator for their failure to comply with the Act's notification requirements. As a result of such actions, the courts may impose injunctive relief and civil penalties, similar to those described earlier under Sections 304 and 311. It is noted that no civil actions or penalties are allowed if the EPA is already in the process of pursuing such actions.

EPCRA AND THE POLLUTION PREVENTION ACT OF 1990

As part of its budget reconciliation package in 1990, Congress included the *Pollution Prevention Act (PPA)*. This law *encourages* industry to minimize the amount of hazardous waste generated during the manufacturing process. While the Act does not specifically mandate waste minimization, it does contain several important reporting provisions. A major objective of the PPA is to expand the use of the TRI. As discussed earlier, the TRI is used as a database and is required under the EPCRA. It is designed to assist the EPA in its efforts to control emissions of hazardous substances. Under the PPA, the EPA will expand its use of the TRI database when evaluating specific facilities and their activities. With the TRI provided by manufacturers in accordance with the requirements established by the EPCRA, the EPA intends to use the data to focus its inspection and compliance activities more effectively.

According to the PPA, the EPA must also establish an independent *pollution prevention office* that must develop waste reduction strategies for use by industry. In addition, the EPA must formulate a strategy for source reduction.

The existing program established by EPCRA requires companies to submit an annual report to the EPA detailing the amount of toxic chemicals they released into the environment during the previous year. These reports are then made available to the public through the TRI. This reporting requirement applies to companies that manufacture, import, process, or otherwise use any of more than 300 listed chemicals. Releases that must be reported include both accidental spills and routine releases, as well as materials that are sent off site to a landfill or elsewhere for disposal.

Before the PPA, companies reported information under EPCRA relating to their waste minimization and toxics reduction efforts *only if* they wished to make that information public. It's no secret that this *voluntary reporting system* was not a tremendous success. In fact, less than 10% of the potentially affected facilities voluntarily revealed their waste minimization or recycling data. Under the PPA of 1990, companies are now required to report such information along with the EPCRA-required toxic chemical release reports (Form R).

Regardless of whether waste was reduced or increased, the reports submitted by companies must include detailed information on all aspects of a company's source reduction and recycling programs, including estimated changes in hazardous waste amounts, production modifications, and the techniques used to encourage employees and management to prevent pollution.

SUMMARY

When the *Comprehensive Environmental Response, Compensation, and Liability Act (CERCLA)* was amended in 1986 under the *Superfund Amendments and Reauthorization Act (SARA),* lawmakers included provisions for emergency planning and community involvement with regard to hazardous substances. Title III of SARA, the *Emergency Planning and Community Right to Know Act (EPCRA),* was intended to be an extension of OSHA's *Hazard Communication Standard* (29 CFR 1910.1200), which requires that employees be made aware of the hazards in their workplace. EPCRA brings this objective into the public sector with specific notification, planning, and reporting requirements.

SARA Title III is divided into three major Subtitles, which are further broken down into Sections. The requirements contained in each Section are primarily aimed at the owners or operators of facilities where hazardous materials are manufactured, used, or stored, and at the state and local authorities that are responsible for coordination of the information provided by these various facilities. The Act requires the governor of each state to appoint a *State Emergency Response Commission (SERC),* which is the focal point for information exchange between the public and the facilities. SERC also oversees the state implementation of Title III requirements. SERCs must designate emergency planning districts and appoint *Local Emergency Planning Committees (LEPCs)* for each district.

The Act specifies separate listings of hazardous substances. Facilities that maintain levels above the established *threshold planning quantity (TPQ)* for each listed chemical must submit annual reports to the SERCs, LEPCs, and local fire departments that show the previous year's activities. These reports, known as the *Tier I* and *Tier II* forms, provide specific information pertaining to the physical and health hazards for listed chemicals. This information can usually be obtained from a chemical's *Material Safety Data Sheet (MSDS).* If a chemical listed as *specifically toxic* is released in amounts above the CERCLA-established *reportable quantity (RQ),* then the facility owner/operator must submit an EPA *Form R* to report the incident.

Title III also contains separate enforcement, penalty, and fining provisions. Under EPCRA, civil and criminal actions are possible, including citizen suits against federal, state, and local authorities.

SARA does provide for the protection of *trade secret* information, except in emergency situations and as long as all specific requirements can be met to justify such a classification for materials.

Under the *Pollution Prevention Act (PPA)* of 1990, the EPA expanded the use of the *toxic release inventory (TRI),* which it compiles using EPCRA Form R data. The PPA requires that facilities report specific details on their waste minimization and recycling data on an annual basis so that this information can be provided to the public.

SARA Title III significantly expanded upon OSHA's idea for communicating information on hazardous substances to those that would or could be affected by exposure to such materials. Where OSHA concerned itself with the worker, SARA carries the objective further and includes the private citizen that may reside adjacent to, in the vicinity of, in close proximity to, or in the community that surrounds a facility where such materials are present. The safety, health, and/or environmental professionals concerned with EPCRA requirements should take steps to ensure that their facility is in compliance with all applicable planning, notification, and reporting requirements, since the deadline for accomplishing these tasks has already passed.

12

Other Agencies and Other Laws

INTRODUCTION

The previous chapters in Part II of this text have focused on the regulatory efforts of the EPA, since it is the primary federal agency concerned with the protection of the U.S. environment. However, other federal agencies are also responsible for the enforcement of laws pertaining to some aspect of environmental protection. Persons who are new to this arena should be made somewhat familiar with these overlapping responsibilities. This chapter will provide a very brief explanation of two important regulatory requirements related to environmental protection that are enforced by federal agencies other than the EPA.

HAZARDOUS WASTE OPERATIONS AND EMERGENCY RESPONSE

As a direct result of the Superfund Amendments and Reauthorization Act of 1986 and the concern it raised over the proper handling of hazardous wastes, the U.S. Department of Labor's (DOL) Occupational Safety and Health Administration (OSHA) promulgated the *Hazardous Waste Operations and Emergency Response (HAZWOPER)* Standard to establish specific requirements for employers who require their employees to handle or come into contact with hazardous waste. The HAZWOPER regulation is located at 29 CFR 1910.120 and became effective on 6 March 1990. OSHA reasoned that hazardous waste poses a serious safety and health concern to anyone required to handle such materials. In addition, since hazardous wastes can cause fires, explosions, and pollution of the air, land, and water, and because so many workers are required to work in facilities or for organizations that engage in the treatment, storage, or disposal of millions of metric tons of hazardous wastes per year, OSHA issued the HAZWOPER Standard to protect workers in this environment and to help them handle hazardous wastes safely and effectively.

The Standard covers workers employed in cleanup operations at both uncontrolled hazardous waste sites and at waste *treatment, storage, and disposal facilities (TSDF)* licensed by the EPA. It is also intended to protect workers who are required to respond to emergencies that involve or may involve hazardous wastes (e.g., as during spill response).

Safety and Health Program

Anyone who is currently familiar with OSHA Standards knows that an effective and comprehensive safety and health program is essential in reducing work-related injuries and illnesses and in maintaining a safe and healthful work environment. In the HAZWOPER Standard, OSHA requires each employer to develop and implement a written safety and health program that identifies, evaluates, and controls safety and health hazards and provides emergency response procedures for each hazardous waste site or TSDF. As a minimum, the HAZWOPER written safety and health program must include specific and detailed information on the following:

1. An organizational written plan;
2. Site evaluation and control;
3. A site-specific program;
4. Information and training program;
5. Personal protective equipment program;
6. Monitoring;
7. Medical surveillance program;
8. Decontamination procedures; and
9. Emergency response program.

HAZWOPER requires the written safety and health program to be periodically updated and made available to all affected employees, contractors, and subcontractors. The employer must also inform contractors and subcontractors, or their representatives, of any identifiable safety and health hazards or potential fire or explosion hazards *before* they enter the work site.

Activities Covered by HAZWOPER

HAZWOPER contains specific provisions that require employer action for any of the following types of activities:

1. Cleanup operations required by a governmental body, whether federal, state, local, or other, involving hazardous substances that are conducted at uncontrolled hazardous waste sites;
2. Corrective actions involving cleanup operations at sites covered by the Resource Conservation and Recovery Act (RCRA);
3. Voluntary cleanup operations at sites recognized by federal, state, local, or other governmental bodies as uncontrolled hazardous waste sites;
4. Operations involving hazardous wastes that are conducted at treatment, storage, and disposal facilities licensed under RCRA; or
5. Emergency response operations for release of or substantial threats of release of hazardous substances.

NOTE: Exceptions are permitted if the employer can demonstrate that the operation does not involve employee exposure or a reasonable possibility of such exposure to hazards.

General Requirements

Aside from the written safety and health plan described above, HAZWOPER requires each employer at a hazardous waste site to develop a safety and health program that identifies, evaluates, and controls safety and health hazards and that provides for emergency response. A preliminary evaluation of the site's characteristics must be conducted by a trained person so that potential site hazards can be identified and appropriate employee protection methods can be selected. Included in this evaluation would be all suspected conditions considered *immediately dangerous to life or health* or that may cause serious physical harm.

Employers must also implement a *site control program*. As a minimum, the program must include a site map, site work zones, site communications, safe work practices, and identification of the nearest medical assistance. Also required is the use of a *buddy system* as a protective measure in particularly hazardous situations so that employees can keep watch on one another to provide quick aid if needed.

Employers must provide appropriate *medical surveillance* at least annually and at the end of employment for all employees exposed to any particularly hazardous substance at or above established exposure levels and/or those who wear approved respirators for 30 days or more on site. This surveillance will also be conducted if a worker is exposed to unexpected or emergency releases.

Engineering controls, work practices, and personal protective equipment, or a combination of these methods, must be implemented to reduce employee exposure below established levels for the hazardous substance involved.

Employers must conduct periodic air monitoring to identify and quantify levels of hazardous substances and to assure that proper protective equipment is being used.

The Standard requires employers to establish an *informational program* that includes the names of key personnel and their alternates that are responsible for site safety and health. The program must also list the requirements of the Standard.

A *decontamination procedure* must be implemented before any employee or equipment may leave an area of potential hazardous exposure. Operating procedures must be developed so as to minimize exposure through contact with exposed equipment, other employees, or used clothing. Showers and changing rooms must be provided where needed.

Prior to beginning hazardous waste operations, an *emergency response plan* is required to address all possible on-site emergencies. These plans must include personnel roles and responsibilities, lines of authority, training and communications, emergency recognition and prevention, safe places of refuge, provisions for site security, evacuation routes and procedures, emergency medical treatment capabilities and requirements, and methods for emergency notification. In addition, an *off-site emergency response plan* must be developed to better coordinate emergency action by the local response services and to implement appropriate control actions.

HAZWOPER Training Requirements

A major function of the HAZWOPER Standard is to establish the minimum training requirements for employees who must work with or around hazardous wastes. Employees must be trained before they are allowed to engage in hazardous waste operations or emergency response that could expose them to safety and health hazards. Experienced workers, however, will be allowed to continue operations, with refresher courses provided as appropriate. The Standard lists specific training requirements for cleanup personnel, equipment operators, general laborers and supervisory employees, and for various levels of emergency response personnel. Persons completing specified training for hazardous waste operations shall be certified. Those employees not so certified, nor with proper experience, shall be prohibited from engaging in those operations, as specified by the Standard. Specific training requirements under HAZWOPER are summarized as follows:

1. *Uncontrolled hazardous waste operations mandated by various levels of government*—Workers engaged in this type of operation must have 40 hours of initial training before entering a site and at least 3 days of actual field experience under a trained, experienced supervisor. *Occasional*

employees visiting the site need only 24 hours of prior training and 1 day of supervised field experience. Managers and supervisors *directly responsible* for cleanup operations must have an additional 8 hours of specialized training in waste management. Annual refresher training of 8 hours is required for regular site workers and the site managers.

2. *Sites licensed under RCRA*—Employees at these locations must have 24 hours of training plus 8 hours of annual refresher training.

3. *Emergency response operations at other than RCRA sites or uncontrolled hazardous waste site clean-ups*—Different levels of initial training are required for employees working at these sites depending on the duties and functions of each responder plus their demonstrated competence, or annual refresher training sufficient to maintain competence, as follows:

   a. *First responders at the awareness level*—These are considered individuals most likely to witness or discover a hazardous substance release and initiate the emergency response. They must demonstrate competency in such areas as recognizing the presence of hazardous materials in an emergency, the risks involved, and the role they should perform.

   b. *First responders at the operations level*—Those individuals who respond for the purpose of protecting property, persons, or the nearby environment without actually trying to stop the release must have 8 hours of training plus *awareness level* competency or must demonstrate competence in their role.

   c. *Hazardous materials specialists*—Individuals who respond to stop the release must have 24 hours of training equal to the *operations level* and must demonstrate competence in several specific areas.

   d. *(Special) hazardous materials specialists*—Those who support the technicians, but require a more specific knowledge of the substances to be contained, must have 24 hours of training equal to the technical level and must demonstrate competence in certain areas.

   e. *On-scene incident commanders*—Persons who assume control of the incident scene beyond the *awareness level* must have 24 hours of training equal to the *operations level* and must demonstrate competence in specific areas.

HAZWOPER, as briefly discussed above, is primarily concerned with the protection of those employees who must perform varying degrees of specialized work with or around hazardous waste materials. OSHA promulgated this Standard as a result of the 1986 Superfund Amendments. The EPA currently manages several hundred million metric tons of hazardous waste each year at licensed RCRA sites. Because someone must *do the dirty work* in order to properly manage such a tremendous amount of hazardous materials, OSHA identified a potentially serious threat to the safety and health of these workers. As with all OSHA requirements, HAZWOPER establishes the minimum acceptable safety requirements for employee protection. Employers who engage in such activities must comply with these requirements to ensure that their employees are afforded the proper protection and training under the law.

HAZARDOUS MATERIALS TRANSPORTATION ACT

The regulation of hazardous materials transportation, which includes hazardous wastes, is authorized by the *Hazardous Materials Transportation Act (HMTA)*, which became effective in 1975. This law provides the *U.S. Department of Transportation (DOT)* the authority to regulate the movement of substances within the United States that may pose a hazard to health, safety, property, or the environment when transported by air, highway, rail, or water (except substances shipped in bulk by water vessel, which are regulated by the U.S. Coast Guard under the Ports and Waterways Safety Act).

Under the HMTA, specific requirements are imposed on shipments of approximately 16,000 hazardous materials, including explosives, flammables, oxidizing materials, organic peroxides, corrosives, gases, poisons, radioactive substances, and etiologic agents. Hazardous substances and wastes that are regulated under other federal laws (RCRA, CERCLA) fall under DOT regulations when they are to be transported.

The HMTA regulations require special packaging, labeling, handling, and placarding when materials *shipped in commerce* are listed as *hazardous*. Specifically, the Act imposes responsibilities on the shipper of the material, the carrier of the shipment, and the manufacturer of the shipping container or packaging material.

DOT Administrative Responsibilities Under HMTA

There are five administrative elements within the DOT, each with a specific responsibility under the HMTA, as follows:

1. *Research and Special Programs Administration*—Under this Administration, the *Materials Transportation Bureau (MTB)* drafts and issues hazardous materials regulations, exemptions, registration certificates, and packaging and container certifications for all transport modes. The MTB also oversees regulation enforcement and pipeline safety. MTB designations for hazardous materials are located at 49 CFR 172.
2. *U.S. Coast Guard*—This Administration conducts all inspections and enforcement activities for hazardous materials being shipped by vessel.

The Coast Guard has regulatory and exemption authority for bulk transportation of hazardous materials by water and the authority (under both the Clean Water Act and Superfund) to respond to releases of oil and hazardous substances into U.S. coastal waters.

3. *Federal Aviation Administration (FAA)*—Conducts inspection and enforcement for air shipments of hazardous materials.

4. *Federal Highway Administration (FHwA)*—Conducts inspection and enforcement functions relating to the transport of hazardous materials by road and the manufacture and use of containers used in bulk transportation by highway. The FHwA also enforces motor carrier safety rules and insurance requirements for hazardous materials and other highway carriers.

5. *Federal Railroad Administration*—Performs inspection and enforcement for all rail shipments of hazardous materials and regulates the manufacture and use of containers used for bulk rail shipments.

General Requirements

With regard to environmental compliance requirements, the HMTA imposes specific regulations pertaining to the shipment of hazardous materials. This includes requirements for cargo classification, packaging, labeling, and placarding. The Act also contains provisions that must be met by carriers of such materials, which includes reporting requirements for emergency/spill incidents.

Because it is the shipper of hazardous materials who initiates actions that will affect those of carriers, emergency response personnel, and others handling hazardous materials, the Act specifies that shippers are primarily responsible for assuring compliance with the hazardous materials regulations. According to HMTA, a shipper is defined as the person who offers a hazardous material for transportation or anyone who performs a shipper's packaging, labeling, or marking function. Briefly, the law stipulates that the shipper must *classify* the shipment according to MTB requirements, select a proper *shipping name,* select authorized and effective *packaging*, properly *mark the package,* label the package as required, fill out the *shipping paper,* *certify compliance* with DOT regulations, and give the materials to the carrier in the proper condition for shipment.

The shipper must determine the proper *classification* of the material to be shipped. Once shipment begins, all regulatory requirements pertaining to the shipment will be based on the classification. The shipment classification serves as visible notification to all those who must handle the shipment or respond to an emergency involving the shipment. Therefore, if the shipper incorrectly classifies a particular shipment, then all other regulations will also be incorrect. The MTB established 22 *hazard classes* and provided definitions for each. A shipper must review each hazard class to determine which will apply to their shipment. If more than one class applies, MTB has established a classification priority list based on the type of packaging required.

Once the proper classification has been determined, the shipper must choose the most accurate *proper shipping name*. The DOT has provided a list of possible names in the *Hazardous Materials Table* located at 49 CFR 172.101. The shipping name must agree with the hazard classification of the material and, as far as possible, must closely describe the identity of the material.

The Hazardous Materials Table is revised frequently to add or delete hazardous materials or to change the requirements imposed on a substance. Approximately 16,000 materials and substances are listed. The environmental compliance practitioner should make it a habit to check the list on a frequent basis to ensure that they are adhering to the most recent requirements. It should be noted that, in addition to packaging and shipping criteria, reportable quantities (RQs) for these materials are also listed on the Table. If an amount of the material at or exceeding the reportable quantity (RQ) is spilled or discharged, the discharge must be reported immediately to the National Response Center (NRC).

Because it minimizes the risks of a release in transit, a great deal of emphasis is placed on proper packaging of shipped materials. For example, the Act specifies that shipping containers must be chosen that are compatible with their contents. After selecting the proper classification and shipping name for a substance, the shipper must refer to the Hazardous Materials Table, which will provide information on the appropriate packaging requirements for that material. During the container selection process, the shipper must ensure that the container chosen is compatible with the material to be shipped. The shipper must first verify that the container will not be degraded or destroyed by the material to be placed in it and that no hazardous decomposition of the container will result when the material is placed into it. The regulations also provide guidance on requirements for reusing certain containers. Containers used for shipping hazardous materials must be manufactured in strict compliance with DOT regulations. In fact, the DOT specifications for packaging are binding on container manufacturers as well. Marking the container with DOT specification letters and numbers is considered to be *certification* of compliance with DOT specifications. Also, those who test, repair, or recondition containers must comply with DOT requirements.

The *proper marking* and *labeling* of packages is also the responsibility of the shipper. One of the most important aspects when marking packages is to use the proper shipping name. The shipping name that is placed on the package must be written exactly as the name taken from the Hazardous Materials Table, which must also match that which is put on the shipping papers. In addition, every hazardous materials package, unless there is a specific exemption, must bear a label denoting its classification and hazard warning. If more than one hazard is possible with a particular substance (e.g., flammable and corrosive), then multiple labels must be used and must appear near each other on the package. DOT shipping labels are recognized symbols in the shipping industry (even on an international level, since they are similar to United Nations labels) and may not be altered in any way. The shipper must place the label adjacent to the shipping name on the package. The label must not be covered or marked in any way so that its intended warning could be missed or confused. Also, carriers must keep a supply of labels in case a warning on a package is lost or damaged during its shipment.

All shipments of *hazardous wastes* must be accompanied by a Uniform Hazardous Waste Manifest. The shipper, or generator, must provide the hazardous waste manifest to the carrier. The manifest must accompany the waste during the entire time it is in transit. Once the shipment arrives at the receiving facility, a signed copy of the manifest will be returned to the shipper. The regulations also require that *placards* be placed on each end and each side of trucks, railroad cars, portable tanks, and any other such containers carrying hazardous materials, including wastes. It should be noted that highway shipments containing less that 1,000 pounds of hazardous materials are generally exempt from the placarding requirement and that aircraft are never placarded. The shipper and carrier share the responsibility of ensuring proper placarding (e.g., the shipper provides the placard, and the carrier places it on the vehicle). When more than one hazardous substance is to be carried, the carrier must determine the proper placard to affix on the vehicle.

Carriers can not accept hazardous material that are not in proper condition for shipment (i.e., shipping name, papers, labels, placards, etc.) or in properly manufactured and certified containers.

Carriers must also submit a report when any *spills* (regardless of quantity) or *accidents* involve hazardous materials in transit. The carrier has 15 days following the incident to submit the required report to the DOT. However, accidents that result in death, severe injury, or environmental damage must be reported immediately to the National Response Center (NRC). The NRC will coordinate emergency response actions.

Another source of emergency assistance is the DOT's *Emergency Response Guidebook*. Also, the Chemical Manufacturers Association's *Chemical Transportation Emergency Center (CHEMTREC)* program is an excellent service for emergency situations. The experts that man the 24-hour service at CHEMTREC provide immediate advice for those at the response scene. They will also contact the shipper of the hazardous materials for more detailed assistance and appropriate follow-up. CHEMTREC can be reached at (800) 424-9300.

It is important to note here that the DOT, under the HMTA, requires carriers to report spills. There are no provisions for cleanup requirements. However, the EPA makes the carrier responsible for the cost of damage and cleanup in cases of spilled hazardous substances or hazardous wastes.

The safety, health, or environmental compliance professional involved in the shipment of hazardous materials, including hazardous wastes, must be aware of the overlap between DOT and EPA regulations under the HMTA. As is the case with the EPA under the many environmental regulations and legislation reviewed in this text, the HMTA allows the DOT to impose civil and criminal penalties, compliance orders, and imminent hazard orders to force compliance with hazardous materials regulations. Civil penalties are common, with fines of up to $10,000 per violation. Shippers and carriers both can be held liable for fines of up to $10,000 per day for continuing violations. Compliance orders are used to require the violator to take specific actions to halt a violation of the hazardous materials rules. Immediate corrective action may be ordered in cases where an imminent public hazard exists.

Appendix A

Sources of Additional Information/Training

The following is a compilation of sources where the interested reader may obtain additional information and/or training in the area of environmental compliance. It should be understood that there are certainly many more excellent references available to the environmental professional than could possibly be listed here. However, those listed below can provide the reader of this *Basic Guide to Environmental Compliance* with more advanced technical information on the growing field of environmental compliance.

PROFESSIONAL ORGANIZATIONS

Numerous national and international professional organizations currently exist that are either totally dedicated to the environmental profession or that have established sections, divisions, or chapters that are designed to serve the environmental professional. Included among these organizations are the following:

1. National Environmental Health Association (NEHA)
   720 South Colorado Blvd.
   Suite 970, South Tower
   Denver, Colorado 80222
   (303) 756-9090
       A national organization dedicated to the advancement of the environmental health professional, NEHA publishes the *Journal of Environmental Health* six times per year for its members and subscribers. The *Journal* includes numerous articles of a technical and scientific nature on a variety of subjects of interest to the practicing environmental health professional. The organization also holds an annual Environmental Health Conference

to provide continuing educational training to attendees and to offer Continuing Education Units (CEUs) for courses attended. NEHA also administers a certification program for those who work in the environmental profession. Certifications are awarded, following an extensive review of an applicant's professional background, work experience, academic accomplishments, recommendations from peers, and the passing of a written examination.

2. American Society of Safety Engineers (ASSE)
    1800 East Oakton Street
    Des Plaines, Illinois 60018-2187
    (708) 692-4121
    The ASSE is an international organization with over 25,000 (1992) members. Organized in 1911 and incorporated in 1915, the ASSE is one of the oldest sustaining professional safety membership organizations in the United States. More recently, the organization established its Environmental Division in an effort to serve the many safety and health professionals that find themselves responsible for environmental compliance as well. The Environmental Division has the distinction of being the fastest growing of all ASSE divisions, perhaps indicative of the existing need in this area of the profession. The ASSE is an excellent source of reference and information on a wide variety of safety, health, and environmental topics. Their monthly publication, *Professional Safety*, often includes articles and information of interest to the environmental profession. The ASSE holds an annual Professional Development Conference, with specialized training and post-conference seminars available on environmental compliance.

3. National Safety Council (NSC)
    1121 Spring Lake Drive
    Itasca, Illinois 60143-3201
    (708) 285-1121
    The NSC is dedicated to ensuring the advancement of safety and health of persons, both on and off the job. Their many excellent programs, seminars, and publications offer the profession quality resources, unmatched on a national level. In addition to a variety of activities in the safety and health arena, the NSC also offers assistance with environmental aspects. Their renowned National Safety Congress, which occurs each Fall, features a host of effective training sessions and meetings, many of which are of interest to the environmental compliance professional.

PUBLICATIONS—BOOKS

Many publications currently exist that specialize in specific areas of environmental compliance. The following are excellent, highly recommended reference sources for those readers interested in intermediate and advanced studies in this field:

1. Title: *Hazardous Waste Site Remediation, The Engineer's Perspective*
   Author/Year: O'Brien & Gere Engineers, Inc./1988
   Publisher: Van Nostrand Reinhold
   New York, New York 10003
2. Title: *Hazardous Waste Management*
   Author/Year: Charles A. Wentz/1989
   Publisher: McGraw-Hill
   New York, New York 10020
3. Title: *Technology, Law, and the Working Environment*
   Author/Year: N. A. Ashford and C. C. Caldart/1991
   Publisher: Van Nostrand Reinhold
   New York, New York 10003
4. Title: *Common Sense Toxics in the Workplace*
   Author/Year: Ilene R. Danse/1991
   Publisher: Van Nostrand Reinhold
   New York, New York 10003
5. Title: *Environmental Decision Making*
   Author/Year: R. A. Chechile and S. Carlisle/1991
   Publisher: Van Nostrand Reinhold
   New York, New York 10003
6. Title: *The Treatment and Handling of Wastes*
   Author/Year: Bradshaw, Southwood and Warner/1991
   Publisher: Van Nostrand Reinhold
   New York, New York 10003
7. Title: *The International Toxic Waste Trade*
   Author/Year: Christopher Hilz/1991
   Publisher: Van Nostrand Reinhold
   New York, New York 10003
8. Title: *Environmental Toxicants*
   Author/Year: Morton Lippmann, Ph.D./1991
   Publisher: Van Nostrand Reinhold
   New York, New York 10003

PUBLICATIONS—PERIODICALS

The dramatic growth of interest in the environmental profession in recent years has led to the publication of many new and informative periodicals. Since these reference publications are published on a frequent basis (monthly, bi-monthly, semi-annually, etc.), they are usually the best method of obtaining up-to-date information on changes and proposed changes of concern to the environmental professional. Some of these magazines are offered free to the practicing professional, while others are available for a modest subscription fee (the reader should inquire to the respective publisher regarding subscription policies). The following are recommended reading for the novice and experienced practitioner of environmental compliance:

1. Title: *Environmental Protection*
   Publisher: Stevens Publishing Corp.
   225 North New Road
   Waco, Texas 76710
   Frequency: 10 times per year
2. Title: *ECON*
   Publisher: PTN Publishing, Inc.
   Suite 21, 445 Broad Hollow Road
   Melville, New York 11747
   Frequency: Monthly
3. Title: *Environmental Careers*
   Publisher: PH Publishing, Inc.
   760 Whalers Way, Suite 100-A
   Fort Collins, Colorado 80525
   Frequency: Monthly
4. Title: *Occupational Health & Safety*
   Publisher: Medical Publications, Inc.
   225 North New Road
   Waco, Texas 76710
   Frequency: Monthly
5. Title: *Occupational Hazards*
   Publisher: Penton Publishing, Inc.
   1100 Superior Avenue
   Cleveland, Ohio 44114-2543
   Frequency: Monthly
6. Title: *Journal of Environmental Health*
   Publisher: National Environmental Health Assoc.
   720 South Colorado Blvd.
   Suite 970, South Tower
   Denver, Colorado 80222
   Frequency: Bi-monthly
7. Title: *Professional Safety*
   Publisher: American Society of Safety Engineers
   1800 East Oakton Street

Des Plaines, Illinois 60018-2187
Frequency: Monthly
8. Title: *The National Environmental Journal*
   Publisher: Campbell Publishing, Inc.
   5636 Whitesville Road, Suite A2
   Columbus, Georgia 31904
   Frequency: Bimonthly

TRAINING SEMINARS/ORGANIZATIONS

There are numerous professional training organizations offering specialized courses that cover a wide variety of topics in the environmental arena. Most tend to focus primarily on hazardous waste management. However, several highly professional training firms have developed courses covering many of the environmental regulations, some of which are referenced below:

1. Sponsor: *Executive Enterprises, Inc. (EEI)*
   Address: 22 West 21st Street
   New York, New York 10010-6990
   EEI is devoted to providing conferences and publications of the highest caliber. They have provided practical, need-to-know information to more than 400,000 business and government executives since 1971. EEI offers on-site seminars, custom designed for a specific facility or location. Their highly diversified training staff provides excellent and informative seminars, with well-organized manuals as handout materials, throughout the country on virtually every aspect of environmental compliance.
2. Sponsor: *Environmental Resource Center (ERC)*
   Address: 3679 Rosehill Road
   Fayetteville, North Carolina 28311
   ERC offers seminars throughout the country designed to simplify the complex environmental regulations facing industry today. Their extremely competent instructors provide a variety of training courses in areas such as hazardous waste management, SARA Title III & OSHA Right-To-Know requirements, the EPA's underground storage tanks, water permitting, environmental audits, and others. A very attractive feature of ERC training seminars is the course manual that accompanies each seminar and the company's follow-up and update service. In most cases, ERC will provide quarterly updates to the course manual for 1 year after completing a specific course.
3. Sponsor: *COMCO, Inc. Environmental & Safety Services*
   Address: 17120 Clark Avenue
   Bellflower, California 90706-5730

COMCO is a full-service safety and environmental consulting firm offering specialized training in safety and environmental programs, covering virtually any environmental issue or concern facing industry today. From OSHA to the EPA, COMCO is capable of helping its clients meet the training criteria specified in applicable federal regulations, as well as inform attendees on the general and specific compliance aspects and requirements of each regulation. The competent professional trainers of COMCO can also design special training sessions for on-site instruction anywhere in the United States.

4. Sponsor: *O'Brien & Gere Engineers, Inc.*
   Address: P.O. Box 4073
   Syracuse, New York 13221

   Although their primary function is in the area of professional site remediation, O'Brien & Gere is also a multi-faceted consulting services firm that can, among other things, provide excellent seminars on any environmental or safety and health issue. The expertise and versatility of their staff enables the company to provide custom-designed environmental training to clients in any industry in any part of the country.

5. Sponsor: *Federal Publications, Inc.*
   Address: 1120 20th Street, N.W.
   Washington, D.C. 20036

   Federal Publications, Inc., is yet another excellent source to obtain professional training on environmental issues. Their many courses are offered frequently throughout the country, and they provide a comprehensive and quite detailed course manual for all attendees. The can also conduct their training sessions on site to facilitate the training needs of its customers.

6. Sponsor: *Institute of Applied Management & Law (IAML)*
   Address: 610 Newport Center Drive, Suite 1060
   Newport Beach, California 92660

   For the environmental or safety and health professional interested in one of the most comprehensive breakdowns of safety and environmental regulations, IAML's week-long session entitled *The Certificate in Environmental Health and Safety Law* is probably the answer. The seminar is taught by representatives from some of the top law firms in the United States. The handout materials and manuals provide detailed explanations of the compliance requirements for most of the primary safety, health, and environmental legislation. The course is offered throughout the country several times per year.

Appendix B

Acronyms and Abbreviations

In the environmental compliance profession, as in the safety and health arena, numerous acronyms and abbreviations are used quite regularly. The following is a reference listing of some of the most frequently used or encountered, either in this text or in the environmental compliance profession in general (Source: U.S. Environmental Protection Agency).

AA&C Abatement and Control
AA&R Air and Radiation
AAAS American Association for the Advancement of Science
AAOHN American Association of Occupational Health Nurses
AAP Asbestos Action Program
AAPCO Association of American Pesticide Control Officers
AARC Alliance for Acid Rain Control
ABTRES Abatement and Residual Forecasting Model
AC Advisory Circular
ACA American Conservation Association, Inc.
ACBM Asbestos-Containing Building Material
ACE Alliance for Clean Energy
ACEC American Consulting Engineers Council
ACFM Actual Cubic Feet per Minute
ACGIH American Conference of Government Industrial Hygienists

ACM Asbestos-Containing Material
ACP Air Carcinogen Policy
ACQR Air Quality Control Region
ACS American Chemical Society
ACSH American Council on Science and Health
ACWA American Clean Water System
ADI Acceptable Daily Intake
ADQ Audits of Data Quality
ADR Alternative Dispute Resolution
ADSS Air Data Screening System
AEA Atomic Energy Act
AEM Acoustical Emission Monitoring
AESA Association of Environmental Scientists and Administrators
AFCA Area Fuel Consumption Allocation
AFRCE Air Force Regional Civil Engineers
AG Attorney General
AGA American Gas Association, Inc.
AHERA Asbestos Hazard Emergency Response Act

AIA   Asbestos Information Association

AIC   Acceptable Intake for Chronic Exposures

AIChE   American Institute of Chemical Engineers

AIHA   American Industrial Hygiene Association

AIHC   American Industrial Health Council

AIP   Auto Ignition Point

AIS   Acceptable Intake for Subchronic Exposures

ALAPCO   Association of Local Air Pollution Control Officials

ALJ   Administrative Law Judge

AMA   American Medical Association

AMC   American Mining Association

AMD   Air Management Division (Regional)

AMSA   Association of Metropolitan Sewerage Agencies

ANEC   American Nuclear Energy Council

ANPR   Advanced Notice of Proposed Rule Making

ANRHRD   Air, Noise, and Radiation Health Research Division

ANSI   American National Standards Institute

AO   Administrative Order

APA   Administrative Procedures Act

APCA   Air Pollution Control Association

APCD   Air Pollution Control District

APER   Air Pollution Emissions Report

APHA   American Public Health Association

API   American Petroleum Institute

APTI   Air Pollution Training Institute

ARAR   Applicable or Relevant and Appropriate Requirements

ARPO   Acid Rain Policy Office

ASCE   American Society of Civil Engineers

ASCII   American Standard Code for Information Interchange

ASHAA   Asbestos in Schools Hazard Abatement Act (1984)

ASME   American Society of Mechanical Engineers

ASSE   American Society of Safety Engineers

ASTM   American Society for Testing and Materials

ATD   Air and Toxics Division

ATERIS   Air Toxics Exposure and Risk Information System

ATSDR   Agency for Toxic Substances and Disease Registry

BACT   Best Available Control Technology

BADT   Best Available Demonstrated Technology

BAT   Best Available Technology

BATEA   Best Available Technology Economically Achievable

BCF   Bioconcentration Factor

BCPT   Best Conventional Pollutant Technology (also BCT)

BCT   Best Control Technology

BCSP   Board of Certified Safety Professionals

BID   Buoyancy Induced Dispersion

BLOB   Biologically Liberated Organo-Beasties

BLP   Bureau of Land Management

BLS   Bureau of Labor Statistics

BMP   Best Management Practices

BOD   Biological Oxygen Demand

BOE   Bureau of Explosives

BP   Boiling Point

BPT   Best Practicable Control Technology

BTU   British Thermal Units

C   Celsius (degrees)

CAA   Clean Air Act

CAAA   Clean Air Act Amendments

CAER   Community Awareness and Emergency Response Program
CAFO   Consent Agreement/Final Order
CAIR   Comprehensive Assessment Information Rule
CAMP   Continuous Air Monitoring Program
CAP   Corrective Action Plan
CAP   Criteria Air Pollutants
CAR   Corrective Action Report
CAS   Chemical Abstract Service
CASAC   Clean Air Scientific Advisory Committee
CBI   Compliance Biomonitoring Inspection
CCAA   Canadian Clean Air Act
CCEA   Conventional Combustion Environmental Assessment
CCHW   Citizens Clearing House for Hazardous Wastes
CDC   Centers for Disease Control
CDI   Chronic Daily Intake
CEI   Compliance Evaluation Inspection
CEM   Continuous Emission Monitoring
CEQ   Council on Environmental Quality
CERCLA   Comprehensive Environmental Response, Compensation, and Liabilities Act
CEU   Continuing Education Unit
CFC   Chlorofluorocarbons
CFM   Chlorofluoromethanes
CFM   Cubic Feet per Minute
CFR   Code of Federal Regulations
CFS   Cubic Feet per Second
CGA   Compressed Gas Association
CHEMTREC   Chemical Transportation Emergency Center
CHESS   Community Health and Environmental Surveillance System
CHIP   Chemical Hazard Information Profile

CHRIS   Chemical Hazard Response Information System
CIAQ   Council on Indoor Air Quality
CIS   Chemical Information System
CMA   Chemical Manufacturers Association
CMB   Chemical Mass Balance
CO   Carbon Monoxide
CO_2   Carbon Dioxide
COD   Chemical Oxygen Demand
CPE   Carcinogenic Potency Factor
CPSC   Consumer Product Safety Commission
CRAVE   Carcinogenic Risk Assessment Verification Exercise
CSI   Chemical Substances Inventory
CSP   Certified Safety Professional
CTD   Control Technology Document
CTG   Control Technique Guidelines
CUS   Chemical Update System
CWA   Clean Water Act
CZMA   Coastal Zone Management Act

DF   Determination and Findings
DARTAB   Dose and Risk Assessment Tabulation
DCO   Delayed Compliance Order
DE   Destruction Efficiency
DEC   Department of Environmental Conservation
DI   Diagnostic Inspection
DMR   Discharge Monitoring Report
DOC   Department of Commerce
DOD   Department of Defense
DOE   Department of Energy
DOI   Department of the Interior
DOJ   Department of Justice
DOL   Department of Labor
DOT   Department of Transportation
DRE   Destruction/Removal Efficiency

EA   Environmental Assessment
EAP   Environmental Action Plan
EC   Effective Concentration
EDF   Environmental Defense Fund, Inc.

EEA   Energy and Environmental Analysis

EEC   European Economic Community

EEI   Executive Enterprises, Inc.

EENS   Emissions Elements Needs Survey

EER   Excess Emission Report

EF   Emission Factor

EHC   Environmental Health Committee

EIA   Economic Impact Assessment

EIS   Environmental Impact Statement

EOP   Emergency Operations Plan

EP   Extraction Procedure

EPA   Environmental Protection Agency

EPC   Emergency Preparedness Coordinator

EPID   Epidemiological Studies

EQR   Environmental Quality Report

ERC   Environmental Resource Center, Inc.

ERP   Enforcement Response Policy

ERT   Emergency Response Team

ESA   Endangered Species Act

ETP   Emissions Trading Policy

EUP   Environmental Use Permit

F   Fahrenheit (degrees)

FAA   Federal Aviation Administration

FACM   Friable Asbestos-Containing Material

FAR   Federal Acquisition Regulations

FAR   Federal Aviation Regulations

FCC   Fluid Catalytic Converter

FDA   Food and Drug Administration

FE   Fugitive Emissions

FEA   Federal Energy Administration

FEIS   Fugitive Emissions Information System

FEMA   Federal Emergency Management Agency

FEPCA   Federal Environmental Pesticides Control Act

FHwA   Federal Highway Administration

FIFRA   Federal Insecticide, Fungicide, and Rodenticide Act

FIP   Federal Implementation Plan

FLP   Flash Point

FM   Friable Material

FML   Flexible Membrane Liner

FNSI   Finding of No Significant Impact

FOI   Freedom of Information

FPA   Federal Pesticide Act

FR   Federal Register

FS   Feasibility Study

FUA   Fuel Use Act

FURS   Federal Underground Injection Control Reporting System

FWCA   Fish and Wildlife Coordination Act

FWPCA   Federal Water Pollution Control Act

GAC   Granular Activated Carbon

GC/MS   Gas Chromatography/Mass Spectrograph

GFF   Glass Fiber Filter

GLC   Gas Liquid Chromatography

GOCO   Government-Owned/Contractor-Operated

GOGO   Government-Owned/Government-Operated

GOPO   Government-Owned/Privately-Operated

GPAD   Gallons per Acre per Day

GPS   Groundwater Protection Strategy

GRGL   Groundwater Residue Guidance Level

GSA   General Services Administration

GW   Groundwater

H_2O Water

H_2O_2 Hydrogen Peroxide

H_2S Hydrogen Sulfide

HAP   Hazardous Air Pollutant
HAZMAT   Hazardous Material(s)
HAZOP   Hazard and Operability
Study
HAZWOPER   Hazardous Waste
Operations and Emergency
Response
HC   Hazardous Constituents
HCFC   Halogenated
Chlorofluorocarbons
HCl   Hydrogen Chloride
HEA   Health Effects Assessment
HEEP   Health and Environmental
Effects Profile
HEPA   High Efficiency Particulate
Air
HHW   Household Hazardous Waste
HI   Hazard Index
HMIS   Hazardous Materials
Information System
HMT   Hazardous Materials Table
HMTA   Hazardous Materials
Transportation Act
HOC   Hazardous Organic
Constituents
HPLC   High Performance Liquid
Chromatography
HRPS   High Risk Point Source
HRS   Hazard Ranking System
HSL   Hazardous Substance List
HSWA   Hazard and Solid Waste
Amendments of 1984
HT   Hydrothermically Treated
HW   Hazardous Waste
HWLT   Hazardous Waste Land
Treatment

IAP   Indoor Air Pollution
ICC   Interstate Commerce
Commission
ICRA   Industrial Chemical Research
Association
ICWM   Institute for Chemical Waste
Management
IDLH   Immediately Dangerous to
Life and Health

IEB   International Environment
Bureau
IG   Inspector General
IP   Inhaleable Particulates
IR   Infrared
IS   Indicator Source
IS   Interim Status
ISMAP   Indirect Source Model for
Air Pollution
ITC   Interagency Testing Committee
IWS   Ionizing Wet Scrubber

JPA   Joint Permitting Agreement

KWH   Kilowatt Hour

LAER   Lowest Achievable Emission
Rate
LC   Lethal Concentration
LCRS   Leachate Collection and
Removal System
LD   Lethal Dose
LDR   Land Disposal Restrictions
LEL   Lower Explosive Limit
LEPC   Local Emergency Planning
Committee
LERC   Local Emergency Response
Committee
LFL   Lower Flammability Limit
LIMB   Limestone Injection,
Multi-stage Burner
LLRW   Low-Level Radioactive Waste
LLWPA   Low-Level Waste Policy Act
LOC   Level of Concern
LPG   Liquefied Petroleum Gas
LRMS   Low-Resolution Mass
Spectroscopy
LRTAP   Long-Range Transportation
of Air Pollutants
LUST   Leaking Underground Storage
Tanks

MACT   Maximum Achievable
Control Technology
MAER   Maximum Allowable
Emission Rate

MATC   Maximum Allowable Toxicant Concentration
MCL   Maximum Contaminant Level
MECA   Manufacturers of Emissions Controls Association
MED   Minimum Effective Dose
MLSS   Mixed Liquor Suspended Solids
MOBILE   Mobile Source Emissions Model
MP   Melting Point
MSDS   Material Safety Data Sheet
MSHA   Mine Safety and Health Association
MTB   Materials Transportation Bureau

NA   Nonattainment
NAA   Nonattainment Area
NAAQS   National Ambient Air Quality Standards
NAEP   National Association of Environmental Professionals
NAR   National Asbestos Registry
NASA   National Aeronautics and Space Administration
NATS   National Air Toxics Strategy
NCAQ   National Commission on Air Quality
NCI   National Cancer Institute
NCO   Negotiated Consent Order
NCP   National Contingency Plan
NCR   Noncompliance Report
NCWQ   National Commission on Water Quality
NEDA   National Environmental Development Association
NEHA   National Environmental Health Association
NEP   National Energy Plan
NEPA   National Environmental Policy Act
NESHAPS   National Emissions Standards for Hazardous Air Pollutants
NFPA   National Fire Protection Association

NGWIC   National Groundwater Information Center
NIMBY   Not In My Back Yard
NMHC   Non-Methane Hydrocarbons
NNC   Notice of Noncompliance
NO   Nitric Oxide
NO2   Nitrogen Dioxide
NOD   Notice of Deficiency
NOI   Notice of Intent
NOV   Notice of Violation
NOx   Nitrogen Oxides
NPDES   National Pollution Discharge Elimination System
NPL   National Priority List
NPR   Notice of Proposed Rule Making
NRC   National Response Center
NRC   Nuclear Regulatory Commission
NRT   National Response Team
NSC   National Safety Council
NSPS   New Source Performance Standards
NSR   New Source Review
NTP   National Toxicology Program
NTSB   National Transportation Safety Board

O3   Ozone
OA&R   Office of Air and Radiation
OCD   Offshore and Coastal Dispersion Model
ODC   Ozone Depleting Chemical
ODES   Ocean Data Evaluation System
OEP   Office on Environmental Quality
OILHM   Oil and Hazardous Material Information System
OLDS   Ozone Level Depleting Substance
OMB   Office of Management and Budget
OP   Operating Plan
ORM   Other Regulated Material
OSC   On-Scene Coordinator

OSH   Occupational Safety and Health
OSHA   Occupational Safety and Health Administration
OWEP   Oily Waste Extraction Program

PA/SI   Preliminary Assessment/Site Inspection
PADRE   Particulate Data Reduction
PAI   Performance Audit Inspection
PAIR   Preliminary Assessment Information Rule
PAL   Point, Area, and Line Source (Air Quality Model)
PAPR   Powered Air Purifying Respirator
PAT   Permit Assistance Team
PC   Potential Carcinogen
PCB   Polychlorinated Biphenyl
PCM   Phase Contrast Microscopy
PDR   Particulate Data Reduction
PEL   Permissible Exposure Limit
PEPE   Prolonged Elevated Pollution Episode
PHC   Principal Hazardous Constituent
PHA   Process Hazard Analysis
PHSA   Public Health Service Act
PLUVUE   Plume Visibility Model
PM   Particulate Matter
PM10   Particulate Matter nominally 10 microns or less
PMN   Premanufacture Notification
POGO   Privately-Owned/Government- Operated
POHC   Principal Organic Hazardous Constituent
POTW   Publicly Owned Treatment Works
PPA   Pollution Prevention Act of 1990
PPB   Parts per Billion
PPE   Personal Protective Equipment
PPM   Parts per Million
PPU   Pollution Prevention Unit
PRP   Potentially Responsible Party
PRTYPOLS   Priority Pollutants
PS   Point Source

PSD   Prevention of Significant Deterioration
PSES   Pretreatment Standards for Existing Sources
PSI   Pounds per Square Inch
PSM   Point Source Modeling
PSNS   Pretreatment Standards for New Sources
PVC   Polyvinyl Chloride

QNCR   Quarterly Noncompliance Report

R&D   Research and Development
RA   Regional Administrator
RA   Remedial Action
RA   Risk Analysis (or Assessment)
RAATS   RCRA Administrative Action Tracking System
RAC   Radiation Advisory Committee
RACM   Reasonably Available Control Measures
RACT   Reasonably Available Control Technology
RAMS   Regional Air Monitoring System
RCRA   Resource Conservation and Recovery Act
RD   Remedial Design
REM   Roentgen Equivalent Man
REMS   RCRA Enforcement Management System
RF   Radio Frequency
RFA   RCRA Facility Assessment
RI/FS   Remedial Investigation/Feasibility Study
RIP   RCRA Implementation Plan
ROD   Record of Decision
RPM   Remedial Project Manager
RQ   Reportable Quantity
RUP   Restricted Use Pesticide

S&A   Surveillance and Analysis
SANE   Sulfur and Nitrogen Emissions
SARA   Superfund Amendments and Reauthorization Act

SCAP   Superfund Comprehensive Accomplishments Plan
SCFM   Standard Cubic Feet per Minute
SDWA   Safe Drinking Water Act
SERC   State Emergency Response Commission
SF   Superfund
SI   Site Inspection
SIC   Standard Industry Classification
SIP   State Implementation Plan
SMCRA   Surface Mining Control and Reclamation Act of 1977
SNAAQS   Secondary National Ambient Air Quality Standards
SNARS   Spill Notification and Response System
SNUR   Significant New Use Rule
SO2   Sulfur Dioxide
SOW   Statement of Work
SOx   Sulfur Oxides
SPCC   Spill Prevention, Containment and Countermeasures
SQG   Small Quantity Generator
SSS   System Safety Society
STP   Sewage Treatment Plant
SWDA   Solid Waste Disposal Act

TAMS   Toxic Air Monitoring System
TAPDS   Toxic Air Pollutant Data System
TCLP   Toxicity Characteristic Leaching Procedure
TCRI   Toxic Chemical Release Inventory
TD   Toxic Dose
TDS   Total Dissolved Solids
THC   Total Hydrocarbons
TLV   Threshold Limit Value
TPQ   Threshold Planning Quantity
TRI   Toxic Release Inventory

TRIP   Toxic Release Inventory Program
TRS   Total Reduced Sulfur
TSCA   Toxic Substances Control Act
TSD   Treatment, Storage and Disposal
TSDF   Treatment, Storage and Disposal Facilities
TSP   Total Suspended Particulates
TSS   Total Suspended Solids
TWA   Time Weighted Average

UEL   Upper Explosive Limit
UFL   Upper Flammability Range
UIC   Underground Injection Control
UL   Underwriter's Laboratories
UN   United Nations
USC   United States Code
USDA   United States Department of Agriculture
USCG   United States Coast Guard
UST   Underground Storage Tank
UV   Ultraviolet

VE   Visual Emissions
VOC   Volatile Organic Compounds
VP   Vapor Pressure
VSS   Volatile Suspended Solids

WAP   Waste Analysis Plan
WBGT   Wet Bulb Globe Test
WHO   World Health Organization
WHWT   Water and Hazardous Waste Team
WQC   Water Quality Criteria
WRC   Water Resources Council
WRDA   Water Resources Development Act
WSO   World Safety Organization
WWTP   Wastewater Treatment Plan

ZRL   Zero Risk Level

Glossary

The following are definitions for many of the terms that appear in this text or are encountered during the normal practice of environmental compliance. Unless otherwise indicated, these definitions have been extracted from the EPA's Information Resources Directory.

Abandoned well   A well whose use has been permanently discontinued or that is in such a state of disrepair that it cannot be used for its intended purpose.

Abatement   Reducing the degree or intensity of or eliminating pollution.

Absorption   The adhesion of molecules of gas, liquid, or dissolved solids to a surface. Used as an advanced method of treating in which activated carbon removes organic matter from wastewater.

Accidental release   The unanticipated emission of a regulated substance or other extremely hazardous substance into ambient air from a stationary source.

Accident   An unexpected incident or occurrence, failure, or loss resulting in a release of hazardous materials.

Accident site   The location of an unexpected occurrence, failure, or loss, either at a plant or along a transportation route, resulting in a release of hazardous materials.

Accumulation start date   That date when the first drop or piece of a waste has been put into the container.

Acid deposition   A complex chemical and atmospheric phenomenon that occurs when emissions of sulfur and nitrogen compounds and other substances are transformed by chemical processes in the atmosphere, often far from the original sources, and then deposited on earth in either a wet or dry form. The wet forms, popularly called "acid rain," can fall as rain, snow, or fog. The dry forms are acidic gases or particulates.

Acid Rain   See *Acid deposition.*

Action levels   1) Regulatory levels recommended by the EPA for enforcement by the FDA and the USDA when pesticide residues occur in food or feed commodities for reasons other than the direct application of the pesticide.   2) In the

Superfund Program, the existence of a contaminant concentration in the environment high enough to warrant action or to trigger a response under SARA and the National Oil and Hazardous Substances Contingency Plan. The term can be used similarly in other regulatory programs.

Activated carbon   A highly adsorbent form of carbon used to remove odors and toxic substances from liquid or gaseous emissions. In waste treatment it is used to remove dissolved organic matter from wastewater. It is also used in motor vehicle evaporative control systems.

Acute exposure   A single exposure to a toxic substance that results in severe biological harm or death. Acute exposures are usually characterized as lasting no longer than a day.

Acute toxicity   The ability of a substance to cause poisonous effects, resulting in severe biological harm or death soon after a single exposure or dose. Also, any severe poisonous effect resulting from a single short-term exposure to a toxic substance.

Administrative order   A legal document signed by the EPA directing an individual, business, or other entity to take corrective action or refrain from an activity. It describes the violations and actions to be taken, and can be enforced in court. Such orders may be issued, for example, as a result of an administrative complaint, whereby the respondent is ordered to pay a penalty for violations of a statute.

Administrative Procedures Act   A law that provides procedures and requirements related to the promulgation of regulations by federal agencies, such as the EPA.

Advanced wastewater treatment   Any treatment of sewage that goes beyond the secondary or biological water treatment stage and includes the removal of nutrients, such as phosphorus or nitrogen, and a high percentage of suspended solids.

Air contaminant   Any particulate matter, gas, or combination thereof, other than water vapor or natural air.

Air pollutant   Any substance in air that could, if in high enough concentrations, harm man, other animals, vegetation, or material.

Air pollution   1) Any undesirable substance mixed with open air (Simonds and Grimaldi 1963). 2) The presence of contaminant or pollutant substances in the air that do not disperse properly and interfere with human health or welfare or that produce other harmful environmental effects (EPA).

Air pollution episode   A period of abnormally high concentration of air pollutants, often due to low winds and temperature inversion, that can cause illness and death (reference Chapter 1).

Air quality control region   An area designated by the federal government in which communities share a common air pollution problem (sometimes several states are involved).

Air quality criteria   The levels of pollution and lengths of exposure above which adverse health and welfare effects may occur.

Air quality standards   The level of pollutants prescribed by regulations that may not be exceeded during a specified time in a defined area.

Airborne particulates   Total suspended particulate matter found in the atmosphere as solid particles or liquid droplets. The chemical composition of particulates varies widely, depending on location and time of year. Airborne particulates include windblown dust, emissions from industrial process, smoke from burning wood and coal, and motor vehicle exhaust .

Airborne release   The release of any chemical into the air.

Alternate method   Any method of sampling and analyzing for an air pollutant that is not a reference or equivalent method, but that has been demonstrated in specific cases to the EPA's satisfaction to produce results adequate for compliance.

Ambient air quality standards   See *Criteria pollutants* and *National Ambient Air Quality Standards.*

Ambient air   Any unconfined portion of the atmosphere (open air, surrounding air).

Antarctic "Ozone Hole"   Refers to the seasonal depletion of ozone in a large area over Antarctica.

Antidegradation clause   Part of federal air quality and water quality requirements prohibiting deterioration where pollution levels are above the legal limit.

Aquifer   An underground geological formation or group of formations containing usable amounts of groundwater that can supply wells and springs.

Area source   Any small source of non-natural air pollution that is released over a relatively small area, but that cannot be classified as a point source. Such sources include vehicles and other small fuel combustion engines.

Article   Under TSCA, a manufactured item that is formed to a specific size and shape during manufacture and whose end use function is dependent in whole or in part on that specific size and shape.

Asbestos   A mineral fiber that can pollute air or water and cause cancer or asbestosis when inhaled. The EPA has banned or severely restricted its use in manufacturing and construction.

Asbestosis   A disease associated with chronic exposure to and inhalation of asbestos fibers. The disease makes breathing progressively more difficult and can lead to death.

Attainment area   An area considered to have air quality that meets or exceeds the National Ambient Air Quality Standards (NAAQS), as defined in the Clean Air Act. An area may be an attainment area for one pollutant and a nonattainment area for others.

Best available control technology (BACT)   An emission limitation based on the maximum degree of emission reduction (considering energy, environmental, and economic impacts and other costs) is achievable by applying production processes and available methods, systems, and techniques. In no event does BACT permit emissions in excess of those allowed under any applicable Clean Air Act provisions. Use of the BACT concept is allowable on a case-by-case basis for major new or modified emissions sources in attainment areas, and it applies to each regulated pollutant.

Banking   A system of recording qualified air emission reductions for later use in bubble, offset, or netting transactions.

Biological oxygen demand (BOD)   A measure of the amount of oxygen consumed in the biological processes that break down organic matter in water. The greater the BOD, the greater the degree of pollution.

Biodegradable   The ability to break down or decompose rapidly under natural conditions and processes.

Biological treatment   The treatment technology that utilizes bacteria to consume waste. This treatment breaks down organic materials.

Bounty hunter provision   Under the Clean Air Act of 1990, a provision that authorizes the EPA to pay a bounty of up to $10,000 to anyone who provides information that leads to a civil penalty or criminal conviction. This provision applies to current as well as past employees.

Bubble   A system under which existing emissions sources can propose alternate means to comply with a set of emissions limitations. Under the bubble concept, sources can implement more than the required controls at one emission point where control costs are relatively low, in return for a comparable relaxation of controls at a second emission point where costs are higher.

Capture efficiency   The fraction of all organic vapors generated by a process that are directed to an abatement or recovery device.

Carcinogen   Any substance that can cause or contribute to the production of cancer.

Catalytic converter   An air pollution abatement device that removes pollutants from motor vehicle exhaust, either by oxidizing them into carbon dioxide and water or by reducing them to nitrogen and oxygen.

Cathodic protection   A technique to prevent corrosion of a metal surface by making that surface the cathode of an electrochemical cell.

Characteristic hazardous waste   Any one of four categories used in defining hazardous waste: ignitability, corrosivity, reactivity, and toxicity.

Chemical abstract system (CAS)   A numerical index that lists chemical compounds and substances, each with its own distinct CAS identification number.

Chemical oxygen demand (COD)   A measure of the oxygen required to oxidize all compounds in water, both organic and inorganic.

Chemical treatment   Any one of a variety of technologies that use chemicals or a variety of chemical processes to treat waste.

Chilling effect   The lowering of the Earth's temperature because of an increased level of particles in the air blocking the sun's rays. (See also Greenhouse effect.)

Chlorinated hydrocarbons   These include a class of persistent, broad-spectrum insecticides that linger in the environment and accumulate in the food chain. Among them are DDT, aldrin, dieldrin, heptachlor, chlordane, lindane, endrin, mirex, hexachloride, and toxaphene.

Chlorinated solvent   An organic solvent containing chlorine atoms, such as methylene chloride and trichloromethane.

Chlorination   The application of chlorine to drinking water, sewage, or industrial waste to disinfect or to oxidize undesirable compounds.

Chlorofluorocarbons (CFC)   A family of inert, nontoxic, and easily liquefied chemicals used in refrigeration, air conditioning, packaging, insulation, or as solvents and aerosol propellants. Because CFCs are not destroyed in the lower atmosphere, they drift into the upper atmosphere, where their chlorine components destroy the ozone.

Chronic toxicity   The capacity of a substance to cause long-term poisonous human health effects.

Cleanup   Actions taken to deal with the release or threat of release of a hazardous substance that could affect humans and/or the environment. The term "cleanup" is sometimes used interchangeably with the terms remedial action, removal action, response action, or corrective action.

Coastal zone   Lands and waters adjacent to the coast that exert an influence on the uses of the sea and its ecology or, inversely, whose uses and ecology are affected by the sea.

Combined sewers   A sewer system that carries both sewage and stormwater runoff. Normally, its entire flow goes to a waste treatment plant, but during a heavy storm, the stormwater volume may be so great as to cause overflows. When this occurs, untreated mixtures of stormwater and sewage may flow into receiving waters. Stormwater runoff may also carry toxic chemicals from industrial areas or streets into the sewer system.

Comment period   Time provided for the public to review and comment on a proposed EPA action or rule after it is published in the Federal Register.

Commerce   Under TSCA, the term means trade, traffic, transportation, or other commerce between a place in a state and any other place outside a state or actions that might affect such trade, traffic, or commerce.

Community water system   A public water system that serves at least 15 service connections used by year-round residents or regularly serves at least 25 year-round residents.

Compliance schedule   A negotiated agreement between a pollution source and a government agency that specifies dates and procedures by which a source will reduce emissions and, thereby, comply with a regulation.

Conditionally exempt   Those small-quantity generators that generate less than 100 kilograms of hazardous waste during any month.

Confined aquifer   An aquifer in which groundwater is confined under pressure that is significantly greater than atmospheric pressure.

Consent decree   A legal document, approved by a judge, that formalizes an agreement reached between the EPA and potentially responsible parties (PRPs) through which the PRPs will conduct all or part of a cleanup action at a Superfund site, cease or correct actions or processes that are polluting the environment, or otherwise comply with regulations that the PRPs had not been in compliance with. The consent decree describes the actions that PRPs will take and may be subject to a public comment period.

Conservation   Avoiding waste of (and renewing when possible) human and natural resources. The protection, improvement, and use of natural resources according to principles that will assure their highest economic or social benefits.

Contaminant   Any physical, chemical, biological, or radiological substance or matter that has an adverse affect on air, water, or soil.

Contingency plan   A document setting out an organized, planned, and coordinated course of action to be followed in case of a fire, explosion, or other accident that releases toxic chemicals, hazardous wastes, or radioactive materials that threaten human health or the environment.

Control technique guidelines (CTG)   A series of EPA documents designed to assist states in defining reasonable available control technologies (RACT) for major sources of volatile organic compounds (VOCs).

Conventional pollutants   Statutory listed pollutants, the nature of which are well understood by the scientific community. These may be in the form of organic waste, sediment, acid, bacteria and viruses, oil and grease, and so on.

Corrosive   A chemical agent that reacts with the surface of a material (including skin), causing it to deteriorate or wear away.

Cost recovery   A legal process by which potentially responsible parties (PRPs) who contributed to the contamination at a Superfund site can be required to reimburse the Trust Fund for money spent during any cleanup actions by the federal government.

Cradle-to-grave   Under RCRA, the common term used to emphasize the extent of hazardous waste management responsibilities. Basically, hazardous wastes must be properly managed, and those who participate in that management are held responsible from the moment it is generated (i.e., its creation) up to the time it is either neutralized, destroyed, or otherwise disposed of properly.

Criteria pollutants   The 1970 amendments to the Clean Air Act required the EPA to set National Ambient Air Quality Standards (NAAQS) for certain pollutants known to be hazardous to human health. The term "criteria pollutants" derives from the requirements that the EPA must describe the characteristics and potential health and welfare effects of these pollutants. It is on the basis of these criteria that standards are set or revised.

DDT   The first chlorinated hydrocarbon insecticide (chemical name: Dichloro-Diphenyl-Trichloromethane). It has a half-life of 15 years and can collect in the fatty tissue of certain animals. The EPA banned the registration and interstate sale of DDT for virtually all but emergency uses in the United States in 1972 because of its persistence in the environment and accumulation in the food chain.

Delist   Use of the petition process to have a facility's toxic designation rescinded.

Derived from rule   Under RCRA, this special rule stipulates that waste generated from the treatment, storage, or disposal of hazardous waste is itself a hazardous waste, unless it does not exhibit any of the hazardous characteristics or is not a listed waste.

Desalinization   Removing salt from ocean or brackish water.

Designated pollutant   An air pollutant that is neither a criteria nor hazardous pollutant, as described in the Clean Air Act, but for which new source performance standards exist. The Clean Air Act does require states to control these pollutants, which include acid mists, total reduced sulfur (TRS), and fluorides.

Direct discharger   A municipal or industrial facility that introduces pollution through a defined conveyance or system; a point source.

Disposal   Final placement or destruction of toxic, radioactive, or other wastes; surplus or banned pesticides or other chemicals; polluted soils; and drums containing hazardous materials from removal actions or accidental releases.

Disposal may be accomplished through use of approved secure landfills, surface impoundments, land farming deep well injection, ocean dumping, or incineration.

Distribution into commerce   Under TSCA, either the introduction, holding, or selling of a chemical substance, mixture, or article into commerce.

Dredging   Removal of mud from the bottom of water bodies using a scooping machine. This process disturbs the ecosystem and causes silting that can kill aquatic life. Dredging of contaminated mud can expose aquatic life to heavy metals and other toxics. Dredging activities may be subject to regulation under Section 404 of the Clean Water Act.

Dump   A site used to dispose of solid wastes without environmental controls.

Ecosystem   The interacting system of a biological community and its nonliving environmental surroundings.

Effluent   Wastewater, treated or untreated, that flows out of a treatment plant, sewer, or industrial outfall. Generally refers to wastes discharged into surface waters.

Effluent limitation   Restrictions established by a state or the EPA on quantities, rates, and concentrations in wastewater discharges.

Emergency (chemical)   A situation created by an accidental release or spill of hazardous chemicals that poses a threat to the safety of workers, residents, the environment, or property.

Eminent domain   Government taking or forced acquisition of private land for public use, with compensation paid to the landowner.

Emission   Pollution discharged into the atmosphere from smokestacks, other vents, and surface areas of commercial or industrial facilities, from residential chimneys, and from motor vehicle, locomotive, or aircraft exhausts.

Emission factor   The relationship between the amount of pollution produced and the amount of raw material processed. For example, an emission factor for a blast furnace making iron would be the number of pounds of particulates per ton of raw materials.

Emission inventory   A listing, by source, of the amount of air pollutants discharged into the atmosphere of a community. It is used to establish emission standards.

Emission standard   The maximum amount of air-polluting discharge legally allowed from a single source, mobile or stationary.

Emissions trading   EPA policy that allows a plant complex with several facilities to decrease pollution from some facilities while increasing it from others, so long as total results are equal to or better than previous limits. Facilities where this is done are treated as if they exist in a bubble in which total emissions are averaged out. Complexes that reduce emissions substantially may bank their credits or sell them to other industries.

Enforcement   EPA, state, or local actions to obtain compliance with environmental laws, rules, regulations, or agreements and/or obtain penalties or criminal sanctions for violations. Enforcement procedures may vary, depending on the specific requirements of different environmental laws and related implementing regulatory requirements.

Environment   The sum of all external conditions affecting the life, development, and survival of an organism.

Environmental assessment   A written environmental analysis that is prepared pursuant to the National Environmental Policy Act to determine whether a federal action would significantly affect the environment and thus require preparation of a more detailed environmental impact statement.

Environmental audit   1) An independent assessment of the current status of a party's compliance with applicable environmental requirements. 2) An independent evaluation of a party's environmental compliance policies, practices, and controls.

Environmental impact statement   A document required of federal agencies by the National Environmental Policy Act for major projects or legislative proposals significantly affecting the environment. A tool for decision making, it describes the positive and negative effects of the undertaking and lists alternative actions.

Environmental Protection Agency (EPA)   Established in 1970 by Presidential Executive Order, the EPA is the primary federal agency charged with ensuring the protection and preservation of environmental resources in the United States.

Evaporation ponds   Areas where sewer sludge is dumped and allowed to dry out.

Exempt solvent   Specific organic compounds that are not subject to requirements of regulation because they have been deemed by the EPA to be of negligible photochemical reactivity.

Exposure   1) The amount of radiation or pollutant present in an environment that represents a potential health threat to the living organisms in that environment. 2) Contact of an organism with a chemical or physical agent. Exposure is quantified as the amount of the agent available at the exchange boundaries of the organism (skin, lungs, etc.) and available for absorption.

Extremely hazardous substances   Any chemical identified by the EPA on the basis of toxicity, and listed under SARA Title III. The list is subject to revision.

Facility   Broadly defined under Superfund to include a structure, installation, equipment, landfill impoundment, storage vessel, vehicle, or any site or area where hazardous substances have been deposited or otherwise have come to be located.

Feasibility study   Analysis of the practicability of a proposal (e.g., a description and analysis of the potential cleanup alternatives for a site or alternatives for a site on the National Priorities List). The feasibility study (FS) usually recommends selecting a cost-effective alternative. It usually starts in tandem with the Remedial Investigation (RI). Performed together, the process is commonly referred to as the RI/FS. The term can apply to a variety of proposed corrective or regulatory actions.

Federal implementation plan (FIP):   Implemented by the EPA when a state fails to implement their own plan for the establishment, regulation, and enforcement of air pollution standards.

Filling   Depositing dirt and mud or other materials into aquatic areas to create more dry land, usually for agriculture or commercial development. Such activities often damage the ecology of the area.

Filtration   A treatment process, under the control of qualified operators, for removing solid (particulate) matter from water by passing the water through porous media, such as sand or a man-made filter. The process is often used to remove particles that contain pathogenic organisms.

Finding of no significant impact (FNSI)   A document prepared by a federal agency that presents the reasons why a proposed action would not have a significant impact on the environment and thus would not require preparation of an Environmental Impact Statement. An FNSI is based on the result of an environmental assessment.

Flash point   That temperature at which a material, liquid or solid, will provide a sufficient quantity of vapors to ignite in the presence of an ignition source.

Fluorocarbon   Any of a number of organic compounds analogous to hydrocarbons, in which one or more hydrogen atoms are replaced by fluorine.

Food chain   A sequence of organisms, each of which uses the next, lower member of the sequence as a food source.

Fresh water   Water that generally contains less than 1,000 milligrams per liter of dissolved solids.

Fungicide   Pesticides that are used to control, prevent, or destroy fungi.

General permit   A permit applicable to a class or category of dischargers.

Generator   An individual, facility, or mobile source that emits or causes or contributes to the emission of pollutants into the air or that releases hazardous wastes into the water or soil.

Germicide   Any compound that kills disease-causing microorganisms.

Global warming   See *Greenhouse effect.*

Gold Book   Common name for an EPA publication known as the Quality Criteria for Water, which was developed as a means of ensuring some level of minimum consistency between the states. The EPA has established minimum criteria for 137 specific pollutants based upon identifiable effects of each pollutant on the public health and welfare, aquatic life, and recreation.

Grandfathering provision   Under the Clean Water Act, any new source that has been constructed to meet current BADT standards will not be subjected to any additional, more stringent standards of performance for as much as 10 years into the future.

Green initiative   Term used to describe the increasing level of environmental awareness to such an extent that the efforts of consumers, insurers, lenders, and the media have begun to focus on issues affecting the environment.

Greenhouse effect   The warming of the Earth's atmosphere caused by a buildup of carbon dioxide or other trace gases; it is believed by many scientists that this buildup allows light from the sun's rays to heat the Earth, but prevents a counterbalancing loss of heat (also known as global warming).

Groundwater   The supply of fresh water found beneath the Earth's surface, usually in aquifers, which is often used for supplying wells and springs. Because groundwater is a major source of drinking water, there is a growing concern over areas where leaching agricultural or industrial pollutants or substances from leaking underground storage tanks are contaminating groundwater.

Halogen   Any of a group of five chemically related nonmetallic elements that includes bromine, fluorine, chlorine, iodine, and astatine.

Hammer provision   Common term for the automatic promulgation of required standards by Congress, usually invoked when a regulatory agency, such as the EPA, fails to promulgate the required standard by an established deadline.

Harmful quantity   With regard to oil and hazardous substances, those that may be harmful to the public health or welfare, including harm to fish, shellfish, wildlife, and public and private property, shorelines, and beaches. The EPA further defines a hazardous quantity of oil as an amount that violates applicable water quality standards or that causes a surface film or sheen or a discoloration of the water or adjoining shoreline.

Hazardous air pollutants   Air pollutants that are not covered by ambient air quality standards, but that, as defined in the Clean Air Act, may reasonably be expected to cause or contribute to irreversible illness or death. Such pollutants include asbestos, beryllium, mercury, benzene, coke oven emissions, radionuclides, and vinyl chloride.

Hazardous Ranking System (HRS)   ™The principle screening tool used by the EPA to evaluate the risks posed to public health and the environment by abandoned or uncontrolled hazardous wastes sites. The HRS calculates a score based on the potential of hazardous substances spreading from the site through the air, surface water, or groundwater and on other factors, such as nearby populations. This score is the primary factor in deciding if the site should be on the National Priorities List and, if so, what ranking it should have compared to other sites.

Hazardous secondary materials   As defined by RCRA, any spent materials, sludges, by-products, commercial chemical products, and scrap metals.

Hazardous substance   1) Any material that poses a threat to human health and/or the environment. Typical hazardous substances are toxic, corrosive, ignitable, explosive, or chemically reactive. 2) Any substance designated by the EPA to be reported if a designated quantity of the substance is spilled into the waters of the United States or if otherwise emitted to the environment.

Hazardous waste   By-products of society that can pose a substantial or potential hazard to human health or the environment when improperly managed. Possesses at least one of four characteristics (ignitability, corrosivity, reactivity, or toxicity), or appears on any special EPA list.

Hazards analysis   The procedure involved in identifying potential sources of release of hazardous materials from fixed facilities or transportation accidents; determining the vulnerability of a geological area to a release of hazardous materials; and comparing hazards to determine which present greater or lesser risks to a community.

Health and safety study   As defined by TSCA, any study of any effect of a chemical substance or mixture on health and/or the environment, including underlying epidemiological studies, studies of occupational exposure, toxicological studies, clinical studies, and ecological studies of a chemical substance or mixture.

Holding pond   A pond or reservoir, usually made of earth, built to store polluted runoff.

Hydrogen sulfide (HS)   Gas emitted during organic decomposition. Also a by-product of oil refining and burning. In heavy concentrations, HS can cause illness.

Ignitable   Capable of burning or causing fire.

Immediately dangerous to life and health (IDLH)   The maximum level to which a healthy individual can be exposed to a chemical for 30 minutes and escape without suffering irreversible health effects or impairing symptoms.

Imminent hazard   A hazardous situation, condition, or circumstance, the nature of which poses a serious and imminent threat to human health or the environment. If actions are not taken to immediately correct or stop the hazard cause, the results could be catastrophic.

Indirect discharge   Introduction of pollutants from a nondomestic source into a publicly owned waste treatment system. Indirect dischargers can be commercial or industrial facilities whose wastes go into the local sewers.

Indirect source   Under the Clean Air Act, any facility, building, structure, installation, real property, road, or highway that attracts or may attract mobile sources of pollution.

Indoor air   The breathing air inside a habitable structure or conveyance.

Indoor air pollution   Chemical, physical, or biological contaminants in indoor air.

Influent   Water, wastewater, or other liquid flowing into a reservoir, basin, or treatment plant.

Injection well   A well into which fluids are injected for purposes such as waste disposal, improving the recovery of crude oil, or solution mining.

Inorganic compound   Chemical substances of mineral origin, not of basically carbon structure.

Interim (permit) status   Period during which treatment, storage, and disposal facilities coming under RCRA in 1980 are temporarily permitted to operate while awaiting denial or issuance of a permanent permit. Permits issued under these circumstances are usually called Part A or Part B permits.

Interstitial monitoring   A technique for monitoring the integrity of the area between the primary and secondary containment systems of underground storage tanks (USTs).

Inversion   An atmospheric condition caused by a layer of warm air preventing the rise of cooling air trapped beneath it. This condition prevents the rise of pollutants that might otherwise be dispersed and can result in an air pollution episode.

Land-ban   Under RCRA, the mandated phasing out of land disposal of untreated hazardous waste.

Landfills   1) Sanitary landfills are land disposal sites for nonhazardous solid wastes at which the waste is spread into layers, compacted to the smallest practical volume, and covered by material at the end of each operating day. 2) Secure chemical landfills are disposal sites for hazardous waste. They are selected and designed to minimize the chance of release of hazardous substances into the environment.

Leachate   A liquid that results from water collecting contaminants as it trickles through wastes, agricultural pesticides, or fertilizers. Leaching may occur in farming areas, feedlots, and landfills, and may result in hazardous substances entering surface water, groundwater, or soil.

Leachate collection system   A system that gathers leachate and pumps it to the surface for treatment.

Level of concern (LOC)   The concentration in the air of an extremely hazardous substance, above which there may be serious immediate health effects to anyone exposed to it for short periods of time.

Listed waste   Wastes listed as hazardous under RCRA, but that have not been subjected to the Toxic Characteristics Listing Process because the dangers they present are considered self-evident.

Local Emergency Planning Committee (LEPC)   A committee appointed by the state emergency response commission, as required by SARA, Title III, to formulate a comprehensive emergency plan for its jurisdiction.

Lower explosive limit (LEL)   The concentration of a compound in air below which a flame will not propagate if the mixture is ignited.

Lowest achievable emission rate   Under the Clean Air Act, this is the rate of emissions that reflects either the most stringent emission limitation that is contained in the implementation plan of any state for such source (unless the owner or operator of the proposed source demonstrates that such limitations are not achievable) or the most stringent emissions limitation achieved in practice, whichever is more stringent. Application of this term does not permit a proposed new or modified source to emit pollutants in excess of existing new source standards.

Major stationary sources   Under the 1990 CAA amendments, any stationary source or group of stationary sources located within a contiguous area and under common control that emits or has the potential to emit considering controls, in the aggregate, 10 tons per year or more of any hazardous air pollutant or 25 tons per year or more of any combination of hazardous air pollutants.

Manufacture   Under TSCA, to import into the customs territory of the United States or to produce or manufacture a chemical substance.

Material Safety Data Sheet (MSDS)   A compilation of data required under OSHA's Hazard Communication Standard on the identity of hazardous chemicals, health, and physical hazards, exposure limits, and precautions. Section 311 of SARA requires facilities covered by the OSHA standard to submit MSDSs under certain circumstances.

Maximum contaminant level   The maximum permissible level of a contaminant in water delivered to any user of a public water system. MCLs are enforceable standards.

Media   Specific environments, such as air, water, and soil, which are the subject of regulatory concern and activities.

Mitigation   Measures taken to reduce adverse impacts on the environment.

Mixed liquor   A mixture of activated sludge and water containing organic matter undergoing activated sludge treatment in an aeration tank.

Mixture rule   Used to determine the hazardous nature of a waste product. Although the EPA has specifically excluded numerous chemical mixtures from this rule, it is still generally true that any mixture of a listed hazardous waste with another nonhazardous waste will render the entire volume of the waste product hazardous and subjected to regulation.

Mobile source   A moving producer of air pollution, mainly forms of transportation, such as cars, trucks, motorcycles, and airplanes.

Monitoring   Periodic or continuous surveillance or testing to determine the level of compliance with statutory requirements and/or pollutant levels in various media or in humans, animals, and other living things.

Monitoring wells   Wells drilled at a hazardous waste management facility or Superfund site to collect groundwater samples for the purpose of physical, chemical, or biological analysis to determine the amounts, types, and distribution of contaminants in the groundwater beneath the site.

Mutagen   Any substance that can cause a change in genetic material.

Mutate   To bring about a change in the genetic constitution of a cell by altering its DNA. In turn, "mutagenesis" is any process by which cells are mutated.

National Ambient Air Quality Standards (NAAQS)   Air quality criteria established by the EPA that apply to outside air.

National Emission Standards for Hazardous Air Pollutants   Also known as NESHAPS, these emission standards are set by the EPA for an air pollutant not covered by NAAQS that may cause an increase in deaths and/or irreversible or incapacitating illness. Primary standards are designed to protect human health, secondary standards to protect public welfare.

National Oil and Hazardous Substances Contingency Plan   The federal regulation that guides determination of the sites to be corrected under the Superfund program and the program to prevent or control spills into surface waters or other portions of the environment. Also known as the National Contingency Plan, or NCP.

National Pollution Discharge Elimination System (NPDES)   A provision of the Clean Water Act that prohibits discharge of pollutants into waters of the United States without a special permit issued by the EPA, a state, or (where delegated) a tribal government on an Indian Reservation.

National Priorities List (NPL)   The EPA's list of the most serious uncontrolled or abandoned hazardous waste sites identified for possible long-term remedial action under Superfund. A site must be on the NPL to receive money from the Trust Fund for remedial actions. The list is based primarily on the score that a site receives from the Hazard Ranking System (HRS). The EPA is required to update the NPL at least annually.

National Response Center (NRC)   The federal operations center that receives notifications of all releases of oil and hazardous substances into the environment. The NRC is operated 24 hours per day by the United States Coast Guard, which evaluates all reports and notifies the appropriate agencies.

National Response Team (NRT)   Representatives of 13 federal agencies that, as a team, coordinate federal responses to nationally significant incidents of pollution and that provide advice and technical assistance to the responding agencies before and during a response action.

Navigable waters   Traditionally, waters sufficiently deep and wide for navigation by all or by specified sizes of vessels; such waters in the United States come under federal jurisdiction and are included in certain provisions of the Clean Water Act.

Neutralization   Decreasing the acidity or alkalinity of a substance by adding to it alkaline or acidic materials, respectively, as required.

New source   Any stationary source that is built or modified after publication of final or proposed regulations that prescribe a standard of performance that is intended to apply to that type of emission source.

New Source Performance Standards (NSPS)   Uniform national EPA air emissions and water effluent standards that limit the amount of pollution allowed from new sources or from existing sources that have been modified.

Nitric oxide (NO)   A gas formed by combustion under high temperature and high pressure in an internal combustion engine. It changes to nitrogen dioxide (NO_2) in the ambient air and contributes to photochemical smog.

Nitrogen oxide (NO_x)   Product of combustion from transportation and stationary sources, as well as being a major contributor to the formation of ozone in the troposphere and acid rain deposition.

Nonattainment area   Geographic area that does not meet one or more of the National Ambient Air Quality Standards (NAAQS) for any of the EPA's listed criteria pollutants designated under the Clean Air Act.

Nonconventional pollutant   Any pollutant that is not statutorily listed or that is poorly understood by the scientific community.

Nonpoint source   Pollution sources that are diffuse and do not have a single point of origin or are not introduced into a receiving stream from a specific outlet. The pollutants are generally carried off the land by stormwater runoff. The commonly used categories for nonpoint sources are agriculture, forestry, urban, mining, construction, dams and channels, land disposal, and salt water intrusion.

Office on Environmental Quality (OEP)   Under the Clinton Administration, a new office created to replace the Council on Environmental Quality (CEQ), which was abolished by Clinton. The OEP is to have more visibility in government policy-making activities.

Off-site facility   A hazardous waste treatment, storage, or disposal (TSD) area that is located at a place away from the generating site.

On-scene coordinator (OSC)   The predesignated EPA, Coast Guard, or Department of Defense official who coordinates and directs Superfund removal actions or Clean Water Act oil (or hazardous) spill corrective actions.

On-site facility   A hazardous waste treatment, storage, or disposal (TSD) area that is located on the generating site.

One-inch Rule   See *Residue Rule.*

Other regulated material (ORM)   Any material that does not meet the definition of a hazardous material, other than combustible liquid in packaging having a capacity of 110 gallons or less, and is specifically listed in the Table of Hazardous Materials as an ORM. A material not listed in the Table may also be considered an ORM if it meets certain characteristics specified in 49 CFR 173.

Outfall   The place where effluent is discharged into receiving waters.

Ozone (O_3)   An unstable allotropic form of oxygen existing in two different layers of the Earth's atmosphere—the stratosphere and the troposphere. In the stratosphere (the atmospheric layer beginning 7–10 miles above the Earth's surface), ozone is found naturally and provides a protective layer that shields the Earth from the harmful effects of the sun's ultraviolet radiation. In the troposphere (the layer extending from the Earth's surface up to 7–10 miles), ozone is a chemical oxidant and a major component of photochemical smog. Ozone can seriously affect the human respiratory system and is one of the most prevalent and widespread of all the criteria pollutants identified in the Clean Air Act. Ozone in the troposphere is produced through complex chemical reactions of nitrogen oxides (which are among the primary pollutants emitted by combustion sources), hydrocarbons (released into the atmosphere through the combustion, handling, and processing of petroleum products), and sunlight.

Ozone depleting chemicals (ODCs)   See *Ozone level depleting substances (OLDS)*.

Ozone depletion   Destruction of the stratospheric ozone layer, which shields the Earth from the sun's ultraviolet radiation, which is harmful to biological life.

Ozone level depleting substances (OLDS)   Substances that lead to the destruction of ozone as a result of the decomposition of certain chlorine- and bromine-containing compounds, such as CFCs (chlorofluorocarbons) or halons, which break down when they reach the stratosphere and catalytically destroy ozone molecules.

Particulates   Fine liquid or solid particles, such as dust, smoke, mist, fumes, or smog, found in air or emissions.

Permissible exposure limit (PEL)   An OSHA-mandated value that represents the level of air concentrations of chemical substances to which it is believed that workers may be exposed on a daily basis without adverse effects. PELs are enforceable by law under the Occupational Safety and Health Act. (See also *Threshold limit value*, or TLV.)

Permit   An authorization, license, or equivalent control document issued by the EPA or an approved state agency to implement the requirements of an environmental regulation.

Permit shield   Under the Clean Air Act, a provision that will allow protection against enforcement actions for operating without a permit for existing sources that submit completed applications in a timely manner.

Persons   1) Under the Clean Water Act, any individual, corporation, partnership, association, state, municipality, commission, political subdivision, or interstate body. 2) Under RCRA, an individual, trust, firm, joint stock company, federal agency, corporation, partnership, association, state, municipality, political subdivision of a state, or interstate body.

pH   A measure of the acidity or alkalinity of a liquid or solid material.

Phenols   Organic compounds that are by-products of petroleum refining, tanning, and textile, dye, and resin manufacturing. Low concentrations cause taste and odor problems in water; higher concentrations can kill aquatic life and humans.

Photochemical smog   Air pollution caused by chemical reactions in the atmosphere.

Plume   1) A visible or measurable discharge of a contaminant from a given point of origin. Can be visible or thermal in water, or visible in the air. 2) The area of measurable and potentially harmful radiation leaking from a damaged reactor. 3) The distance from a toxic release considered dangerous for those exposed to the leaking fumes.

Point source   A stationary location or fixed facility from which pollutants are discharged or emitted. Also, any single identifiable source of pollution, such as a pipe, ditch, ship, ore pit, or factory smokestack.

Pollutant   Generally, any substance introduced into the environment that adversely affects the usefulness of a resource.

Pollution   Generally, the presence of matter or energy whose nature, location, or quantity produces undesirable effects. Under the Clean Water Act, for example, the term is defined as the man-made or man-induced alteration of the physical, biological, and radiological integrity of water.

Polychlorinated biphenyls (PCBs)   A group of highly toxic, persistent chemicals used in transformers and capacitors for insulating purposes and in gas pipeline systems as a lubricant. Further sale of new-use PCBs was banned by law in 1979.

Potentially responsible party (PRP)   Under CERCLA, any individual or company, including owners, operators, transporter or generators, potentially responsible for or contributing to the contamination problems at a Superfund site. Whenever possible, the EPA requires PRPs, through administrative and legal actions, to clean up waste sites they have contaminated.

Preliminary assessment   The process of collecting and receiving available information about a known or suspected waste site or release.

Pretreatment   Processes used to reduce, eliminate, or alter the nature of wastewater pollutants from nondomestic sources before they are discharged into a publicly owned treatment works (POTW).

Prevention of significant deterioration (PSD)   The EPA program in which state and/or federal permits are required that are intended to restrict emissions for new or modified sources in locations where air quality is already better than required to meet primary and secondary ambient air quality standards. (See *Ambient air quality standards.*)

Process   Under TSCA, the preparation of a chemical substance or mixture, after its manufacture, for distribution in commerce.

Publicly owned treatment works (POTW)   A waste-treatment works owned by a state, unit of local government, or Indian tribe, usually designed to treat domestic wastewaters.

Quench tank   A water-filled tank used to cool incinerator residues or hot materials during industrial processes.

Reasonably available control technology (RACT)   The lowest emissions limit that a particular source is capable of meeting by the application of control technology that is both reasonably available and technologically and economically feasible. RACT is usually applied to existing sources in nonattainment areas and in most cases is less stringent than new source performance standards.

Recycle/reuse   The process of minimizing the generation of waste by recovering usable products that might otherwise become waste.

Release   According to CERCLA, any spilling, leaking, pumping, pouring, emitting, emptying, discharging, injecting, escaping, leaching, dumping, or disposing of hazardous substances into the environment. SARA included in this definition the abandonment or discarding of barrels, containers, and other closed receptacles containing any hazardous substances or pollutant contaminant.

Remedial action (RA)   The second phase of the remedial action process that contains the actual construction or implementation phase of a Superfund site cleanup that follows remedial design.

Remedial design (RD)   The first phase of the remedial action process that follows the remedial investigation/feasibility study (RI/FS) and includes development of engineering drawings and specifications for site cleanup. RD is followed by the remedial action (RA) phase.

Remedial investigation   An in-depth study designed to gather the data necessary to determine the nature and extent of contamination at a Superfund site, establish criteria for cleaning up the site, identify preliminary alternatives for remedial actions, and support the technical and cost analyses of the alternatives. The remedial investigation is usually performed in tandem with the feasibility study—hence the acronym "RI/FS."

Removal action   Short-term immediate actions taken to address releases of hazardous substances that require expedited response.

Reportable quantity (RQ)   The quantity of a hazardous substance that triggers reports under CERCLA. When a substance is released in amounts exceeding its RQ, the release must be reported to the National Response Center, the SERC, and the community emergency coordinators for areas likely to be affected.

Residue Rule   Also known as the *One-inch Rule*, it states that any residue left in empty containers will not be regulated under RCRA, provided that all hazardous wastes are removed from the container using the practice commonly employed to remove materials from that type of container and that no more than 1 inch of residue remains.

Response action   A CERCLA-authorized action involving either a short-term removal action or a long-term removal response that may include but is not limited to: removing hazardous materials from a site to an EPA-approved hazardous waste facility for treatment, containment, or destruction; containing the waste safely on site; destroying or treating the waste on site; and identifying and removing the source of groundwater contamination and halting further migration of contaminants.

Response costs   Under CERCLA, those costs associated with the cleanup, removal (including costs associated with emergency response), remedial action (costs associated with permanent remedies), and related enforcement activities.

Risk assessment   The qualitative and quantitative evaluation performed in an effort to define the risk posed to human health and/or the environment by the presence or potential presence and/or use of specific pollutants.

Run-off   That part of precipitation, snow melt, or irrigation water that runs off the land into streams or other surface water. It can carry pollutants from the air and land into receiving waters.

Scrubber   An air pollution reduction device that uses a spray of water or reactant or a dry process to trap pollutants in emissions.

Sediments   Solid, sand, and minerals washed from the land into water usually after a rain. They pile up in reservoirs, rivers, and harbors, destroying fish-nesting areas and holes used by water animals, and cloud the water so that needed sunlight might not reach aquatic plants.

Sewage   The waste and wastewater that is produced by residential and commercial establishments and discharged into sewers.

Significant deterioration   Pollution resulting from a new source in previously "clean" areas. (See also *Prevention of significant deterioration.*)

Significant violation   Violations by point source dischargers of sufficient magnitude and/or duration to be considered a regulatory priority.

Site inspection   As pertains to CERCLA, the collection of information from a Superfund site to determine the extent and severity of hazards posed by the site. It follows and is more extensive than a preliminary assessment. The site inspection gathers the information required to score the site, using the Hazard Ranking System (HRS), and to determine if the site presents an immediate threat that requires prompt removal actions.

Sludge   A semisolid residue from any number of air or water treatment processes. Sludge can be a hazardous waste under certain conditions.

Smog   Air pollution associated with oxidants present in the atmosphere that, as a result of a temperature inversion under no-wind conditions, are brought extremely close to the Earth's surface. Smog has led to air pollution episodes, resulting in serious human illness and death.

Solid waste   As defined by RCRA, any liquid, containerized gas, non-liquid, or nonsoluble materials, ranging from municipal garbage to industrial wastes, that contain simple or complex substances that may or may not be hazardous.

Spent solvent   Under RCRA, a solvent that no longer meets the specifications for which it was originally intended.

Standards   Prescriptive norms that govern action and actual limits on the amount of pollutants or emissions produced. The EPA, under most of its responsibilities, establishes minimum standards. States are allowed to be stricter.

State Emergency Response Commission (SERC)   Commission appointed by each state governor according to the requirements of SARA Title III. The nonsoluble designated emergency planning districts appoint local emergency planning committees and supervise and coordinate their activities.

State implementation plan (SIP)   EPA-approved state plans for the establishment, regulation, and enforcement of air pollution standards.

Stationary source   A fixed, nonmoving producer of pollution, mainly power plants and other facilities using industrial combustion processes.

Storage   Temporary holding of waste pending treatment or disposal. Storage methods include containers, tanks, waste piles, and surface impoundments.

Stratosphere   That portion of the atmosphere that is 10 to 25 miles above the Earth's surface.

Superfund   The program operated under the legislative authority of CERCLA and SARA that funds and carries out the EPA solid waste emergency and long-term removal remedial activities. These activities include establishing the National Priorities List (NPL), investigating sites for inclusion on the list, determining their priority level on the list, and coordinating and/or supervising the ultimately determined cleanup and other remedial actions.

Suspended solids   Small particles of solid pollutants that float on the surface of or are suspended in sewage or other liquids. They resist removal by conventional means.

Technology-based standards   Effluent limitations applicable to direct and indirect sources that are developed on a category-by-category basis, using statutory factors, not including water-quality effects.

Teratogen   Substance that causes malformation or serious deviation from the normal development of an embryo or fetus.

Threshold limit value (TLV)   Represents the level of air concentrations of chemical substances to which it is believed that workers may be exposed on a daily basis without adverse effects. TLVs are developed by the American Conference of Government Industrial Hygienists (ACGIH), which is a nonregulatory agency. TLVs are, therefore, not enforceable by law unless adopted by a federal agency. (See also *Permissible exposure limit,* or PEL.)

Threshold planning quantity (TPQ)   A quantity designated for each chemical on the EPA's list of extremely hazardous substances that triggers notification by facilities to their SERC that such facilities are subject to emergency planning provisions under SARA Title III.

Total suspended solids (TSS)   A measure of the suspended solids in wastewater, effluent, or water bodies, determined by using tests for "total suspended nonfilterable solids."

Toxic   Capable of causing harm to living organisms. One of four characteristics that, if displayed by a waste product, renders that waste hazardous under RCRA.

Toxic characteristic leaching procedure (TCLP)   Testing method established by the EPA used to determine the toxicity of a solid waste. Under specific testing parameters, the waste will be determined toxic and therefore hazardous if certain listed commodities will "leach" out of the waste at levels considered threatening to health or the environment.

Toxic chemical release form   Information form required to be submitted by facilities that manufacture, process, or use (in quantities above a specific amount) chemicals listed under SARA Title III.

Toxic pollutants   Materials contaminating the environment that cause death, disease, or birth defects in organisms that ingest or absorb them. The quantities and length or exposure necessary to cause these effects can vary widely.

Toxic substance   A chemical or mixture that may present an unreasonable risk of injury to health or the environment.

Treatment, storage, and disposal facility (TSDF)   Site where a hazardous substance is treated, stored, or disposed of. TSDFs are regulated by the EPA and the states under RCRA.

Troposphere   The lower atmosphere; the portion of the atmosphere between 7 and 10 miles above the Earth's surface where clouds are formed.

Trust fund   See *Superfund.*

Underground storage tank (UST)   A tank located all or partially underground that is designed to hold gasoline or other petroleum products or chemical solutions.

Urban runoff   Stormwater from city streets and adjacent domestic or commercial properties that may carry pollutants of various kinds into the sewer systems and/or receiving waters.

Variance   Government permission for a delay or exception in the application of a given law, ordinance, or regulation.

Volatile organic compound (VOC)   Any organic compound that participates in atmospheric photochemical reactions, except those designated by the EPA as having negligible photochemical reactivity.

Waste   Unwanted materials left over from a manufacturing process; refuse from places of human or animal habitation; any material determined by the user to no longer serve a useful purpose and will therefore be discarded.

Waste treatment plant   A facility containing a series of tanks, screens, filters, and other processes by which pollutants are removed from water.

Waste stream   Expected wastes resultant from a specific process.

Water pollution   The presence in water of enough harmful or objectionable material to damage the water's quality.

Water quality criteria   Specific levels of water quality that, if reached, are expected to render a body of water suitable for its designated use. The criteria are based on specific levels of pollutants that would make the water harmful if used for drinking, swimming, farming, fish production, or industrial processes.

Water quality standards   State-adopted and EPA-approved ambient standards for water bodies. The standards cover the use of the water body and the water quality criteria that must be met to protect the designated uses or users.

Well   A bored, drilled, or driven shaft or a dug hole whose depth is greater than the largest surface dimension and whose purpose is to reach underground water supplies or oil or to store or bury fluids below ground.

Wetlands   An area that is regularly saturated by surface or groundwater and subsequently is characterized by a prevalence of vegetation that is adapted for life in saturated soil conditions. Examples include swamps, bogs, fens, marshes, and estuaries.

Bibliography

Ashford, Nicholas A., and Charles C. Caldart. 1991. *Technology, Law, and the Working Environment.* New York: Van Nostrand Reinhold.

Berz, David R., et al. 1990. *Certificate in Environmental Health and Safety Law, Block 1* (Seminar Manual). Newport Beach, California: Institute for Applied Management and Law (IAML).

Clean Air Act (CAA) of 1970, 1977, 1990. 42 United States Code (USC), Sections 7401 *et seq.* U.S. Environmental Protection Agency, Code of Federal Regulations (CFR), Title 40, Parts 50 *et seq.*

Clean Water Act (CWA) of 1972, 1977, 1987. 33 United States Code (USC), Sections 1251 *et seq.* U.S. Environmental Protection Agency, Code of Federal Regulations (CFR), Title 40, Parts 112 *et seq.*

Comprehensive Environmental Response, Compensation and Liability Act (CERCLA) of 1980, and *Superfund Amendments and Reauthorization Act (SARA) of 1986.* 42 United States Code (USC), Sections 9602 *et seq.* U.S. Environmental Protection Agency, Code of Federal Regulations (CFR), Title 40, Parts 300 *et seq.*

Emergency Planning and Community Right To Know Act (EPCRA) of 1986 (also known as SARA Title III). 42 United States Code (USC), Sections 11001 *et seq.* U.S. Environmental Protection Agency, Code of Federal Regulations (CFR), Title 40, Parts 350, *et seq.*

Hazardous Materials Transportation Act (HMTA) of 1975. 49 United States Code (USC), Sections 1801, *et seq.* U.S. Department of Transportation, Code of Federal Regulations (CFR), Title 49, Sections 106, 107, 171, *et seq.*

National Environmental Policy Act (NEPA) of 1970. 42 United States Code (USC), Sections 4321 *et seq.* U.S. Environmental Protection Agency, Code of Federal Regulations (CFR), Title 40, Parts 1500 *et seq.*

O'Brien & Gere Engineers, Inc. 1988. *Hazardous Waste Site Remediation, The Engineer's Perspective.* New York: Van Nostrand Reinhold.

Occupational Safety and Health Administration (OSHA). 1990. *Hazard Communication.* U.S. Department of Labor, Code of Federal Regulations (CFR), Title 29, Part 1910, Section 1200.

Occupational Safety and Health Administration (OSHA). 1991. *Process Safety Management.* U.S. Department of Labor, Code of Federal Regulations (CFR), Title 29, Part 1910, Section 119.

Occupational Safety and Health Administration (OSHA). 1990. *Hazardous Waste Operations and Emergency Response (HAZWOPER).* U.S. Department of Labor, Code of Federal Regulations (CFR), Title 29, Part 1910, Section 120.

Resource Conservation and Recovery Act (RCRA) of 1976. 42 United States Code (USC), Sections 1004, 3001, *et seq.* U.S. Environmental Protection Agency, Code of Federal Regulations (CFR), Title 40, Parts 124, 260, *et seq.*

Simonds, Rollin H., and John V. Grimaldi. 1963. *Safety Management.* Homewood, Illinois: Richard D. Irwin, Inc.

Toxic Substances Control Act (TSCA) of 1976. 15 United States Code (USC), Sections 2601 *et seq.* U.S. Environmental Protection Agency, Code of Federal Regulations (CFR), Title 40, Parts 700 *et seq.*

Traister, Matthew. 1990. *The History of Air Pollution and United States Air Policy: Yesterday, Today and Tomorrow.* Syracuse, New York: O'Brien & Gere Engineers, Inc.

U.S. Environmental Protection Agency. 1989. *Information Resources Directory* (OCPA19M-4001). Washington, D.C.: Government Printing Office.

U.S. Environmetal Protection Agency, Office of Air and Radiation. 1991. *Implementation Strategy for the Clean Air Act Amendments of 1990.* Washington, D.C.: Government Printing Office.

Webster's New Dictionary and Thesaurus. 1991. New York: Russell, Geddes & Grossey.

Wentz, Charles A. 1989. *Hazardous Waste Management.* New York: McGraw Hill.

Index